S0-AIB-409

301.0924
B65d

64114

DATE DUE			
Dec 18 68			
Aug 10'83			
GAYLORD M-2			PRINTED IN U.S.A.

WITHDRAWN
L. R. COLLEGE LIBRARY

DIALECTICAL
SOCIOLOGY

DIALECTICAL SOCIOLOGY

AN ANALYSIS OF THE SOCIOLOGY OF GEORGES GURVITCH

Phillip Bosserman

CARL A. RUDISILL LIBRARY
LENOIR RHYNE COLLEGE

EXTENDING HORIZONS BOOKS

PORTER SARGENT PUBLISHER

11 BEACON STREET, BOSTON, MASSACHUSETTS

301.0924
B65d

64114

December, 1968

COPYRIGHT © 1968 BY F. PORTER SARGENT
Library of Congress Catalog Card Number **67-31430**

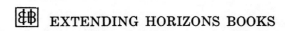 **EXTENDING HORIZONS BOOKS**

Co-editors W. H. Truitt, Dept. of Philosophy,
Suffolk University; A. Engelman, Dept. of
Social Sciences, Franconia College

To
My Father and Mother

ACKNOWLEDGMENTS

Advise and counsel him; if he does not listen,
let adversity teach him.

—ETHIOPIAN PROVERB

In writing this work I have relied on the counsel of many persons. Dean Walter G. Muelder provided the inspiration, challenge, and wise perception necessary for a task such as this. Likewise Professor Irwin T. Sanders' trenchant comments on the manuscript helped to bring much of the material into proper perspective. Professor Gurvitch has throughout this long period given constant encouragement, and patient explanation. Throughout he has been my mentor and for his teaching I owe him an immense debt of gratitude.

Other teachers and colleagues must be recalled for their help during these years of work: Professor Paul Deats, Professors Raymond Aron and Roger Bastide; colleagues, Dean B. A. Gessner, Professors Robert Sellen, Charles Selden, and Robert Greenfield whose critical acumen in discussions of this material always saw easily to the heart of the matter.

To my wife my debt is greatest. Her analytical and incisive mind coupled with a gentle and humanitarian spirit have been continual support in this effort. P. B.

TEMPLE TERRACE, FLORIDA
OCTOBER, 1967

TABLE OF CONTENTS

i

DIALECTICAL SOCIOLOGY

FOREWORD

by PITIRIM SOROKIN

This book introduces to the English speaking world the theoretical system of Georges D. Gurvitch, possessor of a rich sociological imagination which made him one of the most distinguished thinkers of our time.

As a scholar of extraordinary erudition, as a truly creative thinker and builder of one of the most original and significant sociological sytsems in contemporary sociology— "the dialectic, empirico-realistic sociology," as a successor of Durkheim's chair at the Sorbonne and the author of numerous important works in sociology, philosophy, and law, Gurvitch has contributed as much as any other single scholar in this century to the field of sociology.

Gurvitch's theory falls within the scope of dialectic theories of social and cultural systems. His is part of the conspicuous renaissance of dialectic in recent years in the natural and social sciences. A galaxy of eminent physicists and mathematicians, such as Niels Bohr, Louis de Broglie, F. Gonseth, J. L. Destouches, W. Heisenberg, and others,[1] have introduced it, in the form of "dialectic complementarity," into microphysics, nuclear physics, the mathematics of the infinitely great and the infinitely small, and for reconciling opposite theories in these fields. A special international review, *Dialectica,* was established in 1947. In *Dialectica* scientists of various exact sciences endeavor to find, through the dialectic method, a solution to various (conceptual and experimental) difficulties confronting them in their research.

In recent years, we have observed an increasing number of works devoted to the dialectic philosophy and the social sciences and a still more rapidly increasing use of this method in the research of social, cultural, and psychological phenomena by Soviet Marxist scholars as well as by Western philosophers, sociologists, and psychosocial investigators. Representative examples of recent Western works on

---

[1] See, for example, Niels Bohr's article in the *Revue de Metaphysique et de Morale,* Nos. 1-2 (1961), 1-34; L. De Broglie, La Physique nouvelle et les Quanta (Paris, 1937); F. Gonseth, Le Problème du Temps: Essai sur la Methodologie de la Recherche (La Neuveville, Switzerland, 1964); and G. Bachelard, L'Activité rationnelle de la Physique contemporaine (Paris, 1951).

dialectic include the monographs of Merleau-Ponti, Sartre, Gurvitch, and Kühne.[2]

Gurvitch is the most eminent leader of the "empirico-realist dialectic sociology." Mr. Bosserman's book gives us a detailed analysis of his dialectic sociology. What we discover in Gurvitch's theoretical system is a conceptual framework of the total social reality. He gives us an "histology" (in its microsociological analysis of sociability) and the gross (vertical and horizontal descriptions) anatomy and taxonomy of the total social reality, or, in other terms, a systematic theory of differentiation and stratification of this reality. Throughout his analysis Gurvitch continuously stresses the "fluid," ever-changing, precarious equilibria of each of his totalities and their incessant processes of structuration, destructuration and restructuration. In this way his comprehensive theory contributes to the "physiology" of social systems.

Once grasped, the depicted framework of the total social reality easily explains the central features of Gurvitch's special sociologies, like his sociology of knowledge, sociology of moral life, sociology of law, and his theory of social times. The central problem of all these special sociologies is the functional correlation between the specific form of sociability or depth-level or groupings or social classes or social structures or global societies and the specific forms of knowledge, philosophy, ideology, moral phenomena, law, or time conception in each of these social ensembles.

In all of these special sociologies, Gurvitch's principles of the multidimensionality of social phenomena, their precarious equilibria, and their structuration, destructuration, and restructuration are systematically carried on, together with a logico-dialectical analysis of the phenomena studied.

Emerging from this system are several important notions. First, Gurvitch sees socio-cultural reality as a reality *sui generis* different from, and irreducible to physical and biological realities. He views the total socio-cultural reality and socio-cultural phenomena as *multidimensional*, demanding for their adequate cognition a knowledge of all its main aspects as they are combined in the integrated systems (or structured totalities) and the unstructurable and unstruc-

[2] M. Merleau-Ponty Les Aventures de la Dialectique (Paris, 1955); J. P. Sartre, *Critique de la raison dialectique*, Vol. I (Paris, 1960); G. Gurvitch, Dialectique et sociologie (Paris, 1962); and O. Kühne, Allgemeine Soziologie (Berlin, 1958); P. M. Blau, Exchange and Power in Social Life (New York, 1964).

tured ensembles. He regards a real social group or cultural system as a real unity (system) irreducible to a mere nominalistic collection of its members in social groups or of its components in cultural systems. Any real social group or cultural system "is richer than $n + 1$ combinations of its members or elements." Any unified system, social group, or cultural system has its own form of being, its own static and dynamic properties, its own logic, ways of change, and uniformities not found in a mere nominalistic combination of their elements and unaccountable from a nominalistic and singularistic standpoint.

In comparing Gurvitch's system with my own, my conception of the "generic" model of socio-cultural phenomena corresponds to Gurvitch's "microsociology of the manifestation of sociability" as the simplest social phenomenon. My classification of "open and closed," "unibonded, multibonded, and encyclopedic" groups is analogous to Gurvitch's "open and closed," "unifunctional, multifunctional, and suprafuctional" groups and ensembles. Our conception of social classes is similar. My concepts of "organized," "as if organized," and "unorganized and disorganized" social groups are somewhat similar to Gurvitch's "structured," "structurable," and "unstructurable" social totalities. The pluralistic conceptions of social time-causality-space-determinism-liberty in both systems is mutually reconcilable. There is an essential similarity of the main methods of sociology (including dialectic) in both systems. We both stress an urgent need for the close cooperation of sociology and history. There are other similarities.

My disagreement with a number of points in his sociological system (analyzed in my *Sociological Theories of Today*)[3] does not prevent me from regarding his system as significant as any recent system of sociology. His passing away deprived sociology of one of its most eminent cultivators. Personally, I lost an old and most distinguished friend.

Up to now Gurvitch's works have not attracted as much attention among American sociologists as they really deserve. Mr. Bosserman's work fills an important void. His presentation suggests the value of Gurvitch's contributions to general and special sociologies. This volume shows his general theory is so significant as to secure for him one of the most honorable places in the history of sociology of the twentieth century.

---

[3] New York, Harper and Row, 1966, pp. 462-525.

INTRODUCTION

Contemporary scholarship places a high premium on specialization, narrow concentration whereby one becomes an expert in a subject such as ancient Egypt's Middle Kingdom, or a literary savant of the Elizabethan sonnet, or an exponent of small group theory in sociology. Such specializations, though they have certain values for scientific advancement, tend to compartmentalize, disintegrate and distort reality. What Professor Brand Blanshard says about the current state of philosophy holds also for the social sciences:

> Philosophy is in a chaotic state, in which each philosopher does what is good in his own eyes, and someone is badly needed to put their piecemeal results together.[1]

Indeed, the narrow gauged view of social reality results either in leaning too heavily on one aspect of that reality or reaching sterile, simple conclusions which might have been reached more easily through common sense and cursory observation. "A camel is a horse put together by a committee," goes a well-known aphorism. Social reality in the hands of specialists lacking an overarching principle or organization becomes such a curious specimen.

Too often today we don't even possess a camel. All we have before us are disparate bits and pieces of theoretical considerations and research endeavors. Someone is badly needed to put these piecemeal results together. Such a task requires a generalist of the highest order. As Professor Blanshard says, "some people think that knowledge has become so proliferated that the day has already gone by when any mind can repeat for our time what Aristotle and Hegel did for theirs." [2]

This may be true, but in sociological thinking a generalist of impressive breadth and depth has been at work during the past fifty years. Georges Gurvitch, about whom this book is written, has made his studies, presented his theory, given his critical analyses during a period in sociological

---

[1] Review article, of Harry Prosch, *"The Genesis of Twentieth Century Philosophy"* (New York: Doubleday and Co., 1964), *New York Times*, August 2, 1964, p. 7.

[2] *Ibid.*

vii

scholarship when general theory was out of style and such encompassing views were looked upon as detrimental to the scientific enterprise.

At present sociological thinking has reached a point where synthesis is required, an overview is essential. The associations of scholars in sociology are turning more and more to general theory and inquiries into the relationships between philosophy and sociology and between history and sociology. Experiences with nuclear research have led natural scientists to appreciate the indispensability of generalism in science. A general theory is required if specialists are to have any success. To rely alone on specialization is to narrow and limit the very enterprise of science which the specialist wishes to enhance. Without a general principle or principles one is hopelessly caught in the quagmires of minutia, trivia, and non-essentials. One loses perspective and direction for research. As Georges Gurvitch has frequently put it, our age suffers from a crisis of explanation. Social science scholarship often fails to meet the fundamental challenge of answering the question of *why*. Critic Dwight McDonald has trenchantly noted,

> Our mass culture—and a good deal of our high, or serious culture as well—is dominated by an emphasis on data and corresponding lack of interest in theory, by a frank admiration of the factual and an uneasy contempt for imagination, sensibility, and speculation.[1]

The gathering of facts has more prestige than the "artistic, ethical, or philosophical modes of apprehending reality." [2] We think "the mere accumulation of Facts is a sensible activity." [3] Finally, "we want to know how, what, who, when, where—everything but why." [4]

To approach seriously the question of *why* in social science means coming to grips with qualitative analysis as well as quantitative. This inevitably leads to the consideration of values and more importantly of the role of the observer in scientific exploration. Professor Gurvitch's work is valuable here because among other things he sees the im-

---

[1] *Against the American Grain* (New York: Random House, 1962), p. 392.

[2] *Ibid.*, p. 397.

[3] *Ibid.*, p. 397.

[4] *Ibid.*, p. 398.

portant task for sociology of explaining or giving at least some clue as to *why* modern man and society are what they are today. So much sociology is a maudlin endeavor, caught in pompous jargon, elaborating repeatedly the obvious, concerned with the unimportant, convinced statistical tables give it scientific respectability, so often bogged down in tedious rehearsal of factification, and spinning incomplete generalizations. As one wag says, "A half truth is like a half brick; both can be thrown twice as far."

Professor Gurvitch underlines the essential concern of sociology, explanation. He looks at the method by which such explanation is possible. He is aware of the revolutionary changes which twentieth century physics has brought about in the approach to a field of study and to explanation itself. His training in philosophy and history, gives him a wide, encompassing view and erudition sufficient to speak relevantly to the task of contemporary sociology. The compleat contemporary sociologist finds that the generalist's view is now required to offset the limitations of narrow specialization; a philosopher's sensitivity is needed to consider the place of values and see relationships among disparate findings as well as the relationship of the scholar to his field of observation; an historian's understanding of the roots of the past is essential in order to get at the task of explaining why we are what we seem to be.

Professor Gurvitch is such a generalist. He contributes to sociology at this crucial point. His is a significant attempt at bringing contemporary sociological thinking into focus. He raises important issues with which sociology must deal if it is to move from the confining quarters of too narrow a method and perspective to a more relevant and encompassing view of modern society and man.

CHAPTER I

SOCIOLOGY AND SOCIAL REALITY

This book is about the sociology of Georges Gurvitch. Professor Gurvitch held an influential position in mid-twentieth century European sociology. At the Sorbonne he occupied the chair once held by Emile Durkheim. Gurvitch is in many ways his continuator. On the other hand he started a whole new trend in sociology which has important implications for the entire field of theory.[1] This book seeks to give a general survey of his scholarship over the last fifty years; fifty years of prodigious, prolific activity.[2] His theoretical categories and critical acumen throughout this period make his work extremely valuable.

However, the range of Professor Gurvitch's interests and scholarly productivity makes it necessary to concentrate most heavily on a single dimension of his work. Gurvitch's study of groups is one of the most provocative, stimulating, and useful parts of his theory. Our central focus, therefore, is on his treatment of what he terms the macrosociological or horizontal view of social reality.

A dynamic, even revolutionary, contemporary reality is the emergence of numerous newly independent nations of Africa and Asia, all puzzling over the question of national identity as sovereign states. What does it mean to be a nation? Does a nation or group or grouping have a personality of its own? Is there a national consciousness, a reality to a nation or a group which is more than the sum of its individual parts? What is a group? What distinguishes it from an individual? As a newly independent country does such a state immediately possess this national consciousness, or is it developed by a certain reciprocity of perspectives on the part of the individual members and

[1] See Pitirim Sorokin's *Sociological Theories of Today* (New York: Harper and Row, 1966), chapter 14.
[2] Professor Gurvitch died in Paris, December, 1965.

different groups which together create the totality known as the nation? Gurvitch makes certain fundamental contributions in answering these questions. Recent observers of the African scene point to African nationalism and/or socialism as the unifying factor which these new nations are seeking to define and inculcate. History plays a vital part in any form of nationalism. Gurvitch's discussion of the necessary cooperation between history and sociology as well as among all the social sciences is important for an understanding of the current situation in Africa and for relevant scholarship in terms of the discipline of sociology itself.

Gurvitch's notion of the *total social phenomena* illuminates what is happening in Africa and other areas of rapid social change. This concept underlines Professor Gurvitch's notion of a society's totality, its wholeness. Indeed, he calls his approach *Gestalt* sociology. The *total social phenomena* are social reality. With this idea Gurvitch seeks to grasp the meaning of society. It is a symbol, an intermediary means to describe the richness and kaleidoscopic nature of each social whole. Professor Gurvitch emphasizes the basic complexity of social reality. It is manifestly difficult to grasp, comprehend, and understand the diverse, multi-faceted character of society. Yet it behooves the social scientist to try.

In this term, *total social phenomena,* Gurvitch is indebted to Marcel Mauss. In his study of the practice of *potlatch* among certain North American Indians, Mauss arrived at the notion of total social phenomena as a way of explaining this otherwise incomprehensible practice. He discovered that *potlatch* could not be explained by *one factor* alone. It could only be understood as the end product of many factors. Such elements must be seen as a totality. The different aspects must be viewed simultaneously as a whole. Gurvitch takes Mauss' concept, enlarges it both as a descriptive notion and a method. Both of these uses will be described in later chapters.[3]

One remaining aspect of Professor Gurvitch's theory is important for this era of revolutionary change. To describe what is happening in areas where entire culture patterns are disrupted and replaced is a major task of social science. Simplistic, unilateral views are insufficient and ultimately delusionary. Professor Gurvitch attempts to deal with the

---

[3] See Chapters 4 and 5.

revolutionary, irrational, dynamic characteristics of modern nations or societies. He looks at social reality as something more than what one meets on the surface. Below the obvious reside underlying, elemental, powerful forces which irresistibly affect the social body and produce both quiet and revolutionary change. Hence, a depth sociology is required as a companion to *Gestalt* sociology. These two basic views Gurvitch intrcduces and describes. They are the *idées forces* and the *passe partout* in comprehending his theory and its importance for contemporary sociology.

This book describes these notions with the hope certain hypotheses will emerge which will be useful for empirical research. We will subject these ideas to a critical examination in the light of both French and American sociology. Primarily we seek to explain the life work of an important theorist whose approaches to the task of sociology should stimulate and enhance the study of man in society—a study which is increasingly important as the character of contemporary life unfolds in all its richness, its possibilities, and its hazards.

The first part of the book is descriptive. Chapter two sketches briefly Gurvitch's life and background. His cultural heritage and intellectual journey are essential to an understanding of his thought.

The third chapter deals with Gurvitch's general theory, prefaced by Gurvitch's views on the present sociological situation. He outlines in several of his works the false or invalid problems which have sometimes concerned sociologists.[4] He contends these cultural survivals of the nineteenth century have caused undue difficulty for modern sociologists and have spuriously affected their work. This chapter concludes with a brief description of the actual role or task of modern sociology.

The concrete description of Gurvitch's general sociology gets underway in Chapter Four with the examination of the total social phenomena. His method is carefully outlined. Then follows the analysis of depth sociology. This is related to both his philosophical orientation and his work in jural sociology. His debt to Durkheim is particularly apparent in this discussion.

In Chapter Five the horizontal view of sociology, some-

---

[4] *La vocation actuelle de la sociologie* (Paris: Presses Universitaires de France, 1957), I, 29-62; *Traité de Sociologie* (Paris: Presses Universitaires de France, 1958), I, 28-64.

what comparable to Tonnies' *Gemeinschaft* and *Gesellschaft* and Durkheim's organic and mechanical solidarity, comes under scrutiny. Major attention is focused on the macrosociological aspects of this horizontal view, meaning the study of groups from the smallest to the largest. In this chapter we detail Gurvitch's typology of social groupings and social classes.

A precise analysis of the term social structure follows in Chapter Six. Gurvitch's definition of social structure is essentially a reaction to the functional and formalistic theories. His typology of global or inclusive societies concludes the discussion of social structure.

In Chapter Seven we analyze Gurvitch's dialectical method against the backdrop of the total social phenomena both in their vertical and horizontal manifestations. He contends this is the only method which can at once describe the individual parts of social reality while maintaining a view of the whole. His method also is inseparably bound up with sociology's object of study, the nature and essence of social reality.

Chapter Eight critically reviews Gurvitch's whole corpus of thought beginning with his early ideas on social law and natural law and ending with his general sociological theory and dialectical method. The concluding pages show the relevance Gurvitch's theory holds for current American sociology, i.e., how this system of thought challenges certain empirical trends; how this theory provides a valuable clue to the amazing complexity of social reality; finally, how this description of the total social phenomena helps modern sociology to fulfill some of the tasks which it faces in the contemporary world.

The sources for this work come from nineteen months of study with Professor Gurvitch in Paris, numerous letters exchanged in the interim since 1957, when the formal study with him ended, and personal interviews with Professor Gurvitch during the summer of 1960. His numerous publications serve as the focal point for this study. Certain secondary works which have included his theory in their analyses were also consulted.

The aim of this book is to explain an important scholar's ideas on sociology. This work then, is explanatory and analytical. The approach is not comparative, though certain comparisons are made. We seek primarily to fill a

4

void as well as present a challenge to those segments of sociology which are dangerously approaching an orthodoxy which might prevent the imaginative and creative directions to sociological thought in an age when social change is rapid and revolutionary, and demands our best efforts for its comprehension.[5]

One last justification: this century has witnessed a veritable revolution in the intellectual, cultural, and social life of man. Carlton J. Hayes, in his perceptive study, *A Generation of Materialism, 1871-1900,* sums it up:

> Hindsight is notoriously superior to contemporary judgment. Looking backward from 1914, or better from 1939, one can readily perceive a nemesis lurking in the era after 1871 such as was hardly perceptible at all at the fag end of that era in 1900. The mechanistic and materialistic conception of physical science . . . at the base of most of the thinking and much of the action of the era, was proved shortly afterwards to be erroneous. Thanks to the "quantum" theory which Planck set forth in 1901, to ensuing atomic investigations, and to the work of Einstein, the certitudes of physcal "law" eventually gave way to skepticism about "mechanics," "matter," and even "causation." [6]

Relativity and dynamism are the descriptive terms of our time. This new emphasis in the physical and natural sciences has been felt in the social sciences. This new physics has made an equally profound impact on the humanities. Instead of harmony there is emphasis on dissonance; dynamism over against the static, fluidity in place of rigidity, the dialectical in place of the linear, the discontinuous as opposed to the continuous.

In terms of social theory the neat simple explanations of the mid-nineteenth century, those theories resting on single, predominant factors to explain complex events and phenomena in social reality are no longer viable in our age. New concepts must be worked out to fit the knowledge which modern man possesses concerning his natural and

---

[5] Gurvitch's works have had extremely limited circulation in the United States. *The Spectrum of Social Time* (Dordrecht, Holland: D. Reidel Publishing Co., 1964) represented the first time one of his works appeared in English since *Twentieth Century Sociology* (1964), a study he edited with Wilbert E. Moore.

[6] (New York: Harper and Brothers, 1941), p. 339.

social environments. Georges Gurvitch has provided sociology with just this kind of theory. It is a theoretical system which fits the needs of this modern age. It is a theory which goes a long way towards explaining the complexity of man's life in its collective and individual manifestations. This theory in no way denies that there are patterns to man's behaviour, but neither does it try to reduce this patterning to some simple, convenient formula. There has always been a desire to establish the laws which govern society. Moreover, it was the desire of some precursors of modern sociology to establish sociology as a science. They felt this could ·be done through discovering the laws by which society works. Such a position betrays their close affinity with the Newtonian physics of their day. The new physics suggests otherwise. This is important for the social sciences. Social reality is complex and ever-changing; the results gained from research and the postulating of causal laws will necessarily have to be relative. This is depth sociology's greatest merit. Professor Gurvitch attempts to show in his theoretical system the dynamic, fluid, dissonant and dialectical nature of social reality.

In sum, Professor Gurvitch attacks the existential question of social reality. He attempts to present a dynamic theory by which to understand and explain society. He tries to spell out the complexity of this reality and yet retain its tentative, tenuous unity. He indicates how unrealistic and costly it is to treat only one part of human society at the expense of its other aspects. Even if one thinks he is being scientific by compartmentalizing human behaviour into convenient partitions, he is defeating his central purpose of understanding and explaining social reality. Man in his collective and individual life cannot be neatly divided into particular segments. Somehow there must be a wholistic, total approach. In this sense, the dialectical method of Gurvitch is essential. From another point of view, human behaviour cannot be reduced to one factor or to a limited number of factors which can be tested and observed by so-called scientific methods involving statistics and mathematics. This approach overlooks the truly "human" factor. Gurvitch is careful to point out that philosophy still has something to say to the social sciences without their having to espouse any particular, dogmatic philosophical position. Philosophy and history both are correctives to a sterile, cold, and one-sided approach to human behaviour so prevalent among certain students of sociology. Human reality cannot be reduced to mere statistics or sociological mazes, or described in sets of laws, or understood by certain observable functions. One must get below the mere surface of things. It behooves the contemporary social scientist to look at social reality from many different levels of human behaviour, thereby seeing the total social phenomena in their unity and diversity.

CHAPTER II

THE BACKGROUND AND LIFE OF GEORGES GURVITCH

Vivid historical events have a lasting effect on the character of an individual. Experiences through early life and during the formative years provide clues in understanding why a person thinks as he does. E. H. Carr, the British historian, gives the reason.

> The facts of history never come to us "pure" since they do not and cannot exist in a pure form: they are always refracted through the mind of the recorder. It follows that when we take up a work of history, our first concern should be not with the facts which it contains but with the historian who wrote it.[1]

What Carr declares about historians can be applied as well to sociologists. This is particularly important for an understanding of Professor Gurvitch's work. Much of the difficulty with his theory derives from a failure to understand his background.

The categories he uses to express his concepts, the language and symbols which couch his theory are the result of varied influences on his early intellectual life. Gurvitch pleads for explanation in sociology and through sociology. One of its tasks is to explain social reality in all its depths and ramifications. This requires interpretation. The past experience of an individual conditions his manner of interpretation. Gurvitch's particular view of social reality comes from his choice to fish in a certain part of the ocean; it results also from his choice of the type of tackle with which to do this job. The burden of this chapter is to discover

---

[1] Edward Hallett Carr, *What Is History?* (New York: Alfred A. Knopf, 1962), p. 24.

some of the social and psychological phenomena which constitute Gurvitch's personality and life.

Georges Gurvitch was born October 20, 1894, in Norworossisk on the Black Sea in Russia. At an early age his serious intellectual journey began. Gurvitch admits his thinking often shifted from one position to another. It is apparent there are contradictory influences in his intellectual make-up. At the age of fourteen he started reading philosophy and sociology. Early thinkers who influenced him were the Marxists, Kautsky, Plekhanov and Lenin. He read Karl Marx at sixteen but found him difficult to understand. Hegel made an initial impression on him but he became disenchanted with his ultimate synthesis of the ideal in the Prussian conception of the state subsuming at once society and the family.

He encountered after his *baccalauréat* such thinkers as Max Stirner (*L'unique et sa propriété*), Kierkegaard and Proudhon. These writers interested him because they demolished every artificial conception of social reality. He studied Kant and the neo-Kantians during the first years of his university training at Dorpat, Estonia (then part of Russia). He divided those first years, attending winter classes in Russia and summer sessions in Germany, concentrating on juridical studies and readings in Cohen, Cassirer, Richert, Windelband, Renouvier and Hamelin.

During his study with Wundt, Gurvitch became convinced it was impossible to make a direct parallelism between psychology and physiology. They each have their separate domains of study. This period was interlaced with the readings of Henri Bergson. This philosopher made a profound impression on Gurvitch's formative thought. In sum, Bergson eliminated the rigid determinism so evident in Hegel and the later Marx.

During the months just prior to World War I Gurvitch took courses under Emil Lask. He liked this thinker's rigorous dialectic, mostly borrowed from Fichte. Max Weber was an important influence at this juncture. His typological approach will be an important part of Gurvitch's sociological theory.[2]

Gurvitch won top prize in a university-wide essay competition with his monograph, *The Political Doctrine of Theophan Prokopovitch and His European Sources: Gro-*

---

[2] Class lecture by M. Faye, University of Paris, Nov. 27, 1956.

tius, Hobbes and Pufendorf. This victory persuaded him to prepare for a university career. In 1917 he was a *licencié* from the University of Petrograd and soon after completed his *agrégation.*

Certain key notions emerged from these early years of university training. They would stay with him throughout his career.

1) *Realism.* This occupies the primary position in his theory today. It has little to do with the concept of realism as set forth in the ancient controversy between nominalism and realism. Gurvitch means what the common usage of the term denotes, the actual as opposed to an abstraction or a figment. His basic aim is to grasp the real, to see the object so that it becomes absolute rather than relative, in the Bergsonian sense.[3] The intuitionism of two Russian philosophers, Lossky and Frank contributed to this development. Certain Slavophile ideas closely related to Russian Orthodox philosophy made their impact. Especially important were the notions of the real existence of the community (although it never absorbs the individual), the real community of conciliation in the Church (*sobornost*), the concept of a real rural community (*mir*). These are important contributions to Gurvitch's categories of the "We" and the dialectic of "reciprocity of perspectives" between the individual and the collective, and the possibility of an equilibrium between unity and diversity.[4]

Gurvitch distinguished between what is perceived by intuition and what is known (which presupposes a judgment).[5] The idea of a pluralism of realities attracted him. To quote Bergson as he does, "Philosophy requires a new effort for each new problem." [6] Implied here is the belief that each type of experience has an irreducible reality of its own. Moral experience therefore is a unique and separate type; juridical experience is also a certain specific type. This makes possible the separate study of these phenomena. Gurvitch bases the sociology of law and the sociology of the moral life on the concrete reality of certain specific types

---

[3] Henri Bergson, *An Introduction to Metaphysics* (New York: G. P. Putnam's Sons, 1913), pp. 8-9.

[4] René Toulemont, *Sociologie et pluralisme dialectique* (Louvain: Editions Nauwelaerts, 1955), pp. 6-7.

[5] The best discussion of this relationship is found in Gurvitch's *L'experience juridique et la philosophie pluraliste de droit* (Paris: Editions A. Pédone, 1955) pp. 13 ff.

[6] *Ibid.,* p. 13, from *La pensée et le mouvant,* p. 38.

of experience. There is a plurality of realities. One cannot reduce these realities to a monistic unity, to one substance, to make the multiple one. Gurvitch relates he found this absolute realism in the mature Fichte, who saw the multiplicity inherent in reality itself. He handled this diversity by emphasizing the competition and collaboration between intuition and dialectic.

2) Gurvitch's studies in the history of social philosophy and sociology led to his thesis for the Docteur dès Lettres, *L'ideé du droit social*, 1932. These studies concentrated on those thinkers who were both anti-individualistic, meaning those who affirmed the irreducibility of the social, and the anti-statists, those who refused to identify social totalities with one aspect of the whole—namely the state. Gurvitch carefully studied Grotius, Leibnitz, Fichte, Krause and Aristotle. (Indeed, the profound meaning of Aristotle's dictum, "Man is a political animal," coincides with Gurvitch's position.)

The enigmatic Rousseau played a large part in these early studies. Gurvitch noted Rousseau's propensity towards glorifying the State, coupled with a clearly contradictory affirmation of anarchy. Rousseau's thought contains both a radical individualism and a solid argument for the reality of the social fact. This is seen in his intriguing doctrine of the *General Will*. This "will" is not synonymous with the majority but is related to the "whole." Rousseau argued the "General Will" is present in each individual. Gurvitch's conception of the collective mind and its immanence in the individual mind has its inception in this suggestive idea of Rousseau. "The presence of the 'general will' in each individual makes it possible for the individual and society to have a new life thanks to the social contract drawn up between them."[7] Gurvitch notes that Rousseau's difficulty lay in his attempt to prove this social reality through the generality of individual reason. This is inadequate. Reason, says Gurvitch, is only one part of social reality.

Proudhon's contributions to social philosophy are fundamental in Gurvitch's thought. He emphasized the social as part and parcel of the participants' lives (unless these persons were alienated. Karl Marx's debt to Proudhon is apparent here). Social reality is neither transcendent to the

---

[7] Toulemont, *Sociologie et pluralisme* . . . , p. 6. See also Gurvitch's *Rousseau et la declaration des droits* (1917).

individuals involved nor even external to them. This is of fundamental importance to the thought of Gurvitch: Proudhon's basic social pluralism resolved in a constant struggle to attain a tenuous equilibrium among the multiple competing groups. His negative dialectic and a view that every social prognosis was relative coupled with an affirmation of creative humanity had an early influence on Gurvitch. Because of Proudhon's suggestive ideas Gurvitch read the French theorists of revolutionary syndicalism.

3) Precisely at the time he was reading the French syndicalists and Proudhon, the Russian revolutions of February and March, 1917, occurred. For Gurvitch the personal impact of these events was immense. The factory soviets were coming into being. These so-called "councils" elected their own representatives to central soviets (councils) who carried out the larger-scale decision making. More importantly the members of the factory and local soviets began to identify and solve their own problems in a democratic way. Gurvitch observed this process and the gradual possession of political power on the part of the factory soviets which led to the creation of management councils responsible for the economic complex itself. His ideal of a decentralized government and a democratically planned economy comes directly from this experience. This direct contact with the revolutions had a profound effect on his intellectual maturing. In his own words

> In observing, in living through the various reactions of the divergent milieux, groups, classes, syndicates, cells, councils; observing and living the literal formation of new organizations, the activity of established ones, watching the almost total explosion of the prerevolutionary global social structure, I found several ideas which led me to my sociological studies:
>
> 1) Social law being born spontaneously, fully independent of the state and its juridical order and free to enter into various relationships with the law of the state.
>
> 2) The depth levels of social reality in which their hierarchy and their relationships are completely reversed; these levels contradict each other from time to time and interpenetrate at other junctures.

3) The groups seen as a microcosm of forms of sociability.

4) The global society and social classes viewed as macrocosms of groups.

5) The possibility of a collectively planned economy without the rigid control of the state and based on a pluralistic democratic economy with a federalist conception of property.[8]

Gurvitch goes on to relate:

So well I remember a walk with my wife along the banks of the Karpovka in Leningrad. During that spring evening in the year 1920, several months before leaving Russia, I laid out before her the principal conceptions of my sociology upon which I would elaborate; also the principal concepts of my thesis on social law and finally my conception of a decentralized, collectively planned economy.[9]

Gurvitch was to teach one year at the University of Petrograd-Leningrad after receiving his *agrégation*. In October, 1920, he left Russia. He took with him as the sole contents of his luggage, notes for three books: one on Fichte, another on the concept of social law, and a third on the scales and levels of social reality. He felt obligated to leave Russia when all hope vanished that a truly pluralistic state based on decentralized democratic principles could become reality. He also disagreed with the decision to draw up a peace treaty with Germany.

Upon leaving Russia he went to the University of Prague where for five years he taught in the Russian Institute. During these years he concentrated on the phenomenology of Husserl. He had extended conversatons wth Max Scheler whose popularity in Germany was particularly great at that time. Important to Gurvitch's development were the notion of Husserl on the open conscience (intentionality—direction towards . . .) and Scheler's intuitionism at once affective and realist.[10] From these two men Gurvitch gained a fundamental appreciation of the emotional, affective side

---

[8] *Mon itineraire* . . . , p. 7-8.

[9] *Ibid.*, p. 8.

[10] Both Gurvitch's study and the experience of the Russian revolutions had taught him that the irrational factors of social life play a large part in the movement and change which goes on at the interior of social reality.

of social life—an indispensable aspect if one were to succeed in comprehending social reality.

Fichte—primarily the mature Fichte—provided the key for comprehending the complex phenomena of social reality with his concept of dialectical realism. The *sine qua non* of being to Fichte is the realm of the Spirit (the *transpersonal* or *trans-subjective*), the area of the human will which responds to the call of duty. This leads towards the constantly creative aspects of existence. Gurvitch reworks this notion of the transpersonal; it becomes the basis for his sociology of law, religion, morals, etc., falling under the general classification of sociology of the spirit. Such an absolute realism may lead towards the other aspect of the real world, namely the *transobjective* which results in the stability of being and becomes the system of logical essences denoted by Fichte and Gurvitch as Logos. This Logos is anterior to the subject or observer and hence is real. It is beyond the material domain and, in this sense, is ideal. Gurvitch understands the *transpersonal* as the active side, the willing, creative element which becomes the basis for Fichte's ethic. This, in turn, becomes for Gurvitch the spontaneous, effervescent, creative level of social reality, the infrastructure in the vertical view of social life. The *transobjective* (the Logos) serves as the foundation for Fichte's logic and becomes the superstructure, the external, the superficial layer of social reality in Gurvitch's theory. Like Fichte, Gurvitch sees a great conflict being waged between *creation* and *system,* between the *infrastructure* and the *superstructure:* "these two sectors of reality are separated by an *irrational hiatus.* But as a result of these conflicts bridges are thrown over this abyss. They are named conscience, society, and cultural works which are always linked to the superficial." [11]

Finally, Gurvitch discovered through Fichte the impossibility of bridging the abyss between the *trans-subjective* and the *transobjective* without the combined efforts of the dialectic and intuition. The wedding of these two approaches will be the foundation of his method.

In sum, the work with Fichte, the study he had made of Husserl, his conversations with Max Scheler, the influence of the French social philosophers and the intuitionism of Bergson combined with his Russian heritage and the

---

[11] *Ibid.,* p. 9.

indelible impressions of the Russian revolutions make up the tapestry of Gurvitch's formative experience. Thus endowed he had left Russia, sojourned briefly in Prague and located permanently in France. Once settled he began immediately to prepare his thesis on the *Idea of Social Law*. He immersed himself in juridical literature, sociology, socialist thought, and French syndicalist writings. Proudhon came in for another period of careful scrutiny along with Auguste Comte and his followers. Durkheim and his disciples were critically studied. Among them were Marcel Mauss, Lucien Levy-Bruhl and Maurice Halbwachs. Mauss gave Gurvitch the concepts which become the central symbols of his theoretical system: the ideas of *total social phenomena* and the *whole man*.

The philosophers Frederic Rauh, Leon Brunschvicg and Jean Wahl exerted important influence on his thought. Rauh's radical empiricism, Brunschvicg's struggle against every attempt to atrophy reason and idealism, and Wahl's dialectic made their mark.

During this period Gurvitch at the request of Leon Brunschvicg delivered a series of public lectures on "Current Tendencies in German Thought." These were published in 1930 under the title *Les tendances actuelles de la philosophie allemande*.

His central thesis was that the whole tenor of German philosophy had changed from that which existed some thirty years before and up to the First World War. The neo-Kantian philosophy had been supplanted by a new spirit, phenomenology. This philosophical tendency proposed a new and unknown method, a method which opened up avenues of thought and exploration seldom before conceived as supportable. The reworking of Newtonian physics had a profound effect upon philosophy. Freud's early work also entered into this new stream of philosophical thinking.

1. THE JURIDICAL PHASE

The book on German philosophy was only an interlude in the actual program which Gurvitch pursued at this time. His main concern was the preparation of his *L'idée du droit social*, 1932,[12] the main outline of which he had brought with him from Russia. This is a monumental effort to show the real basis for law. His thesis will have to be explored in detail since it stands as the real foundation upon which his

---

[12] (Paris: Recueil Sirey, 1932).

15

future work will rely. Gurvitch's ambition in this project was great. In the broad overview the two theses actually written[13] show first that sociology of law occupies a superior position to that of the more juridical techniques which are a part of any political state; and second, social law, the non-political law so often neglected by jurists, is engendered by each collectivity, each group, each class, sometimes spontaneously and sometimes through customs, precedents and mores. This law can be an explosive and compelling force, as this age attests.

> "What is Law?" has been asked by priests and poets, philosophers and kings, by masses no less than by prophets. A host of answers might be given yet the answer to the question remains one of the most persistent and elusive problems in the entire range of thought. For one may well view the entire gamut of human life, both in thought and in action, as being comprised within the word Law.[14]

This statement by Henry J. Abraham is a good beginning for this consideration of Gurvitch's concept of social law. It suggests the richness of this word. Law is not simply formal in the sense that legislative bodies have made laws and other bodies promulgate those laws and administer them. Law is informal as well. Mr. Abraham quotes from the work of James Coolidge Carter.

> Law, Custom, Conduct, Life—different names for almost the same thing—true names for different aspects of the same thing—are so inseparably blended together that one cannot be even thought of without the other. No improvement can be effected in one without improving the other, and no retrogression can take place in one without a corresponding decline in the other.[15]

This description goes a long way in illustrating what is commonly meant by informal law. The notion of social law is related.

---

[13] *L'idée* . . . and *Le temps present et l'idée du droit social* (Paris: Vrin, 1932) are Gurvitch's two theses for his doctorate. The former was his principal thesis

[14] Henry J. Abraham, *The Judicial Process* (New York: Oxford University Press, 1962), p. 5.

[15] *Law: Its Origin, Growth and Function* (New York: The Knickerbocker Press, 1907), p. 320, quoted in *Ibid.*, p. 5.

Social law is the law created and embodied in collectivities of all types. It is the law which is alongside and underneath individual law. The law of the state itself rests on social law. From all that modern anthropology declares it is apparent civilization derives from the necessary cooperation of persons for survival. Biology has illustrated that the success of the creature, man, comes from his intense sociability. This social solidarity is a result both of biological heredity and the reasoned desire for well-being. The political philosophers who have stressed community purpose and collective values have a long historical record to support them. The present concerns about natural law and world order are in part real longings for that primitive solidarity which has been broken by an irresponsible individualism.

> The sense of common purpose implied in Aristotle's dictum . . . goes back to the earliest beginnings; the inherited instincts of humanity are against an unbridled individualism, and the majority of political thinkers have greatly overestimated the rationality of mankind.[16]

Gurvitch struggles against every anarchical view of social life and any thoroughgoing rationalistic concept of political order. He asserts that historically and at present law must be defined in its widest sense. Examination of the early riverine civilizations indicates the growth of social solidarity intertwined with social law and the more formal manifestations of that law created by the political systems which arose out of organizational necessity.

What then is social law?

> Social law is for us the autonomous law of communion by which each active, concrete, and real totality is integrated in an objective fashion. This social law incarnates a positive value. It is a law of integration. It is distinguished from the law of coordination (the order of individual law) and the law of subordination. These latter two are solely recognized by the systems of juridical individualism and unilateral universalism.[17]

---

[16] John Bowle, *Western Political Thought* (London: Methuen, 1961), p. 4.

[17] *L'idée* . . . , pp. 11-12.

17

There are, then, three great branches of law for Gurvitch: 1) social law which is the law of communion, integration and fusion; 2) individual law which is based on interpersonal, interindividual relationships; and 3) subordinative law which is the law characteristic of non-democratic states. This last type is founded on a heterogeneous system of individual law. For example the rule of a paternalistic owner over the interior organization of a factory or a capitalist industry is for Gurvitch a perversion of the social law which is immanent to the "whole" of the factory. This rule of the owner is based on the individual law which is derived from the interindividual relationships of the owner and the other members of the factory.

As a clue to the total thought of Gurvitch concerning law it should be noted his general polemic is against an individualism which neglects the social facts of life. More precisely, he contends against every kind of juridical individualism. A way of summing up his general aim would be to say he is seeking a synthesis between individualism and universalism (autocracy and dictatorial legal arrangements) by way of a *transpersonalism*.[18]

Gurvitch sees the whole as distinct from the sum of its individual members. The social group is real. This is in keeping with the Durkheimian tradition. He parts company with Durkheim when the latter asserts the totality is transcendant to the individual persons. The social group is not an entity against which they struggle nor in which they find the means to identity; it is not a superior personality nor an element which goes beyond the self. Rather it is a superconscious activity, immanent in each person and derived from the ensemble of their actions.

> In this sense of reciprocal co-penetration between superconscious activity and conscious action, the transpersonal whole symbolized by the term 'We', can be characterized as an immanent totality.[19]

The key word to describe this real social whole is the "We." It is distinguished from those coordinative relationships which serve as the basis for individual law or the juridical arrangements based on legal commerce between persons. The pronouns which illustrate this type are "I," "you," "he," "they" and "them." The "We" feeling or sense

---

[18] *Ibid.*, p. 111 for a particularly fine discussion of this synthesis.
[19] *Ibid.*, pp. 9-10. Footnote 3.

gives rise to integration or communion or extensive cooperation which alone make possible social law.[20] Moreover Gurvitch feels this law of integration, or social law, is important because it alone can grasp the essential problems which are present in the new types of institutions of the present era: vast labor unions, industrial democracies, federalism, social parliamentarianism, the growing importance of international law over national law plus socialism without *étatism*. This suggests a pluralism to juridical orders which are simultaneously interdependent and mutually limiting in their activity. These various juridical entities (in the broad sense here) collaborate on an equal footing within national and international communities. "This pluralism and all the institutions which cause it cannot be understood juridically apart from the idea of social law." [21]

This means that a new conception of power is implicit in the theory of social law. The state cannot alone provide the naked force sufficient to bring autonomous groups into a cooperative endeavor. This was the dream of Proudhon that the balance of power be effected between the state and the economic groupings. This is possible because a new type of justice resting on the transpersonalism of the "We" activity comes into being. It is the justice of social law; such a justice brings about a synthesis between commutative justice (the outcome of individualism) and distributive justice (the product of universalism) resulting in an integrative, transpersonal justice carried out by social law. There are seven essential parts to Gurvitch's definition of social law:

1) The general function of social law: an objective integration of a totality by provision for the fusion of all its members.

2) The foundation of its obligatory force: the dynamic creation of this law in a direct manner by the very same totality which integrates it.

3) The object of social law: the regulation of the internal life of the totality.

4) Intrinsic structure of the corresponding juridical relationship: a direct participation by the whole in the functioning of the law without the necessary intermediary of an organization.

5) Its external manifestation: a social power which

---

[20] *L'idée* . . . , p. 18.
[21] *Ibid.*, p. 14.

is not normally linked with unconditional coercion. 6) Its realization in certain organizations: the primacy of the unorganized expressions which give an equal opportunity to participation. 7) The subject to which organized social law addresses itself: the complex collective person.[22]

Each of these characteristics needs to be expanded. The following discussion will take up each of these attributes of social law:

1. *The general function of social law.* Integration is the general function. This function is opposite to that of coordination which characterizes individual law. The concept of integration is closely allied to the idea of *totality.*

> The social "whole" represents in its essence a mobile and concrete system of equilibria based on a fusion of "reciprocal perspectives," a system which is dynamic and where the irreducible elements of multiplicity and unity, individual and universal, tend to be synthesized in a fashion which is perpetually changing.[23]

Integration into this social whole results in its ideal form, in a real social group which is dynamic and immanently a part of each member. It cannot be reduced to a simple unity, nor is it a conglomeration of dispersed atoms which have as their sole link some common abstract law to which they have submitted. Integration is mutual participation and implication. Coordination is merely cooperation. Put another way, integration is an attempt to realize at the empirical level the values of the transpersonal spirit. This concept of Fichte is the means by which a synthesis is realized between the multiple and the one, between the individual and the universal. The synthesis resides in the *moral ideal,* in the superconscious creator Spirit (the "We"). The creator Spirit is composed of persons, values in themselves, who participate in its activity. This transpersonal Spirit is the *immanent* totality, "where the one and the multiple are produced reciprocally in a continuous movement of mutual participation."[24] This is not simply a moral ideal but an essential tendency of all real social beings.

---

[22] *L'idée* . . . , p. 17.
[23] *Ibid.,* p. 17.
[24] *Ibid.,* p. 17.

To be integrated in this totality is to be a part of the production of this totality. "The members integrated in a totality, participating in its dynamic unity . . . enter into certain relations of communion, of partial communal fusion in what is called the 'We' and not into relationships of opposition (me, you, him) which are characteristic of coordination." [25]

In other terms, integration is a centripetal movement experienced in an immediate and direct way. Coordination and subordination are movements in the opposite directions resulting in multiplicity or centrifugal action. [26]

One might say this conflict between integration and coordination is the perpetual battle waged at the heart of every group. The unity of the group is dependent upon a moving, dynamic equilibrium serving as the foundation of group life.

Law in its integrative function goes beyond negativism, restraint and coercion. It is positive. Its work is towards peace, union and order.

2. *The problem of authority.* The very essence of the real group's social cohesiveness is the obligatory force it maintains over its members. Such an authority comes from the totality itself. An interior order, derived from some outside source and imposed on a group, is no longer the law of integration but the law of subordination. "Social law always derives its obligatory force from the direct authority of the whole by which it regulates the interior life of that totality." [27]

This source of authority or obligatory force comes from what Gurvitch calls the *normative facts.* These will be discussed later with the relationship of law and justice. Suffice it to say these normative facts are derived from the totality and become at the same time the basis for that totality's cohesion.

3. *The object of social law.* Its unique object is to integrate the totality, to make it into a whole whereby it may enter into the external affairs of group life. Such an entry into these affairs will take one of two avenues: either the group will be treated as an individual or it will be integrated into a larger unity. In the first instance it will submit to an individual law; in the second it will be subject to

---

[25] *Ibid.,* p. 18.
[26] *Ibid.,* p. 19.
[27] *Ibid.,* p. 19.

a social law, but one which is different from that of its own making.[28]

4. *The structure of social law.* There is a unique type of relationship belonging to the concrete social grouping. The members participate mutually and directly in the totality of this group. This participation itself serves as the basis for their regulation and creates a liaison or bond among the various members which has a character all its own. The essence of that liaison is discovered in the mutual penetration of obligations and claims on the part of the members. Again one can note Gurvitch's debt to Fichte. In summary

> the group holds together because this is a con-
> crete system in which the individual participates;
> where the part is no longer a part but a function-
> ing and dynamic element and where unity and
> multiplicity are produced mutually in a recipro-
> cally functional relationship. This category of the
> *concrete system* precedes all juridical construc-
> tion.[29]

There is no need for an intermediary structure, though such an organization is not precluded. "That which imposes these mutually cooperative acts is not some nonexistent organization but the value of the life in common, the total as an equilibrium for all its members." [30]

5. *Social power as its external manifestation.* The power which the group holds over its individual members is derived from the totality itself. The social whole incarnates this social power. It is "a function of 'social service' to the end of maintaining the totality itself." [31] This power once again does not depend upon the existence of certain organizations to be effective. Such power can use unconditional coercion but it is infrequent. Every collectivity can impose obligations on its members. Such force does not rest on power alone. It comes from the element of unity within the totality. As Talleyrand counseled Napoleon, "It is difficult to sit for a long time on a naked sword." No group can depend upon raw power alone for any length of time. The element of the social law, which is the product of the collectivity, will ultimately contain the foundation of legitimacy.

---

[28] Toulemont, *Sociologie et pluralisme* . . . , pp. 86-87.
[29] *Op. cit.*, p. 23.
[30] *Ibid.*, pp. 21-22.
[31] *Ibid.*, p. 23.

Such a legitimacy may be expressed as a majority action or as a direct action of a group representing the collectivity. Individual law cannot express social power. Subordinative law, because of its mixed character, can express a social law of domination, which is a perverted type. The concept of legitimacy is a crucial problem today. Gurvitch contends some notion of social law is needed to resolve this question. So many jurists and students of law have placed an excessive and sometimes exclusive emphasis on the role of individual law; this invariably tempts them to place some sort of power above the law. They have gone so far as to declare this power essential to the very existence of law. This has led to the distorted estimation of the state as that power over and above the law. "Only the theory of social law which finds the precise place of power in the juridical system and constructs this power as an immanent structure of 'the law of integration' is master of the situation." [32]

Gurvitch makes some crucial observations on the nature of social power in a democratic state.

> The power in a democratic state is not a power of domination but of integration in the subjacent, political community. It is founded on the social law which emerges from this community and not on a subordinate law. Because this law of political integration is sanctioned by an unconditional constraint does not transform it into a law of subordination, but only condenses it into a social law of an altogether particular kind: *social law condensed and opposed to pure social law.*[33]

6. *The relationship of unorganized social law to the organized level of social reality.* This characteristic merely underlines the well-spring from which come the *normative facts,* those transpersonal values which are products of the totality and are also products of that level of social life which is unorganized. "The impersonifiable authority of social law is completely independent of the existence of organization, and the organized social power relies on the purely objective social power of the unorganized, subjacent community." [34] This subjacent community is vastly

---

[32] *L'idée* . . . , p. 25.
[33] *Ibid.*, p. 28.
[34] *L'idée* . . . , p. 29.

different from its organized levels. It is richer, more irrational, and remains impervious to all attempts to capture and categorize it definitively. What one is able to see of this unorganized level is only a portion of what is really there. "It is limitless in content—this substructure upon which all the rest stands." [35]

7. *The subject of organized social law is the complex collective person.* The law of coordination is interindividual or intergroup. These are simple unities. However, the law of integration or social law deals with complex systems of interaction. These complex persons are unities "in which the members conserve their partial personalities at the heart of the total personality." [36] Cooperatives and economic and political federations and confederations are examples of what Gurvitch means by complex collective persons.

Thus social law seeks to bring unity out of multiplicity without denying such a plurality. It finds this unity in the common values in which it directly participates. These *normative facts* hold together the interior life of the collectivity by a social power that is most generally free from necessity to use unconditional coercion. This social law finds obligatory force in these *normative facts* which are the products of an unorganized level of activity characterized by a reciprocal relationship among the members, involving both claims and obligations on the part of all.

What is social law about? What is its underlying purpose? Before these questions can be answered, one must deal with the problem of justice. Law and justice are intertwined.

I. JUSTICE.

Gurvitch sees justice as more than either commutative or distributive. In fact social justice synthesizes the two and transcends them. It reaches the transpersonal, collective level while preserving the integrity of the individual. The history of this concept of justice is long. It extends back to the Greeks, to Hebrew religion and to the Christian fathers. From earliest times two strains developed: first, an individualistic interpretation leading to commutative justice, and second, a universal conception espousing certain timeless principles and leading to the idea of distributive justice or "to each his due." Leibnitz, Grotius, and Wolff are early

[35] *Ibid.*, p. 28-29.
[36] *Ibid.*, p. 32.

formulators of the contemporary concept of social justice. Society involves the cooperation of beings endowed with reason. Justice is communal. There is no conflict between the individual and the universal, or the microcosm and the macrocosm. Rather justice is the synthesis of the whole with its parts. Such a justice is objective since an objective equilibrium of certain principles is imposed on the individual consciousness; it is superior to every individual or collective will.[37]

Proudhon, in the tradition of Leibnitz, Fichte and Krause, proposed the socialization of justice. For him justice makes possible the conciliation of the whole with its parts. Both are equally real. There is then a balancing of personal and transpersonal values which are equally positive.

> Justice is at once objective and subjective, real and formal, or rather it transcends these opposites because it integrates individuals in a transpersonal, antihierarchical order, in which every individual maintains his own dignity precisely to the extent that he is an indispensable member of a community that cannot be reduced to the sum of its parts. Justice demands the realization of an order which is neither communism nor despotism, nor atomism, nor anarchy, but Liberty in order and independence in unity. It is through "mutualism," the interplay of collaborative associations and their federations, through the humanization of property by its transformation into a social function in the hands of cooperative associations and through counterbalancing of the state by organized economic societies that justice can best be approximated.[38]

Gurvitch's debt to Proudhon becomes obvious in this conception of justice. His course at the Sorbonne on Proudhon, published under the title, *Les fondateurs français de la sociologie contemporaine: Saint-Simon et P. -J. Proudhon,* makes this even more explicit.[39] Proudhon's concept of justice as a positive and dynamic element leads Gurvitch to see justice as the way of resolving conflicts and anti-

---

[37] Georges Gurvitch, "Justice" in the *Encyclopedia of Social Sciences*, Seligman, ed. (New York: The Macmillan Company, 1930), VIII, 512.

[38] *Encyclopedia* . . . , VIII, 512.

[39] (Paris: Centre de Documentation Universitaire, 1955), pp. 4-6.

nomies at the heart of every society. Simple explanations of
the causes of these conflicts will not do.

> Only the principle of the synthesis of individualism
> and universalism, which excludes any tendency to
> reduce the a priori values of the whole and of the
> individual, the one to the other, but which recog-
> nizes them as equivalent, can permit the problem
> of justice to be grasped in all its importance.[40]

Where does the problem of justice lie? It resides in the
discrepancy between the ideal realm of the moral where
there is a perfect synthesis of the personal and transpersonal (individualism and universalism) and the real world
where a fierce conflict takes place between these values. The
gap between the ideal and the actual is the problem area.
This gap is filled in a tentative way by justice. "Justice is
an essential medium for the moral ideal, an a priori condition for its realization. It is its necessary ambiance, it
shines with its reflected light; in its shelter alone the moral
ideal may display its richly individualized and complex tis-
sues." [41] The moral ideal and the tentative arrangement of
justice are inseparably bound together. Yet they are clearly
distinguishable from each other. They have different structures which make it possible for this distinction to be made.

The moral ideal is alogical or irrational as Fichte expressed it. Justice is that step towards rationalization.

> The moral ideal is accessible only through action,
> through a "volitive intuition," consisting in the
> participation on the transpersonal plane of pure
> creative activity, in which each must act in a man-
> ner absolutely dissimilar from that of all others,
> discovering by that very fact his place in the whole
> of creative activity.[42]

This immediate moral ideal needs to be translated into
real life, into general terms. The means of logic cool off
the white heat of this moral experience and put it into
defined categories for application in the life of society. "It
(logic) arrests the intuition-action and amalgamates it
into a judgment. Justice is midway between morality and
logic." [43] Intuition changes to recognition in the act of

---

[40] *Op. cit.*, p. 513.
[41] *Loc. cit.*
[42] *Ibid.*, p. 513.
[43] *Experience juridique* . . . , p. 100.

judgment. This is very different from the direct experiencing of this moral value. Gurvitch gives the example of listening to a symphony concert. One may not like the music but this does not stop him from feeling a sense of injustice when certain noises are made which disturb the listening of this music for others.

> It is precisely to this act of recognition of the moral ideal that justice applies itself, and the values which depend on it are consecutive to moral values. Through this act of recognition, strongly impregnated with intellectual elements and presenting the amalgam of a judgment and an action, the logicalization and the generalization of the irrational qualities of the moral ideal are achieved.[44]

These moral experiences are individualized and incomparable. Justice generalizes from these experiences, which is indeed necessary if these moral values are to be relevant. Hence a "certain schematic stability is substituted for creative movement; a quantitative element for the ensemble of pure qualities." [45] Justice derives its creative force from the very fact that it never cuts itself off from its source, but it utilizes the elements of quantification, generalization and stability in order to be relevant. Clearly, moral experience has its own structure which is different from this of justice. Thereby the two can be distinguished and recognized, though they must never be separated. There are certain affinities between this concept of justice and that of Reinhold Niebuhr.[46] His theory that justice is a tentative approximation of order reflecting the ultimate value of Agape is similar to this idea held by Gurvitch.

II. LAW.

"Law is always an attempt to realize justice." [47] This attempt to realize justice depends upon the variables in the given social milieu. This is the basis for Gurvitch's relativism which forces him to rule out the existence of natural law. Law remains law only so long as it seeks to realize

---

[44] *Op. cit.*, p. 514.
[45] *Experience juridique* . . . , p. 100.
[46] Reinhold Niebuhr, *An Interpretation of Christian Ethics* (New York: Harper and Brothers, 1935), is his clearest statement on justice.
[47] *L'idée* . . . , p. 96.

justice. It becomes something else, something deformed and perverted, if justice is not its goal. The logic of the idea runs like this: one cannot define law without first defining justice; justice is tied to values which make it axiological; the values closest to justice are moral ones, based on the Fichtean criterion of the moral ideal. Starting then with law, what are its characteristics?

1. According to Gurvitch the "rule of law is distinguished from the moral rule by a deterministic or precise and final character. Moral precepts are indefinite and infinite by nature." [48] The juridical rule is general in its expression and stable in form. The moral rule is creative, dynamic and individualized. Law has a more defined logical and rational structure than justice. It is both a norm and a judgment showing the necessary liaison between the law and the moral truth. "In other words the law is a judgment of value and a judgment of reality." [49] To explain more clearly the relationship of justice, moral value and law, Gurvitch has this to say:

> The relationship of justice and law is much nearer that between a logical category and the object constituted by that category. Justice plays the role of the Logos rather than of the ideal of law. The moral ideal is essentially opposed, inasmuch as it is unrealizable, to empirical morality and cannot be embodied in the latter; by its nature it can only exercise a "regulative" function with regard to the moral point of view. Justice on the contrary inasmuch as it is strongly impregnated with logical values, has the faculty of forming law directly: it does not oppose law so much as constitute it. Justice cannot serve as a basis of criticism and appreciation of the law because it is one of the elements of it.[50]

This clarification helps to sharpen the distinction between these levels of juridical life. Such a life has as its goal justice which in reality deals with the relationships of persons.

2. Law seeks to establish a perfect correspondence between the duties and claims of all the members of a given

---

[48] *Ibid.*, p. 104.
[49] *Loc. cit.*
[50] *Encyclopedia* . . . , p. 514.

collectivity. "The structure of juridical rule is essentially bilateral or more precisely, multilateral, while the structure of the moral rule is unilateral." [51] For order to prevail each person shares certain obligations and claims with the other persons of his totality. This is the task of law. Gurvitch calls this the imperative-attributive character of law. The great legal philosopher, Petrazhitsky, developed this notion.[52] Even earlier Fichte had described this relationship in detail. Moral values are uniquely imperative. This underlines the social character of law. When these values are relativized and generalized they take on their multilateral character (imperative-attributive) and in this way become social. The real intent of law is justice, which is interpreted by Gurvitch to mean security, peace and a stable social order. The beginning of a conciliation between the personal and the transpersonal values occurs at this point.

> The interdependence of reciprocal duties and claims forms in its achievement social order. The achievement of juridical reciprocities, supposing the reality of the other self, as far as a center of desires and claims and its interdependence with duties give law in general its character of a phenomenon linked essentially to the social life.[53]

Gurvitch in this statement shows once again his reliance on Fichte and Scheler for this understanding of the other self and the activity of the self as the center of claims and duties.[54]

Such a law incorporating within it the interdependence of claims and duties can be expressed in three different ways:

a. It can be *coordinative*. These claims and duties are expressed in a subject-object relationship, in an interpersonal, intergroupal manner.

b. This law can be *subordinative*. The corresponding

---

[51] *L'idée* . . . , p. 104.

[52] In the Encyclopedia of Social Sciences, XII, Gurvitch wrote the article on Petrazhitsky and his work. He points out that Petrazhitsky indicated "while moral emotions and their immediate data have a 'unilateral' and simple 'imperative' character, juridical emotions have a bilateral or imperative-attributive character." p. 103.

[53] *Op. cit.*, p. 105.

[54] See the footnote in *L'idée* . . . , p. 105, for an explanation of this idea of Fichte.

claims and duties are expressed in a master-servant, ruling elite-obeying community relationship.

c. The law can be *integrative*. This is the level of social law where the claims and duties of the whole and its members are affirmed in common. The interdependence is intensified since there is a partial fusion of all in the totality.[55]

3. The hint of this third characteristic has already been given. Each rule of law is the element of a system, a whole, a complex order. "An imperative-attributive rule detached from the social system in which it is incorporated would not be able to realize its multilateral relationship." [56] The existence of the imperative-attributive relationship implies the existence of a social order. Order is impossible without it. Law is pre-eminently social.

4. The same order of positive law must recognize the same values if the imperative-attributive relationship is to exist. The same rules of law must be obeyed in the same given social milieu. This becomes the fourth characteristic of law. Here Gurvitch affirms the notion that the rule of law cannot be above, beyond or autonomous from the given social setting. If it is, it is ineffective, which means it fails to realize justice. This leads inexorably to its ceasing to be law. Because law must be relevant to the given social setting, law is made positive. It cannot be otherwise or it becomes autonomous. This in reality is Gurvitch's way of resolving the problem of the normative and the relative. The *normative facts* or the common values of a given totality are expressed through positive law in two different ways: the formal statement of these *normative facts* through the techniques of law Gurvitch calls formal positive law; to the direct and immediate apprehension of these *normative facts* he gives the name of intuitive positive law.[57] It is Gurvitch's belief this latter form is the "natural law" about which contemporary jurists and theorists speak. When he denies the autonomous nature of law, Gurvitch does not mean to deprive law of all normative content. This would reduce it to mere techniques and systems, which has so plagued the conceptions of law since the last of the nineteenth century. In fact this error has given rise to the renewed discussions on "natural law." There was a deep

---

[55] *L'idée* . . . , p. 106.
[56] *Loc. cit.*
[57] *L'idée* . . . , p. 107.

awareness that something was amiss. In reality, the law is a complex phenomenon which plays an intermediary role. It is an attempt to move between heteronomy and autonomy, between the normative and the totally relative. "Law is an intermediary as justice is an intermediary between the moral ideal and the Logos." [58]

5. The fifth characteristic of law is its option to use coercion as a means of effecting its rule. Moral laws on the other hand can never use constraint since they have an indeterminate character and an irrational aspect to their existence. This option to use coercion does in no way imply such constraint is necessary. There are numerous laws which never require physical coercion for their compliance. For instance the laws regulating the Houses of Congress are adhered to from a sense of obligation and "lawabidingness." "In fact one may go so far as to say law which is sanctioned by physical force finds its underlying authority in a level of law which is not so sanctioned, and that all organized law rests on non-organized law." [59] Gurvitch proceeds to give some of the best arguments ever assembled to refute the validity of force as the basis for compliance to law. He uses as a source Petrazhitsky in his *Théorie generale du droit et de l'état.*[60] In *L'idée*, Gurvitch cites Rousseau's splendid argument on the futility of reducing the legitimacy of political power to that of coercion. Logically it would follow that law, since it is not dependent upon physical coercion, is not dependent upon the state. The theories of *étatism* always forget that the *conditional* coercion of the non-political organizations exerts a preponderance of influence over the citizens and leads directly to their propensity towards compliance. "Obviously custom, tradition, education and indoctrination play a prominent part in developing habits of compliance in the citizens of the political community." [61]

These five characteristics lead to this definition of law.
The law is a positive order which represents an attempt to realize Justice in a given social milieu

---

[58] *Ibid.*, p. 108.
[59] *L'idée* . . . , p. 109.
[60] *Ibid.*, p. 111.
[61] Peter H. Odegard, Robert K. Carr, Marver H. Berstein and Donald H. Morrison, *American Government: Theory, Politics and Constitutional Foundation* (New York: Holt, Rinehart and Winston, 1961), p. 14.

by an ensemble of multilateral rules with an imperative-attributive character. It insists on a strictly determined interdependence between corresponding duties and claims, deriving their obligatory force from the "normative facts" and admitting in certain cases the possibility of being affected by coercion without its absolute requirement, however.[62]

This notion of law makes it impossible to separate the motive from the action, the internal from the external. This is the true sense of the relationship between the whole and the individual persons, the moral value and its external manifestation in the law, the individual and the universal, the normative and the positive. All are necessarily linked together. One without the other is the death of both. This goes a long way to sustain the Christian ethic based on commandments written on the heart.

Law has a positive function as well as a negative one. "It aids as well as restrains; it fulfills an educational role along with a preventative one." [63] Law keeps social life from becoming anarchical; it also seeks to ameliorate in a positive and effective way.

The final statement on the role of law concerns Gurvitch's idea of the presence of law as a totality. The synthesizing role of law brings together individualism and universalism. This synthesis is possible through the "reciprocity of perspectives," a concept developed by Gurvitch. This notion is especially important in his method and general sociological theory. The concept of reciprocity shows the dialectical relationship between the individual and the whole, between the multiple and the one. His principle of order is the multilateral structure of the juridical precepts. Mutuality is possible through the imperative-attributive relationships embodied in the law. This is what gives law its social character. The imperative-attributive complex would be impossible without the reality of the other "self" which leads to the interdependence of claims and duties. Yet these claims and duties must be the same. Therefore the social milieu must be the same. All these factors lead to the conception of the "whole." This is the essence of law.

[62] *L'idée* . . . , p. 111.
[63] *Ibid.*, p. 112.

The prejudice of seeing law as necessarily individualistic and purely abstract has to be rejected for
the juridical sphere in general. The idea of the
"whole," of the "concrete universal," is indispensable for grasping the general notion of law. The
door is open, thence, for the idea of social law.[64]
The obligatory force of law is the next step in this idea.

III. THE NORMATIVE FACT.

Law never stands alone. It is the product of the social
whole. Law attempts to realize justice. What then gives
law its obligatory force? Why is it obeyed? It is apparent
that law does not depend upon naked force. Something else
sheathes the bare sword of power. Something makes compliance to the law acceptable and even pleasant at times.

In Gurvitch's structure of thought the essence of "law-
abidingness" is the *normative fact*. Some middle concept
is needed to placate the disruptive tensions implicit in the
following dichotomies: autonomy versus heteronomy, normative duty versus the practice of duty, rights versus force,
idealism versus realism, formal law versus the spontaneous
law which underlies force.[65] To repeat, law is neither totally
heteronomous nor autonomous. It is likewise neither totally idealist nor realist, nor totally any of the extreme
points on these continua. Law is the middle ground, the intermediary between these various endpoints. Law rises
above these to an impersonal or transpersonal level. "In
other words (law) goes beyond this dialectic to find its
obligatory force in the objective facts which incarnate certain intrinsic positive values (juridical and moral in character)." [66] This impersonal character gives these objective
facts an authority for establishing the rule of law. This
is the authority which underlies the law. The force of
obligation flows from the *normative fact*. This is the fundamental notion of law. It is a difficult idea, but its explanation is essential to an understanding of Gurvitch's entire
system of thought.

Gurvitch rejects total reliance upon force for the authority of law. Still, law must have sufficient force to be effective. The search then is for the *real* force, if coercion has
been eliminated as the viable source of authority. Force and

---

[64] *L'idée* . . . , p. 113.
[65] *L'idée* . . . , p. 114.
[66] *Ibid.*, p. 114.

law are related. To set them over against each other is an error. To make them identical is also wrong. It is necessary to go beyond this impasse. This leads to the *normative fact*, which raises a question. Is law an ideal element opposed to the real? Gurvitch says law is neither. If strictly ideal, it is removed from reality; this would overlook its "positive" character. On the other hand, if juridical realism is the only essence of law, this reduces it strictly to the empirical level and repudiates all values which give that law content and a "specific reality as law." [67] Gurvitch quotes Kant: "A doctrine of law which is purely empirical can be like the wooden head in the fable of Phaedra, a beautiful head indeed, but, alas, without any brains." [68]

Gurvitch takes the middle position, adopting what he calls the ideal-real method in order to get at the phenomenon of law. This phenomenon incarnates "certain positive, extratemporal values" [69] which make it different in structure from all other realities such as morality, religion and politics. This peculiar content of juridical experience leads to the essence of the *normative fact*. The *ideal-real* method is the means by which this "ultimate reality of legal authority" is grasped. The route the method takes is something like this:

a. Beneath every social organization exists the spontaneous law of the unorganized subjacent community.

b. This unorganized community's law is based on a normative fact, an object, transpersonal authority. To state this law exists is insufficient. To be legitimate the law must be valid; it must be effective.

c. Only active communities can engender or make law. Passive ones are incapable of this, e.g., friendship communities or those groups based on adoration or love. A community must be active, must have something to accomplish. Ideas are the product of action. Thinking is action. (Fichte is present again.) Values are creative and the products of creative action. The efficacy of this *normative fact* comes from the following sequence: in order for an active community to create the law, it must be impregnated by it; and the law, in order that it be a real law, must be created by the given community and given authority by that commu-

---

[67] *L'idée* . . . , p. 116.
[68] *Ibid.*,
[69] *Ibid.*, p. 117.

nity. In other words, at one and the same time the communities create the law and base their very existence upon it. "The communities create their being in engendering the law, which also serves as their foundation." [70]
To be more explicit:

> One cannot say either that the law pre-exists the community or the community the law, but that they are born and affirm each other *together*. They are inseparable in their existence and their validity. These communities, within which the constitution by the law and the generating of a law coincides, are precisely the *normative facts*.[71]

These *normative facts* are derived from the concept of justice. Justice is the search for stable order, peace and union. To realize justice requires the creation of certain values which are held in common. The *normative facts* are the core elements of juridical life; they are the components of law. Law is not a set of abstract rules which can be examined piece by piece in a legal laboratory. Law is more than this. Underneath are those elements "which are at once more concrete and more objective than rules of law; these are the normative facts." [72]

In sum, the authority of law rests on certain common values derived from the community and of necessity binding the community together, in other words, establishing justice. These values are translated into law; they are the components of law although the law is the more formal, logicalized expression of these basic values. The *normative fact* raises the question of the source of law. Positive law contains two basic elements: 1) the *normative fact* as the source of its obligatory character and 2) its actual existence as the guarantee of its real effectiveness as a rule.[73] Gurvitch rejects the popular notion that law rests on custom, juridical practice, convention and precedence. He says it is necessary to go below and find the sources of the "sources." Hence, there are in his terminology primary sources and secondary sources. The former would be the *normative facts;* the latter would include the level of informal law, e.g., custom and convention plus the formal expres-

[70] *Ibid.*, p. 119.
[71] *Loc. cit.*
[72] *L'idée* . . . , p. 119.
[73] *Ibid.*, p. 133.

sion of law itself. "The primary sources are the *normative facts* which unite authority and effective guarantees. Hence, what were once considered the sources of law become the 'techniques' for implementing and stating the *normative facts.*" [74]

These secondary sources are relative and tentative in character. They do not have the stability of the primary level. The dialectical relationship between the two levels gives law its continuity on the one hand and its flexibility on the other.

However, Gurvitch finds it unnecessary that the primary level express itself solely through secondary means. He distinguishes, therefore, between *formal positive law* (which includes every type of means through which the *normative fact* may be channeled) and *intuitive positive law,* which is a direct and immediate apprehension of the *normative fact* without recourse to the mediary level. [75] This leads logically to a consideration of natural law.

IV. NATURAL LAW.

Gurvitch defines natural law as "that law which, grounded in the innermost nature of man or of society, is independent of convention, legislation or other institutional devices." [76] The principle of natural law tries to find a solution to the persistent problem of the relationship between the ideal and the real.

> The problems which it (natural law) raises are as old as the earliest speculation regarding law; for it is a reflection of the antinomies inherent in the realm of jurisprudence itself, wherein the ideal norm is confronted with the deviations of reality, apriorism with empiricism, autonomy with heteronomy, stability of the established order with the dynamic of moral progress, justice with security, ideal with social necessity and immobile organization with the elastic continuity of life. [77]

Natural law has taken many forms to deal with these critical questions. It has been seen as a metacultural ethic for law as a whole, or the "*a priori* element antecedent to

---

[74] *Ibid.,* p. 134.
[75] *L'idée* . . . , p. 135-136.
[76] "Natural Law" in the *Encyclopedia of Social Sciences,* XI, 284.
[77] *Loc. cit.*

all law" [78]; or the ideal source of law providing the constant test for positive law. Others have seen natural law as the "invariant rules of law in contrast with the changing," [79] or a species of autonomous law which is detached from the positive realm and contains its own verification; finally, as a spontaneous law "differentiated by its living and organic properties from the law promulgated in advance by the state or its agents." [80]

Gurvitch inquires whether there can be a natural law. His answer is negative. Social reality contains certain antinomies, certain conflicts which are real and undeniable. "The natural law theorists have resolved all the antinomies contained in the juridical sphere by transposing these contradictions into an entirely detached sphere." [81] This merely begs the question. The real goal must be to do away with every type of artificial abstraction. The only way to do this, suggests Gurvitch, is to bring idea and fact into some kind of synthesis.

A purely autonomous law is a contradiction in terms. If there is any correspondence between claims and duties, this means a common value has been agreed upon in a given social milieu, and from that value has sprung a law which has validity and authority. Hence "if a law is effective in the life of a totality, this means its *purely normative* character has been destroyed." [82] In more explicit terms:

> The law cannot seek to serve justice, which demands the establishment of security and peace without becoming positive. A purely autonomous law is no longer a law, but a moral postulate, an opinion on the law, rising from a point of view concerning the moral ideal, but not the law itself.[83]

If justice is the attempt to establish order, security and peace, or simply the making of a society, and such an order is realized by instituting an equilibrium between claims and duties of all persons in the social whole, then this particular type of "equilibrium" is only viable for a given social milieu. Natural law as an abstract theory floating above such

---

[78] *Loc. cit.*
[79] *Experience juridique* . . . , p. 103.
[80] *Loc. cit.*
[81] *Experience juridique* . . . , p. 116.
[82] *Loc. cit.*
[83] *Loc. cit.*

particular and peculiar contingencies is irrelevant; it cannot exist as law since law, to be law, must be *effective*.

Gurvitch's analysis of natural law has been attacked frequently. His position was introduced in *L'idée*. He answers his critics in *L'experience juridique*.[84] His argument denies the possibility of identifying justice and natural law. Seeing natural law as purely transcendent law, synonymous with justice, is attempting to make it a criterion for judgment. This is a contradiction in terms.[85] A law to be effective must function within the domain of the empirical, within a concrete social milieu. Natural law fails to do this. Justice is the mid-point between the moral ideal and the real. According to Gurvitch justice is also the substance of all law. Law, it must be remembered, seeks to realize justice. Justice and natural law are never the same. It is impossible to deduce "from a logical category the object which it constitutes." [86] Justice fails to serve as the basis for judging existing law since "it is the constitutive element of all law." [87]

Gurvitch uses the following analogy:
> One cannot decide if a chair is good or bad by applying the logical category of the substance of which the object is made. It is evident one can criticize and judge existing law according to a moral ideal. One can say that this law is morally better than another, but that is precisely because the moral is different from the law and one is beyond the categories of both law and justice.[88]

Natural law theory creates an artificial abyss between what is called natural law and positive law or the ideal and the empirical. The three suggested answers for bridging this gap lead to difficulty. The first affirms that natural law is the superior of the two. This results in anarchy, on the one hand, since each person has the right to decide when a particular juridical regulation is against his conception of natural law; on the other hand, if one judges that a particular social group, such as the church, possesses a superior positive law, then it is free to interpret the natural

---

[84] Cf. pp. 103-137.
[85] *Experience juridique* . . . , p. 116.
[86] *Ibid.*, p. 118.
[87] *Loc. cit.*
[88] *Loc. cit.*

law as it sees fit. This becomes a form of collectivist anarchy.

The second answer affirms that positive law is superior to natural law. This leads to the conclusion that positive law always can do that which "is permitted by natural law; but even more, it is permitted to do those things which are condemned by natural law." [89] Natural law is reduced to a nonentity in such a system.

The third "solution" recognizes that each order of law is equal to the other. This would lead to an impossible impasse since there would be no third order of law to arbitrate between natural law and positive law when conflicts would arise.[90]

Gurvitch therefore rejects natural law because of the impossible problems it poses. He points out that there are those theorists of natural law who would relativize it by putting it into different categories according to time and place. Harry Emerson Fosdick's aphorism is recalled here: "The eternal truths must be put in changing categories." Yet this would give to natural law an almost infinite variation, while recalling its supposed immutability and its entirely *a priori* character. Gurvitch asks, "What are some fundamental rules of natural law?" [91] When one begins to examine these so-called rules, he soon discovers they are based firmly "on the authority of a given social milieu making them actually rules of positive law. The only difference is that these *normative facts* are expressed in an immediate and intuitional way without going through certain formal means." [92] Often natural law is confused with this intuitional positive law. All the concrete, particular rules supposedly included in it are really dogmatized, intuited positive laws which have validity only in the social milieu of the particular theorist.

Remember the role of justice is to establish order, security and peace. Who is to say such a social order did not exist among the Dahomeans, for instance, who sacrificed the most beautiful members of the clan to placate their gods? It is always necessary to see the particular expres-

[89] *Experience juridique* . . . , p. 129.
[90] *Loc. cit.*
[91] *Ibid.*, p. 127.
[92] *Ibid.*, p. 128.

sion of justice within its own setting. Failure to do this leads to a new expression of arbitrariness.[93]

> In effect, Justice provides only a tentative recon-
> ciliation of conflicting equivalent moral values; it
> is a mobile and unstable equilibrium, infinitely dy-
> namic and changing.[94]

The idea of justice, concludes Gurvitch, is so variable it is impossible to use this as the universal criterion by which to judge empirical, positive law, even if it were admissible to assume that justice is a metacultural ideal.

V. THE JURIDICAL EXPERIENCE.[95]

The previous discussions on the idea of social law including the nature of law, justice, the *normative fact* and natural law have set the stage for a general overview of juridical experience as conceived by Gurvitch.

A fundamental notion throughout his presentation is the concept of reality. There is an irreducible reality to every form of experience. This makes it possible to study morals, law, religion. All such experience is divided into two levels: a) the surface level of intellectual reflection and construction and, b) the spontaneous or immediate level, the ground of all experience.

Juridical reality contains then a conceptual structure, including certain provisions to reduce the conflict of various competing interests. Underneath these secondary features are the intuitive acts of recognition. The juridical experience is a complex of these ingredients.

The juridical subject is always collective. True, an individual can promulgate the law, as Pharoah from his throne or a factory owner from his oak-paneled office. However, the law which he promulgates or announces was the product of a community, a collectivity.

Moreover, it is only by a collectivity that a *normative fact* can be grasped and be the source of authority. This is linked with the need for social order, the content of justice. In turn justice must be established in the common values, the *normative facts*, which are intuited by a living community. These values become the basis for the claims and duties of each person. Justice is the balance of these claims

[93] *Ibid.*, pp. 120-121.
[94] *Ibid.*, p. 120.
[95] The writer is indebted to René Toulemont's summary of this material in his volume previously cited. See especially pages 78-80.

and duties. Such an equilibrium results in a social order. The law seeks to establish justice, to provide the construction or the means by which security, peace and unity may be acquired by the commonwealth.

In summary: "a) the individual can promulgate the law as does the collectivity; b) only a collectivity can *create* the law, but c) the *juridical given* which results from this can be individual as well as collective." [96] This latter step means the result may be an individual law in accordance with Gurvitch's notion of contractual or coordinative law as distinguished from integrative law. However, to be more precise, individual law is never purely individual. It implies the imperative-attributive relationship which is part and parcel of the *normative facts* whether those facts be the products of the integrative community or of relations with others.

Juridical experience is fraught with antinomies and conflicts. This leads at once to its complexity and its pluralism.

> The antinomic character of juridical experience has another aspect which distinguishes it from other experiences, also antinomic in character, that is . . . conflicts surge forth at the very interior of each immediately perceived given. In each of these . . . an unrelenting conflict occurs between the infinite and the finite, the irrational and the rational, the individual and the general, quality and quantity, the moral and the logical, the dynamic and the static, the creative and the rigid, all these tensions forming the very essence of the spiritual data of juridical experience.[97]

In the midst of this conflict comes juridical experience as the arbiter. It affirms both the ideal and the sensate. Juridical experience sees the two as equal. To recognize the existence of specific juridical experience permits the researcher to grasp the reality of law. Law is related to moral experience since it is comprised of justice; the reality of law finds its expression in the intuitive and formal avenues of positive law. Yet the specific juridical experience cannot be identified with either the underlying value or the purely sensible. In Gurvitch's words:

> While the given reality of moral experience has a

---

[96] *Sociologie et pluralisme* . . . , p. 79.
[97] *Experience juridique* . . . , p. 64.

character which is ideal, the reality of law grasped
by the juridical experience is intermediary between
the realm of sensible facts and the ideal world;
the juridical experience, being a midpoint between
the sense experience and the experience of the
spiritual, has for its basic data neither ideal values
nor the facts donated by the senses but certain
normative facts, certain sense facts which incarnate by their very existence certain values.[98]

Gurvitch explains the law as an intermediary between
the ideal or moral and the logical, between the creative impulse itself and the stable system which produces continuity. Law operates between the purely quantitative and
the qualitative, between the strictly individualized and the
universal; in sum, the juridical experience is the midpoint
between the moral experience and the logical ideas which
define and delimit. To repeat, the task of the juridical experience is that of a go-between, an arbiter, a builder of
equilibria, a means for establishing justice.

Obviously such a task means these equilibria will vary
according to the different social milieux. As Gurvitch often
states, there are varying equilibria within a given society,
within a particular totality. This then, is a radical pluralism, the direct result of Gurvitch's radical empiricism. This
pluralism is inherent in the juridical experience. Basically
this pluralism can be traced to two main sources; a) the
plurality which results from the spiritual data of juridical
experience, namely, the diversity of juridical values, "the
multiplicity of aspects under which is lived the idea of justice in all the richness of its infinite totality," [99] and b) the
irreducible plurality of the centers of juridical experience
resulting in a plurality of juridical orders, each of which
must be taken into consideration.

The question remains as to how this pluralism is handled.
Gurvitch makes several helpful distinctions: first, the depth
of juridical experience can be separated between the organized law and the spontaneous law. In other words the
mode of expressing the *normative facts* can be either direct
or through formal means. The former is *intuitive positive
law;* the latter is *formal positive law.* These two distinctions intersect each other but in no way does Gurvitch iden-

---

[98] *Ibid.,* pp. 17-18.
[99] *Experience juridique* . . . , pp. 77.

tify intuitive positive law with the spontaneous level of law or the formal law with the organized plane.

It is wrong to think that a technical process necessary to state a law needs to have an organization thereby implying that spontaneous or unorganized law can only be expressed by direct intuition. Many technical processes do not require an organization, e.g., custom, precedent, codes, programs, etc. Stated by these unorganized formal processes, unorganized law becomes a formal positive law and thereby remains unorganized.[100]

Second, there is the distinction between the *normative facts* derived from a fusion in the totality and those arising from the "relations with the other." This distinction helps to explain the opposition between individual and social law. At the most profound level of juridical life, the level of *normative facts,* there are two types of *facts* which are juxtaposed: the individual and the integrative. The first type describes the intuitive acts which remain apart and affirm an interdependent relationship; the second type sets forth the intuitive acts leading to a participation of all in one and the same act.[101] Gurvitch upholds the priority of the latter over the former. Personal values belong to the individual type, transpersonal values to the law of communion. Commutative justice becomes the essential expression of the former, distributive justice of the latter. However, the integrative form rises above both commutative and distributive justice in its support of transpersonal values, values which are both subjective and objective, both individual and universal. The dialectic is once again present. The tension is resolved by accepting it and showing the principle of mutuality. One other type completes the corpus of law. This one has a mixed character. It is the law of domination, a perversion of social law. The perversion comes from its reliance on a subject-object dichotomy, best illustrated in an absolute monarch or a patronizing factory owner. These three forms of law, then, become the system of law: 1) social law or the law of integration; 2) individual law or interindividual, intergroupal law; and 3) subordinative law or the law of domination.

Gurvitch states repeatedly that in these distinctions he

---

[100] *Ibid.,* p. 133. See also pp. 136-139 in *L'idée du droit social.*
[101] *Experience juridique* . . . , p. 74.

does not in any way mean to suggest that one type is superior to the other forms. He has been criticized for this seeming lapse in his claim to objectivity. Certain critics have declared the spontaneous, unorganized law appears to be favored by Gurvitch. He refutes this with vigor. The spontaneous community subjacent to the democratic society can be good or bad. This is why democracy must continue to place a great emphasis on education. The law of integration is no better than the law of coordination. It is necessary to have coordinative law in order that the external relationships of the subjects of a community are regulated. "I have always sought to show these two kinds of law, integrative and coordinative, as irreducible to each other; they are of equal value, hence spontaneous social law does not have priority over individual law on any scale of value." [102] They are both essential.

When Gurvitch uses the words perversion or deformed to describe subordinative law, he does not make a value judgment. He merely seeks to qualify the distinction. History shows subordinative law has at certain periods been the best solution for particular situations. Who is to say that a Nyerere is not the best solution for Tanzania or a DeGaulle for France? They both wield considerable power and would fit this category of subordinative law. Certain periods of martial law are essential in the life of every nation. A president of a democracy during war must assume such powers. Subordinative law, then, is merely a descriptive term for certain types of rule.

There is some criticism of Gurvitch's category of intuitive law. It would appear he has entered the back door of natural law. He counters that this charge is unfounded. Intuitive law can be detrimental to a totality. For instance the intuited law of the whites in the Southern United States would maintain racial segregation. The formal law, on the other hand, has expressed the *normative facts* of the entire nation in a much more rational and moral way.

The final problem of juridical experience concerns the pluralism of values. What is the principle of their unity? Gurvitch asserts unity is immanent to the juridical values and groups which engender them. In the case of values, they cease to exist if they are separated from their parent groups. Each group, if it exists as a particular entity, does

---

[102] *Experience juridique* . . . , p. 75.

so within the wider context of the totality which encompasses it. This principle can be seen as a series of concentric circles moving from the smallest social unit out to the widest unity, which is the international community in its broadest sense. The *normative facts* of the nation, therefore, can only be real as they are made effective within the wider context of the international community. All of these circles of law or, more specifically, groupings engendering law, are dependent upon each other. In this sense, the unity is implicit within the multiplicity. The principle of unity is integration raising the question how well are the values integrated into the task of justice or how well is each group integrated into the next wider social unit.[103]

VI. THE KINDS OF SOCIAL LAW.

Among the kinds of social law it is necessary to mention only those which have a direct bearing on Gurvitch's sociology of the total social phenomena.

1) *Subjective social law and objective social law.* Subjective law concerns the ensemble of claims and rights belonging to the complex collective personalities, the specific subjects of social law. Objective social law deals with the whole gamut of institutions (normative facts) and rules which make up a juridical system. This distinction takes into consideration the imperative (objective)—attributive (subjective).[104] Subjective social law can be expressed as the organized level since the division of social power in an organization is in reality a consignment of rights and, hence, of duties. This subjective type can also be expressed in certain unorganized ways such as in the right to join or leave a group or assuming the right to act for a group in a crisis.

2) *Spontaneous or unorganized social law and organized social law.* The spontaneous level is absolutely essential to all organized expressions.

3) *Particular social law and common social law.* This distinction points to the superiority of a commercial social law for example which seeks to serve the general interest over and above the particular social law which is "ethnocentric" in its expression.[105]

One final contribution which Gurvitch makes in his dis-

---

[103] *L'idée* . . . , pp. 47-48.
[104] *L'idée* . . . , pp. 47-48.
[105] *Ibid.*, p. 51.

cussion of social law is his description of the relationship between positive law and the state. Gurvitch begins by suggesting what that relationship is *not:* 1) The state cannot be elevated above the law. This is an "imperialist conception" of the state. 2) The state cannot be identified with the law. This is the error made by Kelsen and others.[106] 3) The state cannot be seen independent of the law and law independent of the state. Gierke was wont to make this error. 4) The state cannot be seen as inferior to the law, which was the misconception of Duguit. 5) Lastly, the state cannot be interpreted as only partially intersecting the world of law. Even the most autocratic type of political

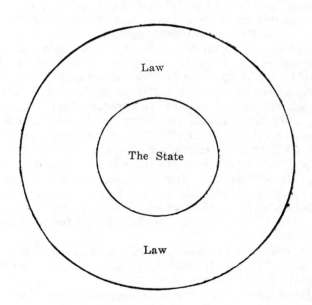

[106] *L'idée* . . . , p 151. See Gurvitch's treatment of Kelsen in his *Le Temps present et l'idée du droit social,* Part I, Section 11, Chapter 11. Cited in a footnote in *L'idée* . . . , p. 151.

46

system is founded on law. Hence, there is only one positive way to see this relationship between the state and positive law.

The state must be considered as a defined circle of law inscribed in an infinitely larger circle of non-political law. In the juridical life, the state is as a small, deep lake in the immense sea of law which encloses it on all sides.[107]

Gurvitch uses the preceding diagram[108] to illustrate this dialectical relationship between the state and positive law.

This concludes the description of Gurvitch's juridical phase. The emphasis in his work shifted after this long preoccupation with the law. However, the roots of his sociological theory are here. This will be patently clear in the chapter to follow.

2. THE SOCIOLOGICAL PHASE

These preoccupations with the concept of social law and especially its relationship to the state led Gurvitch to make some assessments of the political scene. He attempted to correlate his sociological analyses with his strong political convictions about the superiority of the decentralized planned economy based on democratic structures. He approved of the factory councils and representative councils which held a firm hand over the economy. He considered that the regulatory and disciplinary power of management operative in most factories and enterprises was based on a "perverted social law". As described previously, such a subordinative system was submissive to an artificially derived individual law of property which "by itself failed to serve juridically as the basis for any social power." [109] In his L'experience juridique, Gurvitch includes two long discussions on socialism and democracy. These were written in the period between the two World Wars, but his introduction to these chapters in the book brings his thought up to date.[110]

Gurvitch states, "I had to distinguish more clearly in my work between value judgments and descriptive statements." [111] This he did in 1944, at New York, when he made

---

[107] L'idée . . . , 152.
[108] Loc. cit.
[109] Mon itineraire . . . , p. 12.
[110] The third part, pp. 235-296.
[111] Mon itineraire . . . , p. 12.

a deliberate effort to put down his ideas for a program of political-social action in his *Declaration of Social Rights*.[112] His goal was to write a work which would inspire the formulators of the Fourth Republic's constitution. He comments, "Alas in vain! However, a beginning can be observed in the Popular Federalist Republic of Yugoslavia during these recent years." [113]

Obviously Gurvitch raised some important questions in his two theses on the idea of social law. Some of these questions were sociological and philosophical as well as doctrinal. His theory of the *normative facts* as the source and authority for all law came under special attack. Hence, he felt he had to answer his critics. This he did in *L'experience juridique*.

Other interests attracted him. After he defended his thesis and received his doctorate, he taught for several years as a professor at the College Sevigne. He also taught sociology as a replacement at the University of Bordeaux. In 1935, he followed Maurice Halbwachs at the University of Strasbourg as a professor of sociology. His interests now were focused almost entirely on general sociology. He began his analysis of general sociology in a surprising manner by undertaking a study of a subject which had long fascinated him, namely, the relationship between the sociology of the moral life and moral philosophy. This is one of the clearest examples of how the European approach differs so widely from the empirically oriented American school. "If it's logical, it's true," is the way a professor friend somewhat derisively described European sociology's philosophical tradition. On this subject of moral philosophy, Gurvitch published a small volume entitled *Moral Theory and the Science of Morals*.[114] He tried to show the possibility of a fruitful cooperation between the two disciplines. Both have as their domain of study, *moral experience*. Such experience has an irreducible reality which calls for uniquely characteristic methods to study these phenomena. Moral experience is full of variations and surprises. Such experience contains the relationships of duties, values and creative freedom. Such experience is studied by moral philosophy.

---

[112] New York: Editions de la Maison Francaise, 1944, and Paris: Vrin 1946.

[113] *Op. cit.*, p. 12.

[114] Paris: Presses Universitaires de France, 1937. A revised edition appeared in 1948 and a third edition in 1961.

Sociology on the other hand, describes the infinite variations of this moral experience. Philosophy's domain is the interior life of this experience. Sociology tries to understand the role of this experience in social reality. It does this by establishing a typology of moral experiences which is then applied to given social milieux at once integrating this experience with the total social phenomena.

In 1948, Gurvitch said that while preparing the second edition of this book, he discovered that he had, without realizing it, linked sociology of moral life to a particular philosophical position:

> In the first place I had supposed that a person could attain the immediate moral experience and secondly, I had admitted to a stable hierarchy of the kinds of morality, which accorded a preeminence to the morality of creative liberty. I promised myself therefore to return to this question.[115]

In 1938, Gurvitch had published his first book dedicated solely to sociology, the *Essais de sociologie*.[116] In this collection of essays he made for the first time the distinction between microsociology, sociology of groupings and the typology of global societies. This work also contained his thesis, latently present in his books on social law, that of the reciprocal immanence of the individual consciences and the collective consciences. He designated this by the term he borrowed from Theodor Litt, *reciprocity of perspectives*. He notes, "Unhappily, I committed the error of only developing in detail the microsociological typology (in particular, mass, community and communion) without providing as extended a study of the typology of groupings and global societies." [117] This led to his critics' assertion that he favored the microsociological elements as having the most important position in social reality. "In reality, I am inclined to put the emphasis on the types of global societies, all the while insisting on the dialectical tension among all three scales." [118]

In his *Elements de sociologie juridique*,[119] 1940, he tried to spell out this necessary dialectic among all three and to give some concrete evidence for this theory. As he moved

---

[115] *Mon itineraire* . . . , p. 14.
[116] Paris: Libraire du Recueil Sirey, 1938.
[117] *Monitineraire* . . . , p. 14.
[118] *Ibid.*
[119] Paris: Aubier, 1940.

more and more in the direction of being a "full-time" sociologist, he made an effort to rid his theory of any philosophical overtones which would belie a particular position. He admitted he didn't always succeed in this effort. The ideal-realist position which was borrowed more from Proudhon than Fichte had a remarkable staying power. He asserted he would only be rid of this tendency later on. There is a real question as to whether he has ever fully succeeded. This will be analyzed in a later critical chapter.

After the armistice and the demobilization of France in 1940, Gurvitch had an opportunity to go to the United States. He was invited by the New School of Social Research of New York to come there and teach. He arrived in New York in mid-October, 1940, scarcely knowing how to read English and possessing no facility to speak the language. His teaching at the New School was mainly in the area of the history of French sociology. The first two years he taught in French. In 1941, he participated in the formation of the École Libres des Hautes Études at New York under the leadership of the French government. Gurvitch had the task of heading up the French Institute of Sociology within this school. Gurvitch comments that the discussions held under the auspices of the Institute were especially influential in his thinking. Both American and French sociologists participated. Among the problems considered by the persons participating in these meetings was the question of the future of France. What would be the social and political structure of the Fourth Republic? It was this setting which provided the impetus for Gurvitch formulating his own ideas in the *Declaration of Social Rights*, 1944.

Gurvitch was impressed by American juridical philosophy. Roscoe Pound and his school made a real impact on this twice-expatriated scholar. It was a result of this confrontation with American leaders in sociology of law that Gurvitch decided to rework his own sociology of law from a more realist position. This effort was published in 1942 as *Sociology of Law*.[120] The content of this volume will be incorporated into later chapters dealing with the development of his sociological thought.

At this point Gurvitch's interests and thought were turning in other directions. He was becoming increasingly con-

---

[120] New York: Philosophical Library, 1942. A revised edition appeared in London: Kegan Paul, 1947 and 1953.

cerned with the relationship between empirical research and t.ieory in sociology. Gurvitch was struck by the disproportionate amount of descriptive and experimental effort among certain elements of the American school of sociology and the paucity of scientific results. He was also impressed by the lack of sophistication on the part of many American research scholars. They appeared to be without any conceptual tools and a general inability to distinguish between the important and the accidental. They seemed to have an even lesser notion about the right questions to ask. Finally he was appalled by the over-use of technical skills, such as surveys, questionnaires and statistics, which could only lead to superficial descriptions. This necessarily sacrificed every effort at real understanding. Moreover, such a reliance on techniques deprived them of coming to grips with sociological theory. Certain American approaches to sociology surprised him by their lack of substance and depth. It was his feeling that empirical research in sociology had declined in quality during the previous twenty-five years. It is at present clearly inferior to the classic work done by Znaniecki and Thomas in their *The Polish Peasant in Europe and America* (1918-1921), and that by the Lynds in *Middletown* and *Middletown in Transition*. It is even of a lesser quality than the work of Le Play and his school in France. To fill this void Gurvitch suggested a symposium on sociological theory and its applications in the twentieth century. This effort was published in the United States in 1946, and in France in 1947, under the title *Twentieth Century Sociology.*[121] It was done in collaboration with Wilbert E. Moore of Princeton and included contributions from American and European sociologists. Outside a recognition of the "false problems" inherited from the nineteenth century, which had handicapped the progress of sociology, "this collection," according to Gurvitch, "has scarcely been of value beyond serving as a work for listing in bibliographies. I was the least satisfied of all with the project." [122]

Gurvitch returned to France in 1945. He immediately took the initiative to organize in 1946, the *Centre d'Études Sociologiques* within the framework of the *Centre National de la Recherche Scientifique,* in the hope that he could make a contribution toward the joining of general sociological

---

[121] New York: Philosophical Library, 1946. The French translation, Paris: Presses Universitaires de France, 1947.

[122] *Mon itineraire* . . . , p. 16.

theory and empirical research in France. Gurvitch said he counted heavily on the systematic spirit of the French and on their precise philosophical training.[123] This observation says considerable about the differences in orientation between the French and American schools. However, Gurvitch continues,

> I was, alas, too optimistic. Some interesting public discussions were sponsored by the center; the three "Weeks of Sociology" produced some worthwhile reports and discussion (*Industrialisation et Technocratie*, 1948, under my direction, *Villes et compagnes*, 1952, and *Sociologie de la famille contemporaine*, 1955, under M. Sorre's direction). Several research studies achieved some success resulting in some valuable publications. Still the Center has failed in realizing the indispensable conjunction between theory and empirical research which sociology so needs.[124]

Gurvitch left the direction of the Center in 1949. His health and pressing responsibilities made it necessary to curtail some of his outside activities. He was involved in teaching regular classes at the Sorbonne and at the École Practique des Hautes Études, to which he had been invited in 1948. He decided at this stage in his work to concentrate his total effort on the task of bringing theory and empirical research into a fruitful relationship. With this goal in mind he helped to found in 1946, the *Cahiers Internationaux de Sociologie*. This has been one of the most influential sociological journals in France. It was with this same purpose that he published his systematic sociological theory under the title *La vocation actuelle de la sociologie*, in 1950.[125] A new revised and expanded edition of this work in two volumes has recently appeared. The first volume was published in 1957. It deals with Differential Sociology. This contained at last an equal treatment of microsociology and macrosociology.

It is in this work that Gurvitch pushes his relativism and empiricism to their extreme limits. This results in what he

---

[123] *Ibid.*, p. 17.

[124] *Loc. cit.*

[125] Paris: Presses Universitaires de France, 1950, and Volume I of the new revised edition, 1957. A third edition has been published in 1963 along with the first edition of Volume II on problems in general sociology.

calls *dialectical hyperempiricism*. The terminology designates about as concisely as possible the nature of his methodology. The components of this dialectical approach include complementarity, mutual implication, ambivalence or ambiguity, polarity and reciprocity of perspectives. The dialectical tensions are observable among the microsociological types, the types of groupings, social classes and the global societies. These tensions exist among the depth levels of social reality, the hierarchies of which vary with each type of partial or global structure. This dialectic occurs among the total social phenomena, the astructural elements, the structures and organizations; the dialectic describes the way in which sociology, history and ethnology are related to each other. These factors give an idea of the dynamic quality of social reality which requires an equally dynamic approach for its study. Finally, this method seeks to achieve an adequate understanding of the phenomena of social reality, the necessary step to realize certain causal explanations. When it seeks causal explanations sociology will require help from history. "One of the secrets of cooperation between theory and empirical research in sociology is utilizing the very precious materials which come to sociology from history." [126] History, on the other hand, has need of the findings of sociology. The typology of sociology is essential for the study of global social structures. Gurvitch declares that this is where the thought of Marx again becomes important in his understanding of social reality.

This same dialectical hyper-empiricism served as a guide for Gurvitch's study, *Les determinismes sociaux et liberté humaine*, 1955. Here he showed how determinism and freedom interact. This is the relationship between biological and environmental heredity and freedom. Gurvitch sought to study sociologically the pathways of freedom as they crisscross the different social frameworks. "The pluralism of social determinisms which are always partial and their relative unification in the sociological determinism necessary to carry out certain efforts in common, change (as scales of determinism) with each type of global society." [127] This leaves a large place for human freedom, both in its individ-

---

[126] *Mon itinéraire* . . . , p. 18. On this subject see Gurvitch's "Continuité et Discontinuité en Sociologie et en Histoire", which appeared in the *Annales*, 1957, and "La Crise de L'Explication en Sociologie", in *Cahiers Internationaux de Sociologie*, XXI, 1956.

[127] *Mon itinéraire* . . . , p. 18.

ual and collective expressions, in social life. Such freedom is the source of the unexpected, the unpredictable. In this same work Gurvitch confronts the problem of the multiplicity of social time, a problem which he took up in a public lecture course at the Sorbonne during the academic year, 1957-1958. There are a number of types of social time. Each global structure or social grouping hierarchizes these times according to its character and historical situation.

During his sojourn in the United States, Gurvitch gained a particular interest in the sociology of knowledge. For a long time it had been apparent to him that one could not study the sociology of the moral life or the sociology of law with sufficient relativism and realism without recourse to a study of the sociology of knowledge. Earlier he had been impressed by the work of Scheler and Levy-Bruhl in this whole area.[128] The study of symbols and signs as a means of expression and diffusion further enforced his interest in the sociology of knowledge. Also ideology as a separate concern of Marx had influenced the thought of Karl Mannheim. Thus Gurvitch felt forced to follow the same lead. In 1944-1945, he gave a course at Harvard on the Sociology of Knowledge. He made a constructive critical analysis of all the conceptions formulated up to that time. In the following years the problem was pursued further in his public lectures at the Sorbonne and in his advanced seminars at École Pratique des Hautes Études. In several of his publications he included sections on the Sociology of Knowledge.[129] He saw the necessity of distinguishing between different kinds of knowledge: perceptive knowledge of the external world, knowledge of the "other" or the "we," of groups and societies, common sense knowledge, political knowledge, technical knowledge, scientific knowledge, and philosophical knowledge. He showed their functional correlations with the various social frameworks. The intensity of those correlations and the hierarchization of the kinds of knowledge into a functional framework vary ac-

---

[128] See Max Scheler, *Philosophical Perspectives*, Oscar Haac, translator (Boston: Beacon Press, 1958), Chapter II, "The Forms of Knowledge and Culture," pp. 13-50.

[129] "La problème de la sociologie de la connaissance," *Revue Philosophique*, Part I (Octobre-Décembre, 1957), 494-502; *Revue Phil.*, Part II (Octobre-Decémbre, 1958, 438-451; *Revue Phil.*, Part III (Avril-Juin, 1959), 145-168; "La problème de la sociologie de la connaissance," *Traité de sociologie*, ed. Georges Gurvitch (Paris: Presses Universitaires de France, 1960, II, 103-136.

cording to the types of partial and global structures. Hence, these dichotomies emerge: mystical and rational knowledge, intuitive and reflective knowledge, speculative and positive knowledge, symbolic and adequate knowledge, individual and collective knowledge.

He described the multiple points of rapport among these forms and kinds as they operate within a particular global structure. This is the basis for an empirical and concrete study of the problem of the sociology of knowledge. Furthermore, such an approach, Gurvitch claims, removes sociology of knowledge from any competition with epistemology. The sociology of knowledge poses certain questions for epistemology but makes no effort to provide a solution, since that is outside its domain. Gurvitch once again sees these two disciplines as mutually enriching one another; in fact they need each other if they are going to be creative and relevant.

Gurvitch's last work *The Social Frameworks of Knowledge*, appeared posthumously.[130] Very interestingly, following these considerations, he was led to study the phenomena of social classes, the suprafunctional macrocosms of groupings which remain as partial structures. The problem of social classes was the subject of a public lecture course at the Sorbonne during 1952-1953. These lectures served as the corpus of a book. *The Concept of Social Class from Marx to the Present Day.*[131]

The approach which he followed in his sociology of knowledge took him to the sociological study of the moral life. Again, a public lecture course at the Sorbonne, 1956-1957, gave him the opportunity to develop in detail this subject. He had previously outlined his thoughts in his lectures called "Introduction to the Sociology of the Moral Life," given in 1948. Again he distinguished several *kinds* of moral life: traditional morality, finalistic morality, morality of virtues, judgment after the deed, imperative morality, morality of symbolical and ideal images, and creative morality. These kinds of morality are engaged in a much more profound relationship with social reality than the parallel kinds of knowledge. Hence the sociology of the moral life can establish functional correlations among social frameworks and the different kinds of morality on a much larger

---

[130] Paris: Presses Universitaires de France, 1966.
[131] Paris: Centre de Documentation Universitaire, 1954.

scale than was possible with the sociology of knowledge. The microsociological elements and the nonstructured groupings are important social frameworks for the analysis of moral life. The most concrete and complete study comes from juxtaposing the moral life with the social classes and above all the types of global structures. This enables the researcher to describe the different scales incorporating the various kinds of morality as well as describing the changing accentuations of the *forms of morality,* e.g., rational or mystical, intuitive or reflective, rigid or natural, atrophying or expanding, strongly followed or defeatist, collective or individual.

Finally, the sociology of the moral life, in calling for empirical research in this area, does in no way enter into competition with moral philosophy. It does propose certain new problems for moral philosophy to consider.

In recent years Gurvitch's publications have followed the general patterns delineated in this summary. It was only fitting that he should have been chosen by the Presses Universitaires de France to edit the two volume symposium by a team of French sociologists. Entitled *Traité de sociologie,* Volume I appeared in 1958 and Volume II in 1960. The format of this symposium follows the general lines of Gurvitch's systematic thought. He wrote the sections dealing with the object and method of sociology, the history of sociology, the problems of general sociology (an excellent summary of his whole system), the problems of the sociology of knowledge, problems of the sociology of the moral life, problems of the sociology of law, and an introductory statement suggesting the relationship between psychology and sociology.

He continued to be active in various sociological organizations in France and elsewhere. He participated in the third annual Colloquium sponsored by the Association Internationale des Sociologues de Langue Francaise, held in Geneva in May, 1960. He gave the general conclusions and summary of this conference which dealt with the *Structures sociales et democratie economique.*[132] He was at the time of his death president of this organization of French language sociologists.

A 1962 publication, *Dialectique et sociologie*[133] considers

[132] Brussels: Free University of Brussels Press, 1961.
[133] Paris: Flammarion, 1962.

in detail his methodology. This will serve as the basis for the later chapter here on his approach to sociology.

Gurvitch has always related his teaching and theoretical thought to an active involvement in political concerns. In the summer of 1962, an attack was made on his life by right wing extremists. They bombed his apartment but he and his wife escaped serious injury. The attack was the result of his strong stand against terrorism in Algeria.

This final statement from his autobiographical notes explains the driving force behind his work as an academic and a citizen of the world.

Destiny seems to desire that in my reflection and work I go "against the current." The rhythm of my thought has nearly always been in contrast to that which was à la mode. I am therefore "excluded from the horde." For the most part, American and French sociologists consider me a "philosopher" who has entered the wrong door, and the "philosophers" regard me as a traitor who changed camps long ago. However this sense of isolation, at times discouraging, appears very natural: my position implies the necessity of an intimate collaboration, not only between theory and empirical research, but also between sociology and philosophy. Both must renounce their dogmatism and sense of superiority. While both explore the nature of human life, they must mutually criticize each other. At the same time they must maintain their complete autonomy. Each needs constantly to ask the other certain basic questions which only an incessant dialogue is capable of answering.[134]

---

[134] *Mon itineraire* . . . , pp. 21-22.

CHAPTER III

AN OVERVIEW OF GURVITCH'S SOCIOLOGICAL THEORY

General theory deals with the basic theoretical framework by which specializations in sociology can be pursued. "It pertains to the body of knowledge and involves the issues and concerns that are common to all sociologists, regardless of the specialized fields in which they work." [1] Certain theoretical problems have survived the nineteenth century. Gurvitch contends these problems vitally affect sociology today. To understand his thought we must define the questions he confronts and the concerns he holds important. Hence, our exploration begins with Gurvitch's estimation of the current scene in sociology.

1. THE CURRENT SCENE IN SOCIOLOGY

Sociology at present is passing through a period of crisis. This crisis is caused by several factors. It is, therefore, patently necessary to define the task, method and limits of this social science. Sociology is a new discipline, relatively speaking. Its whole history encompasses the difficult decades of the nineteenth century and the disruptive, volatile years of the present century.

> However, it is wrong to consider the history of sociology as being the same thing as the history of the social philosophies popular during the nineteenth century. Sociology's need is to become a science in the full sense of the term. Thence, it must cut all ties with social philosophy. It must go beyond it.[2]

---

[1] Theodore Abel, "Comments on Sorokin's 'Practical' Influence of 'Impractical' Generalizing Sociological Theories," *Sociology and Social Research*, XLVII (January, 1963), 211.

[2] Notes on a lecture given by Dr. Georges Gurvitch at the University of Paris on December 11, 1956.

These are the opening words of a course Gurvitch offered at the Sorbonne on the History of Sociology during the year 1956-1957. The statement indicates the general plan which sociology must follow to extricate itself from the residual problems inherited from the nineteenth century. Since its inception during the first half of the past century, sociology has had a difficult time. Mainly, this difficulty has come at the point of trying to liberate itself from any liaison with dogmatic philosophy. This has meant rejecting all historical dogma which described social reality in terms of "order" or progress." [3] However, the overthrow of such philosophies of history led to an equally errant emphasis on "predominant social factors." [4] Examples Gurvitch suggests are the so-called "schools of sociology" which place almost total emphasis on the geographic, biological, anthropological, demographical, technological, economic, psychological, idealistic or formalistic factors.[5] Thus at the close of the last century a dedicated effort was made to free sociology from every dogmatic premise. At this juncture the critical spirit came to the fore, paving the way for empirical study of the social facts which could give a common basis of exploration for sociologists. It is necessary to mention that Durkheim did much to clarify the specificity of social reality by insisting the method of approach be one of seeing "the social facts as things." [6] W. G. Sumner and C. N. Cooley in the United States, and Hobhouse in England made important contributions to the clarification of sociology's task during the early part of this century.[7]

Following their work, sociology took on the special characteristics of the different countries. Gurvitch explains that in France,

> the categories of Durkheim's school of sociology were broadened and refined by the work of Lucien Levy-Bruhl and his students Marcel Mauss and

---

[3] Georges Gurvitch, *La vocation* . . . , I, 2. All references are to Gurvitch unless otherwise indicated.

[4] *Ibid.*

[5] "La crise de l'explication en sociologie," *Cahiers internationaux de Sociologie*, XXI (Janvier-Juillet, 1956), 3.

[6] Emile Durkheim, *Les règles de la mèthode sociologique* (quatrième édition; Paris: Felix Alcan, 1907), p. 20. Durkheim declares: "La première règle et la plus fondamontale set de considerer les faits sociaux comme des choses."

[7] *La vocation* . . . , I, 2.

Maurice Halbwachs. . . . But they soon showed a marked preference for the archaic societies and showed a desire to reform the spirit of certain social sciences.[8]

Germany, despite the work of Max Weber and the phenomenological school of Max Scheler, stayed on a purely speculative level. Its theory has been formalistic in nature (for example, L. von Weise). This ultimately led to the acceptance of the totalitarian ideology of the National Socialists.[9] The United States has been captivated by scientific technique, empirical research, and statistical methods.[10]

Now Gurvitch asks:

What is going to be the destiny and orientation of sociology in this present historical setting, where, after the military defeat of totalitarian fascism, the battle is engaged but not resolved between the different types of global structures: organized capitalism, communism, technocracy, collectivism, pluralism, etc.; where resultant conflicts are arising between national and international planners, brought about either by trusts and cartels, nation-states, or by the producers and consumers themselves; where atomic energy must ultimately be substituted in industrial production for black or white oil.[11]

In 1960 Gurvitch observed that there has never been a time exactly like the present when the social structures of modern civilizations are threatened totally by technology. This becomes clear upon examining the relationships between technology, the cultural works of civilization and the social structures. "Before, social structures challenged technology; now, the contrary is true." [12] At the time this statement was made, the summit meeting between Eisenhower and Khrushchev had just been cancelled over the "U-2 incident." Gurvitch noted that this summit meeting failed because political power was dominated by the military; the leadership of the state was virtually in their hands. There is a "formal" democratic structure but underneath

[8] *Ibid.*
[9] *Ibid.*
[10] Lecture notes, January 11, 1967.
[11] *La vocation* . . . , I, 3.
[12] Personal conversation with the author, August, 1960.

private interests prevail: workers are dominated by their own technicians, "trusts" by their own kind of economic planners, politicians by party bureaucrats and the bureaucracies of the state; the latter is more and more dominated by an army which is day by day increasing its destructive power. This holds for the U.S.S.R. as it does for the western world.[13] Add to this the condition of sociology: "It has abandoned its real task; it has capitulated to the 'test-o-mania' and 'quantophrenia' to use Pitirim Sorokin's terms; this occupation with tests and measurements has made it impossible to offer any sociological explanations to certain grave problems such as fascism and technocracy." [14]

Gurvitch raises four basic questions concerning sociology: (1) If sociology depends on the interaction of certain concrete social structures, can it be considered a science in the full sense of the word? (2) If the answer is yes, then what are the limits of sociology as a science? (3) If one separates the indicative and the normative, in other words, the objective "facts" from judgments of what should be, does this eliminate all possibilities of practically applying the findings of sociology? (4) With what important issues should sociology be occupied?[15]

Gurvitch presents answers to these questions from the position of his philosophical and juridical background. The questions Gurvitch raises fit within the context of "being." The ontological nature of social reality is undeniable. Individual existence is part and parcel of social existence. Social existence is indissoluably linked with individual existence. Attempts to separate the two are useless. Gurvitch comments on Reinhold Niebuhr's *Moral Man and Immoral Society.* In a lecture on the "Sociology of the Moral Life," [16] he contends that Niebuhr denies real contact between society and morality. Social life for him would be amoral. Neither collective nor social morality exists.

> The domains of the moral and the social are such strangers to one another, [in Niebuhr's thought] that a post factum application to society of ethical criteria valid in the individual conscience, would be perfectly inoperative.[17]

---

[13] *Ibid.*
[14] *Combat* (Paris), January 23, 1957, p. 7.
[15] *La vocation* . . . , I, 3.
[16] Gurvitch, course given at the Sorbonne, 1956-1957.
[17] Lecture notes, University of Paris, December 6, 1956.

Gurvitch indicates such a position would reduce all attempts to realize ethical criteria to a bitter cynicism. Moreover all human behavior would be relegated in advance to the amoral or even immoral.

> Further, this position excludes artificially from social reality the majority of the elements which are included in it, such as non-conformist behaviour, cultural patterns, attitudes, symbols, creative innovating behaviour, collective ideas and values, and the collective mind which is expressed in certain mental acts such as intuition and judgment.[18]

There is a dialectical relationship between the individual and the collective which such a position ignores; rather it puts them in virtual isolation. This dialectic is necessary to the understanding of social reality as it is existentially conceived. Gurvitch, therefore understands the orientation of sociology to be concerned with the inescapable involvement of "all existence" in a plurality of social situations which is often paradoxical.[19] Such contradictory situations can be illustrated by the rapport between the individual and society, the relations of "I," "Alter Ego," and "We," [20] These various relationships or involvements in the social situation itself can only be put in bold relief by the operative processes of "complementarity," "ambiguity," "polarization," the dialectic of "mutual implication" and "reciprocity of perspectives." [21]

Gurvitch believes that sociology is faced with the growing pluralism of groups which oppose one another in the struggle for equilibrium. Moreover, knowledge itself has become a valid field of scrutiny for sociology.[22] He points to the ineffectiveness and "fatigue" of a great number of present social symbols. This problem needs to be confronted since the requirement for "active" symbols is particularly cru-

---

[18] *Ibid.*
[19] *La vocation* . . . , I, 4.
[20] *Ibid.*
[21] *Ibid.* See below, section five.
[22] *Ibid.*

cial.[23] He registers a concern for an increasing dearth of reflection on the "rhythm of social reality." [24]

This is the existential situation facing sociology today. Gurvitch emphasizes the theoretical spadework required if such problems are to be answered. The vast empirical work done by American sociologists is deceiving. The enormous amount of accumulated material has to be selected according to specific criteria which are not available due to the lack of agreement among sociologists. This is particularly disconcerting when it is readily admitted a conceptual scheme, serving as a point of departure, is indispensable.[25]

One concern repeatedly appears in Gurvitch's writings. Sociology is faced above all with a crisis of explanation and its subsequent communication. It is summed up in one word, *l'explication*.[26] This problem of explanation takes different forms:

1) *Over-explanation.* There are times when too much explanation is offered based on too little factual matter. An example of this is evolutionary theory which seeks to give a "sense of history" or answer the question, "Where is society going?" This is not a legitimate task for sociology.[27]

2) *A false interpretation.* This results when an explanation is given that is not supported by the evidence available. Seeing social reality in terms of one predominant factor is an illustration.[28]

3) *Overly simple explanation.* This problem in explanation is due to an inadequate view of the complexity of social reality. An example of this exaggerated approach is the desire to make too broad a generalization from a limited field of research.

> The typological or monographic techniques, if they are used too narrowly, deny the dialectic between

---

[23] *Ibid.*

[24] *Ibid.* See especially the whole of his *Déterminismes sociaux et liberté humaine;* also, *The Spectrum of Social Time,* of *La multiplicité des temps sociaux,* translated by Myrtle Korenbaum and C. P. Bosserman, Dodrecht, Holland: D. Reidel and Sons, 1964.

[25] *Ibid.,* pp. 4-5. Cf. his "Le concept de structure sociale," *Cahiers Internationaux de Sociologie,* XIX (Juillet-Décembre, 1955), 3-44.

[26] *Cahiers Internationaux* . . , XXI, 4.

[27] *Ibid.,* p. 5.

[28] *Ibid.,* p. 6.

microsociology, the sociology of groups and social classes, and the study of inclusive societies.[29]

4) *Over-emphasis on empirical research.* *United States* social science researchers have actually renounced every possibility of explanation by transforming *sociology* into *sociography*.[30] When mechanics of sociological research become an end in themselves, when the researchers fail to rely on an adequate theoretical framework for making generalizations and explanations, then the crisis of "interpretation" is especially severe.[31]

Such a crisis of explanation can threaten the very life of sociology. First, its very autonomy as a science is threatened. It is in danger of becoming a common denominator for the social sciences. Second, it is in danger of becoming an auxiliary science to help keep recalcitrant groups in line with existing structures. Third, it is in danger of becoming subservient to technocracy. "The sociologist's advice must be profitable for industry. Empirical researchers are becoming technocrats." [32] This is very close to the thesis pursued by Loren Baritz in his book, *The Servants of Power: A History of the Use of Social Science in American Industry.* He maintains that social scientists have armed management with powerful new weapons with which to manipulate their workers. They have shown industrial managers the Rorschach tests and Thematic Apperception tests—by which workers unknowingly tell things about themselves which they would not have otherwise revealed if they had been left to the usual methods of "communication." A practiced device is to share with the workers why management decisions were made as they were. This gives the workers a false sense of belonging, according to Mr. Baritz. They are merely tools in the hands of manipulators who have obtained their power from the social scientists who have sold themselves to the highest bidder.

Gurvitch concludes that this crisis in explanation has arisen out of five misinterpretations: first, the attempt to encase in rigid formulas of determinism the causes of social reality; second, the failure to understand the dialectical relationship between comprehension and explanation. Weber has had a great deal to do with this misinterpretation. His

---

[29] *Ibid.*
[30] *Ibid.*
[31] *Ibid.*
[32] *Ibid.*

suggestive concept of "Verstehen" (the understanding of the internal sense of behaviour) reduces comprehension to introspection and subjectivity. Third, the tendency has been for each branch of sociology to enclose itself in self-made limits which fail to see the total social phenomena. Fourth, the repudiation of the dialectical process in sociology has led to the compartmentalization of different factors in social reality, making it impossible to grasp the total social phenomena *en marche.*[33] Fifth, this crisis of explanation is "due to the crisis in general theory. All science must explain *through*[34] *theory.* Science must have certain hypotheses for guidance in research." [35] Bad theory is preferable to none at all. Explanation is impossible without a general sociological theory ; the more theory is neglected, the more impossible it is to conquer the problem of explanation.[36]

This assessment of the present scene in sociology then serves as the impetus for defining a systematic theoretical scheme. However, before a discussion of Gurvitch's general theory is undertaken, it is necessary to understand the historical approach he makes.

2. FALSE PROBLEMS FROM THE NINETEENTH CENTURY

Certain fundamental problems concerned sociology during the century of its birth. These have largely been resolved, but they are significant as an historical background against which Gurvitch builds his theoretical system.

I. SOCIOLOGY OR PHILOSOPHY OF HISTORY?

When sociology was founded, one of its prime considerations had to do with the end of society. "Where are we going?" or "Where is society going?" or "Where goes the world?" However, to ask such questions is to become deeply involved in the time-worn considerations of philosophy of history. This has no place in sociology. Comte, in declaring sociology to be the positive science of the social facts seemed at first to separate himself from such philosophy of history. However, he went on to declare sociology to be the science of sciences and also pointed to the inevitable achievement

---

[33] *Ibid.,* p. 10.
[34] Italics mine.
[35] *Ibid.,* p. 12.
[36] *Traité* . . . , I, p. 241.

of man (by virtue of this new science) which would culminate in the "positive phase," according to Comte's theory of development. Moreover, the great founders of twentieth their disappearance in a society without class.[37]

Durkheim declared society developed in the sense of growth in organic solidarity and from there, in the sense of liberty, equality and fraternity. Hobhouse, Dewey and Mead believed society progressed without pause towards the total triumph of reason. Saint-Simon announced the coming of the era of social solidarity, Proudhon, the perfect realization of social justice. Marx was convinced that the varied 'alienations' of man, which he described, were only temporary and he promised their disappearance in a society without class.[1]

Gurvitch gives four basic reasons why all pretension towards a philosophy of history must be eliminated in sociology. (1) Value judgments are confused with descriptive judgments of reality when a certain goal or end for society is discussed. (2) Society does not develop unilaterally, as certain philosophies of history imply. Social reality illustrates clearly the discontinuity of movement and development in its various structures and levels.[38] (3) A philosophy of history often implies a monistic interpretation of social reality. There is not one society, but there are many "societies." [39] (4) Finally, philosophy of history destroys sociology's competence to analyze the present situation by placing an emphasis upon the transformation of society.

It is only in renouncing the illusions concomitant with a philosophy that must point to some end and which includes a unilinear and continuous social evolutionary theory, that sociology can concentrate on the really scientific description of such structure or concrete social situation. It does this by tracing the diverse possible perspectives, often antinomic in nature which are revealed in a society that is constantly being remade. It is then free to

[37] *La vocation* . . . , I, 30.
[38] *Ibid.*
[39] *Ibid.*, p. 32.

utilize the results of these analyses in a practical way.[40]

II. SOCIOLOGIES OF ORDER AND PROGRESS.

This second false problem inherited from the nineteenth century deals with those interpretations of the social reality which would reduce its character to one or two simple formulas: either social reality can be defined by its stable, crystallized order of structures, or there is observable in the social system a movement towards inevitable progress. Bonald, de Maistre and Ballanche are representatives of the former position. Condorcet, Saint-Simon, Proudhon, Marx and Cournot are proponents of the latter. The division between *static* and *dynamic* social structures, first formulated by Auguste Comte, is an artificial distinction.[41] These are dialectical and interpenetrating in reality. Such a reduction of social reality to either one of these descriptive terms smacks of a value judgment; it is also a naïve appraisal of the complexity of the dynamic, fluctuating, social configuration. It amounts to an arbitrary reduction of this complexity to over-simplified conceptual abstractions. Such abstractions are usually made by social philosophers or sociologists who are influenced by a particular period in history in which such easy assertions as these could be made. Every social structure contains the forces of order and progress; present also are the static and the dynamic, the centripetal and the centrifugal. Lord Acton's aphorism is descriptively correct, "the only absolute is change." What forces will prevail, how they are arranged, the manner in which they are expressed will differ in each given milieu and epoch.

III. THE FALSE CONFLICT BETWEEN THE INDIVIDUAL AND SOCIETY.

It is equally false to place the individual over against society or to maintain that every social grouping is reducible to its individual members. It is likewise false to maintain society has a psychological and moral preeminence over the individual person. Moreover, to insist that the two abstractions simply interact is to deny the actual situation. Ac-

---

[40] *Ibid.*, pp. 32-33.
[41] *Ibid.*, pp. 35-36.

cording to Gurvitch there is a dialectic once again set up between the individual and society. They are not "exclusive entities, exterior to one another." [42] He goes on to say, in the first place,

> Neither the individual nor society is able to exist without the other. . . . The individual is immanent in society and society is immanent in the individual. From this reciprocal immanence one finds society anew in the depth of the 'Me,' and discovers once again the 'Me' in the depth of the 'We' of society. [43]

In the second place, the reason for this conflict arising between the individual and society has its "origin in certain optical illusions which have been compounded by false interpretations." [44] There is a tendency to consider the conflicts observed in both oneself and society as conflicts between the collectivity and its individual members. The study which Durkheim made on suicide underlines how false abstractions can lead to equally errant conclusions.

> Durkheim placed in opposition to one another "psychological causes" for suicide . . . and "social causes," giving to these latter factors the predominant role. Maurice Halbwachs—his continuator—reached the conclusion that each suicide could be explained both from the point of view of the individual and that of the collectivity without having to discover conflict between the two. [45]

Thus, this conflict is an artificial one. The complexity of social reality points to the necessity of seeing the total social phenomena and the total psychological phenomena. To isolate one level of social life and declare this as being the whole story is to view complex social reality in an unrealistic way.

> To desire to separate completely "Mine," "Thine" and "Ours" and more largely the tension between the individual, the interpersonal, and the collective (We, groups, global societies) is to dissolve or destroy, as such, the conscience itself. The collective conscience and the individual conscience con-

[42] *Ibid.*, p. 37.
[43] *Ibid.*
[44] *Ibid.*, pp. 37-38.
[45] *Ibid.*, p. 38.

sist precisely in the interpenetration of these three factors and in their dialectical relationships, from which come all cultural works (in particular symbols).[46]

In the total psychological phenomena neither the individual conscience, the conscience of others, nor the collective conscience can take a dominant role. They all three form the *whole man.* The problem of conflict between the individual and society is poorly put. It is both artificial and unrealistic.[47] An individual is by definition a member of a society or probably many societies. A contemporary historian lends support to Gurvitch's contention.

The facts of history are indeed facts about individuals, but not about actions of individuals performed in isolation, and not about the motives, real or imaginary, from which individuals suppose themselves to have acted. They are facts about the relations of individuals to one another in society and about the social forces which produce from the actions of individuals results often at variance with, and sometimes opposite to, the results which they themselves intended.[48]

Probably one of the most striking illustrations of this indissoluble link between the individual and society appears in Bergson's *Les deux sources de la morale et de la religion.*[49] He points to the celebrated story of Robinson Crusoe. This is supposedly about a man totally isolated on an island in the middle of the sea. Yet Crusoe is never free from his society, Bergson suggests, since each day he uses those tools and goods which were saved from the shipwreck. Without them he could not exist. With them he is able to subsist and by virtue of using them he maintains a constant contact with the very society in which he was born and by which he was "socialized."

---

[46] *Ibid.,* p. 40. The distortion of social reality by psychologists is aptly described by Talcott Parsons in the introduction to Max Weber: *The Theory of Social and Economic Organization* (New York: Oxford University Press, 1947), p. 27.

[47] Cf. Gurvitch's "Is the Antithesis of 'Moral Man' and 'Immoral Society' True?," *Philosophical Review,* LII (November, 1943), 533-552.

[48] E. H. Carr, *What Is History?,* p. 64.

[49] Paris: Presses Universitaires de France, 1932, the first edition. 1953, the 66th edition.

DIALECTICAL SOCIOLOGY

IV. THE RELATIONSHIPS OF SOCIOLOGY AND PSYCHOLOGY.
Sociology and psychology are not opposed to each other. It is false to assume they can exist independent of each other or that an ultimate choice must be made between the two, though such a demand is often made. The substantive material of society cannot be adequately studied by either individual psychology or a collective psychology or sociology alone. The disciplines are interdependent and the task requires a joint effort.

However, this conflict between the two areas of study continues to the present day. In America certain scholars, such as the psychologist Kardiner in his *The Individual and His Society*,[50] assert there can be no possible contact between psychology and sociology. The school of Durkheim has made the opposite mistake by reducing all their study to collective psychology, to the neglect of the more individual phenomena.[51] Both disciplines have their particular material to study: psychology, for example, has the abnormal phenomena of the human mind and the mind's physiological characteristics; sociology deals with the basic material of social organizations, social structures, and the cultural works which constitute civilization, e.g., knowledge, religion, law, art, and morality.[52]

Yet they find a common meeting place.

> The living drama of increasing and decreasing tension towards the spontaneous which is manifested in the unpredictable, the instantaneous, the fluctuating, takes divergent directions moving between the poles of the Me, Alter-Ego or the Collective (We, Groups, Societies) ; this tension is only possible within the context of the same mental process or, as we would prefer to say, within the concept of the total psychological phenomena. In the total psychological phenomena . . . the three directions of these living tensions are revealed to be as intimately linked as are the same poles in the total so-

[50] New York: Columbia University Press, First edition, 1939, third edition, 1946.
[51] *La vocation* . . . , I, pp. 44-45.
[52] *Ibid.*, pp. 45-46.

cial phenomena, in which they are integrated, be it partially or completely.[53]

This illustrates clearly that both disciplines study the human condition; in such a study the lines between the disciplines are far from distinct and only relative. Man is a whole, and "the We, Groups, Classes, and Societies in which he participates militate against his being cut into fragments."[54] The total psychological phenomena and the total social phenomena must be treated as a whole. Since they interpenetrate, are interdependent and remain bound together in an inextricable totality, this requires a method of study which takes into account this dialectical tension. This method will be described in the seventh chapter. Suffice it to say that psychology can take the researcher either in the direction of the more spontaneous levels of psychical life, which can be expressed collectively, interpersonally or individually (usually all three at the same time), or towards the collective of the We, groups, classes and global societies.

The psychical phenomena are total. The point is, whether they move in the direction of the spontaneous or towards the organized, they are inextricably related to the total social phenomena. Within the total psychic phenomena, three disciplines operate: collective psychology, social psychology and individual psychology. The partitions between these three are relative. The social psychologist, as he studies interpersonal and intergroupal relations, is dependent upon collective psychology (whose domain is the collective mind) since the collective conscious is prior to every type of "human relations". Language is a case in point. A *We*, a group or a society is essential for language to have any meaning.

It is the same for individual psychology. This discipline depends on the collective mind "since neither the individual, whether unconscious or conscious, can be isolated from the interindividual psychical relationships or the collective psyche."[55] Every person, though singularized by the psychologist, is the kind of person he is because of his interaction with the given social milieu. Be it understood this primacy of the social is more latent than manifest. The following diagram helps to show the relationships among these three psychologies:

[53] *Ibid.*, p. 46.
[54] *Traité* . . . , II, 334-336.
[55] *Traité* . . . , II, 336.

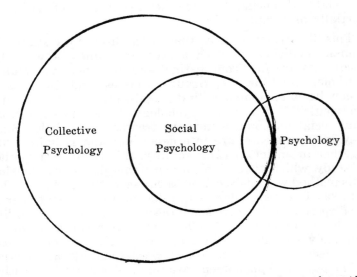

Every conflict situation arising from the dynamic activity of social reality has its effect upon the total psychical phenomena. A psychological reality exists as well, whose interaction with the social gives rise to further conflict situations, all of which make an impact on the psychical phenomena.

Finally, the cultural works of a society or a group are at once the products and molders of these total psychical phenomena. Hence, there is a possible psychology of language as well as a sociology of language. "Psychology looks for the phases of the spontaneous, and sociology the degrees of crystallization." [56]

Gurvitch rejects the American school of cultural anthropology, since to him it reifies culture to such an extent it drains it of all content. Moreover, cultural anthropology forgets that culture is the product and producer of social reality and psychical reality. They cannot be separated. The rapport between these two realities is dialectical. Such a dialectic, which tries to inscribe the psychical within the social, makes possible an understanding of the complex interdependence of the total psychical phenomena with culture.

Gurvitch includes two other diagrams which help to ex-

[56] *Ibid.*, p. 337.

plain these relationships. The first is an ideal conception as yet unrealized by either sociology or psychology: the psychical phenomena are inscribed within the social. The second is realistic, presenting what actually obtains in current research.

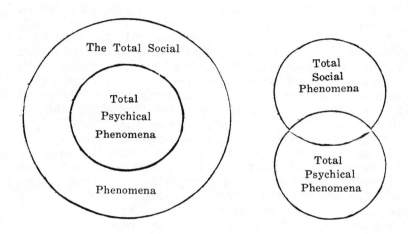

In both conceptions it is understood there are areas of the total sociological phenomena which are entirely outside the interests of the psychical, e.g., the morphological, organizations, technological means and patterns, and social structures. The importance of the psychological explorations into such areas as the Ego, "the relations arising from *Mine, Yours* (singular), and *Ours* varies according to the manifestations of the total social phenomena in their different types and structures." [57]

V. THE DIFFICULTY OF THE SINGLE PREDOMINANT FACTOR.

If there is one problem which plagues sociology more than any other, it is the problem of the single predominant factor. From the most sophisticated scholars to the most naive laymen, this error seems more likely to frustrate the development of a thoroughgoing science than anything else. Any so-called school of sociology which puts a particular emphasis on geography, biology, technology, psychology, eco-

[57] *Traité* . . , , II, 338.

nomics or culture illustrates this error. Reductionism to a simple predominant causative factor is too simple. It is too neat. It does not take into consideration the dynamic and complex nature of social reality. Such a reduction is seductive. In periods of stress people want easy answers. They are confused, distraught and weary. There is an increasing presence of fear. Simple solutions to complex problems are demanded. It is then that radical politics of the "right" or "left" gain recognition and support. Moreover, the cloistered halls of the universities have harbored the skilled researcher and scholar who after all his labor comes forth with a thesis that purports to explain the total social phenomena by either a materialistic determinism, or a "survival of the fittest," or the influence of the Protestant ethic, or the role of climate . . . *ad infinitum.*

Gurvitch gives two examples of outstanding thinkers in the history of sociology who failed to escape this error of the single predominant factor, Emile Durkheim, the founder of modern sociology, saw the importance of social reality as a phenomenon which cannot be reduced to the sum of its parts, a reality which has a unique quality of its own and therefore cannot be identified with any other reality. He goes further to show there are various levels to this reality: the superficial or morphological, the institutional, incorporating symbols, values, and ideas which are at one and the same time the content of social reality and are produced by that society itself, and at the deepest level Durkheim observed the *"free currents* of the collective *conscience."* [58] Three branches of sociology interpenetrate and mutually support each other in their attempt to examine the data of these several layers. Those branches are social morphology, social physiology and collective psychology. It would seem Durkheim had solved the problem of the single predominant factor. However, he and his followers fall into the trap by giving too much importance to the collective conscience, and thence, to collective values and ideas. His innovating concepts degenerate into a new *spiritualism.*

Karl Marx is Gurvitch's second example. He contends that Karl Marx in his early years and at the end of his life "never considered economics as a 'predominant factor' to explain social reality." The works of his youth described a society as a collective activity, a collective effort which is

---

[58] *La vocation* . . . , I, 52.

both spiritual and material. Social reality is irreducible. It is a whole which produces the very elements which become its content. These productive forces cannot be separated from their social frameworks, nor from the individual and collective consciences nor their cultural works. They make up a totality, albeit an *active* totality. It was only later that Marx tried to simplify his conception and directly identified the economic life with social reality. This error was made when he integrated the "productive forces" of society and the "relationships of production" so completely that they could be described in economic terms: "the ensemble of the productive forces and the relationships of production is that which we call society." [59]

Gurvitch goes on to say that what both Durkheim and Marx lack is a sufficient relativism.

> Durkheim . . . would have escaped the danger of returning to the very conceptions he proposed to combat, if he had admitted the morphological base, the organizations, institutions, the symbols, values and collective ideas, and finally the "free currents" of the collective mentality have an importance which differs according to the types of society, in particular according to the diverse *social structures;* at times, even the simple social conjunctures cause them to fluctuate perceptibly in their relationships. The same holds for Marxism. If Marx would escape from the single predominant factor, he would have to admit the relative importance of the "material productive forces", the "relationships of production," the "reality of the collective conscience," cultural works, and "ideology." All of these are essentially variable in different types of societies whose "natures" are not all the same. [60]

This solution for Durkheim and Marx is characteristic of Gurvitch. His concept of relativism as it relates to the types of global society will be a recurring notion in his own thought. Such a relativism calls for a "radical empiricism" to uncover all "predominant factors" which are couched in quasi-scientific terms but are nothing more than simple dogmatisms. In sum, the espousal of a predominant factor is a two-fold error: 1) it tends to immobilize and harden

---

[59] *Ibid.*, p. 55.
[60] *Ibid.*, p. 55.

that which is essentially variable and dynamic; 2) it destroys the object of sociology, which is "to know a specific social reality as an ensemble of its hierarchical [depth] scales, levels and myriad aspects, whose hierarchies depend upon the type of society and its structure!" [61]

VI. THE ROLE OF LAWS IN SOCIOLOGY.

This final problem inherited from the nineteenth century is particularly difficult to eliminate. There has always been a desire to establish the laws which govern society. Moreover, it was the desire of some precursors of modern sociology to establish sociology as a *bona fide* science. They felt this could be done by discovering the laws by which society works. This assumption was a natural outgrowth of the enlightenment. Their hope, however, was based on a close affinity with the Newtonian physics of their day. Now, the natural sciences are *teaching* the social sciences. Physics declares it is impossible to establish causal laws.

> In microphysics . . . following experiments with electrons and quanta, the equation of uncertainty was introduced. Since then one is more and more reluctant to seek strict regularities and even causal liaisons.[62]

Gurvitch feels it is impossible "to formulate in sociology so-called causal laws since the discontinuity between cause and effect is so great." [63] However, there still remains the need for "causal explanations." This type of research must be done within the context of the total social phenomena. Gurvitch explains why:

> The only laws which could be valuable in sociology are the laws of probability founded on statistics. But they are only applicable in very occasional and restricted situations, preferably at the material base (morphological and ecological) or at the level of external collective behaviour which can more or less be predicted, that is regular, habitual, and traditional.[64]

If it is impossible to speak of hard and fast causal laws, it is useful and necessary to assert there are "tendencies

---

[61] *Ibid.*
[62] *Ibid.*, p. 57.
[63] *Ibid.*, p. 60.
[64] *Traité*, p. 61, I.

towards regularity." [65] This means there are direct, observable integrations of various elements within a social whole. These integrations are what might be termed *functional correlations*.[66] Observable are certain correspondences between two groups of social facts. These cannot be relegated to any other period or any other place. They reveal that these ensembles of social facts are integrated into the same framework of the total social phenomenon. There is no assurance they will remain so. The single certainty is that they are *integrated* into the same framework. This means that the realities of certain cultural works such as knowledge, art, religion, law and education are not mere products of the social frameworks. If they were, they would lose their specificity as an irreducible reality. The dialectical method, so essential to sociology, is the only way of assuring that this perspective is maintained. The tendencies towards regularity are only applicable at the macrosociological level. Only here does the sociologist observe certain *patterns* or directions towards which the ensembles point. He must necessarily withhold final judgment as to the final outcome or endpoint of these patterns or directions. This discussion will be more detailed in both the next chapter and Chapter Seven where Gurvitch's methodology is analyzed. In summary, direct integration is the key step in the process of sociological explanation. Under certain circumstances it will be impossible to discover any real tendencies or precise functional correlations due to the difficulty of the phenomena with which the sociologist is working. This in itself is an element of explanation. This kind of honesty is sorely needed at the present hour.[67]

This discussion of the invalid problems inherited from the nineteenth century, some of which have been almost totally eliminated, others of which are constantly reappearing in various disguises and forms, shows clearly the questions and the issues which Gurvitch faced. It is important to remember these as the outline of his theory develops. He is reacting against certain false problems and assumptions. They are historically discernible yet often hidden

---

[65] *Traité* . . . , I, p. 244.
[66] *Ibid.* Gurvitch uses the same meaning for functional correlation that a mathematician gives to the term. See Robert Merton, *Social Structure and Social Theory* (Glencoe, Illinois: The Free Press, 2nd ed., 1957), pp. 21-25.
[67] *Ibid.*, pp. 244-245.

under new categories or put into attractive garbs. Their artificiality and falseness remain. One of the tasks of contemporary sociology is to unveil these false problems and to clarify the real role of the sociologist.

3. THE ACTUAL TASK OF SOCIOLOGY

The field of study for sociology is social reality "taken in all its levels, all its aspects, all its strata in depth." [68] Elsewhere Gurvitch writes:

> The object of sociology is the typology of the total social phenomena: the microsociological types, the types of groupings, the types of social classes, and the types of global societies. [It studies them] within their movements of structuration and destructuration at the interior of these various types located in the time segments which are reconstructed according to their discontinuity.[69]

This statement reveals Gurvitch's distinction between sociology and history. Sociology is not interested in continuity. In fact it emphasizes the discontinuity of the types in order to observe the total social phenomena in all their flux and movement. These are the irreducible elements of social reality. They give birth to various manifestations which become the characteristics of the given reality. These total social phenomena parallel the "normative facts" of juridical experience. These are the elements which express that subjacent totality that is constantly changing, constantly building, destroying and rebuilding. "These phenomena are the homes or reservoirs which create and stimulate, which provide the means by which the We, groups and societies are at once creating and being created, changing and being changed." [70] In another volume Gurvitch defines social reality as the center where man participates in mankind.[71] This reality is irreducible to any other reality. The total social phenomena affirm this reality more than anything else. Sociology studies these social phenomena within the context of their ceaseless movements between "structuration" and "de-structuration" seen in the microsociological, groupal, and global types. It is particularly

---

[68] *La vocation* . . . , I, p. 4.
[69] *Cahiers Internationaux* . . . , XXI, 15.
[70] *Traité* . . . , I, p. 20.
[71] *Spectrum of Social Time* . . . , p. 1.

imperative that sociology accentuate their contingency. It, therefore, needs to call attention to the ruptures between the various types, between past, present and future, between different time segments and continua of reconstructed time periods, with the ultimate purpose of grasping the total social phenomena in their processes of development, retardation and recovery.[72]

Sociologists of the nineteenth century tended to be unidimensional in their approach. "Twentieth century sociology is above all multidimensional. It is sociology in depth." [73] It is "existential sociology." What does the depth sociologist see?

> The social reality to the practiced eye of the sociologist is arranged in levels, strata, planes, or in layers. These strata, or levels, interpenetrate and mutually impregnate each other. Moreover, they do not cease to enter into conflict: their rapport is tenuous, paradoxical, and dialectical. This has to do with the inextricable tensions inherent in all social reality, which one can qualify on a vertical scale. To these relative polarizations are added, at each depth level, the horizontal conflicts and tensions; the antagonism of classes is a good example.[74]

Sociology seeks to bring all these conflicts and tensions to the surface. It tries to see them in their specific social context. The acuteness of these tensions varies according to the multiplicity of the structures involved, the pluralism of types and even of their conjunctures. "It no longer . . . belongs to sociology to resolve or camouflage these conflicts." [75] Sociology's vocation is to develop its capacity for unmasking the contradictions and latent tensions existing in any given social reality, the framework of which is the total social phenomena.[76]

> The intellectual honesty of the researcher in sociology is measured by the steadfastness with which he finds proof in a struggle without mercy against

---

[72] *Determinismes sociaux* . . . , p. 37.
[73] *La vocation* . . . , I, 63. Notice the rapport this concept has with depth psychology. In fact, another descriptive term for Gurvitch's sociology is depth sociology.
[74] *Ibid.*
[75] *Ibid.*
[76] *Ibid.*

every endeavor destined to mask or silence the acute drama, which, at each instant of society's existence, is played out between the different strata of society and at every level of these strata.[77]

Several thinkers have seen the multi-dimensional character of social reality. Significantly their backgrounds are varied. For Gurvitch the most important are Proudhon, Marx, Durkheim, Hauriou, Bergson and the phenomenologists. All went far towards uncovering the various levels of social reality. Each may have intended to do something else. The point is that each revealed a pluralism and depth to social reality which calls for an adequate methodolgy to examine such complex phenomena.[78] That methodology will be the next step in this study.

Gurvitch emphasizes that these precursors of depth sociology represented diverse philosophical positions. Though they saw the multidimensional nature of society, they were unable to renounce all tendencies favoring particular philosophical theses. This serves as a warning.

Nothing will undercut the vocation of depth sociology more than to utilize the analysis of the different levels to the end of defending a particular philosophical thesis. It is necessary to renounce even the use of such methods as "inversion" or "phenomenological reduction" since sociology as science can have nothing to do with a particular philosophical position.

It will be part of the task ahead to see if Gurvitch successfully avoids this pitfall he describes. Remembering his philosophical heritage and an admitted awareness of his own propensities towards certain philosophical doctrines, it should be interesting to follow the development of his method. He is quick to assert all particular systems of thought must be overcome if sociology is to carry out its vocation as a science. This requires a radical empiricism, one which is scrupulously relative in its analysis of the different relationships at the interior of social reality.

---

[77] *Ibid.* Cf. his *Determinismes sociaux* . . . , pp. 37-38; 60-61.

[78] *Ibid.*, p. 64. See especially Edmund Husserl's "Phenomenology," in *Encyclopedia Britannica* (14th edition), XVII, 699-702; and Gurvitch's *Les fondateurs français de la sociologie contemporaine: Saint-Simon et P. J. Proudhon* (2 volumes; Paris: Centre de Documentation Universitaire, 1955) ; and the whole of *Les tendances* . . .

[79] *Ibid.*, p. 65.

CHAPTER IV

GURVITCH'S SOCIOLOGY OF THE
TOTAL SOCIAL PHENOMENA

James Baldwin has entitled a book of essays, *Nobody Knows My Name.*[1] It is a poignant title suggesting the depths of uneasiness which he faces as an individual. These essays, though written by an American Negro, coming out of a definite social milieu, have a universal ring to them. The search for identity goes on for humanity in general, and the individual in particular. This is a world-wide search involving individuals, groups and nation-states.

The very shaping of history now outpaces the ability of men to orient themselves in accordance with cherished values. And which values? Even when they do not panic, men often sense that older ways of feeling and thinking have collapsed and that newer beginnings are ambiguous to the point of moral stasis. Is it any wonder that ordinary men feel they cannot cope with the larger worlds with which they are so suddenly confronted? That they cannot understand the meaning of their epoch for their own lives? That—in defense of selfhood— they become morally insensible, trying to remain altogether private men? Is it any wonder that they come to be possessed by a sense of the trap?[2]

In concluding these introductory remarks to his book, *The Sociological Imagination,* C. Wright Mills goes on to say that information is not lacking for modern man. This is an age of fact. Reason is not missing either. It is available in large part. What modern man needs is a "quality of mind." [3] It is the kind of mind which will help persons use creatively and imaginatively the information, the knowl-

---

[1] New York: Dial Press, 1961.
[2] New York: Oxford University Press, 1959, pp. 4-5.
[3] *Ibid.,* p. 5.

edge which they possess, "in order to achieve lucid summations of what is going on in the world and of what may be happening within themselves." [4] This, Mills calls "the sociological imagination."

Pick up any issue of *American Sociological Review* or *American Journal of Sociology* and examine the contents. It becomes readily clear that on the one hand "information" is not lacking. It is also patently clear that "scientific" exploration is being done in bits and pieces. What exactly is meant by this statement? Simply this, that social scientists in general and sociologists in particular have failed in recent years, since the advent of statistical know-how and grand acceptance of the social scientists and their wares by the power centers of industrial society, to ask the important questions or wrestle with the encompassing perspective that belonged to the classical thinkers in social thought. It is out of style, so to speak. Yet a curious thing is happening. The physical sciences are moving in the direction of greater synthesis in knowledge, while the social sciences seem to be breaking and disintegrating the social totalities into a myriad of disparate parts. Granted, this must be done in order to understand the integral workings of the social whole. But it is false to leave the social body dissected on the laboratory table without realizing at the same time there are just as many, if not more, factors at work which unify that body and cause it to function as a whole. The two processes must be conducted at one and the same time. To leave out one is to distort the picture.

This search for identity with which James Baldwin is concerned and which characterizes the condition and concerns of peoples all over the globe, raises other problems. Is not this question the real one being raised by the emerging nations of Africa, Asia and South America? Now this search for selfhood and nationhood invariably involves the study of history. Yet the modern social scientists in America have little sense of the historical dimension. Furthermore, historians distrust social scientists. This creates an unfortunate abyss, since both need each other and are hopelessly inept in the long run without this mutual support. To quote C. Wright Mills once again:

The sociological imagination enables us to grasp

---

[4] *Ibid.*

history and biography and the relations between the two within society. That is its task and its promise. To recognize this task and this promise is the mark of the classic social analyst. . . .

No social study that does not come back to the problems of biography, or history and of their intersections within a society has completed its intellectual journey.[5]

History gives depth to the study of present day cultures and societies. "We are what we are today because of what we were yesterday" may be a cliché, but there is considerable truth in it. The common attitude of an American branch of sociology is reflected in this statement by Robert Merton:

Social scientists believe it no longer sufficient to describe the behaviour, attitudes, values and social relations obtaining in a complex society simply on the basis of a large but scattered array of documents, both public and private, and on educated guesses about what people are thinking and feeling. Studies of the historical past, of course, have no alternative. But in the study of present-day societies, these procedures are giving way to systematic, though far from perfected, methods.[6]

There is much to be commended in this statement, much that is acceptable. However, there is an implicit denial of the historical reference. This emphasis on systematic methods for the study of present-day societies by-passes unconsciously the necessary reference to the well-springs of the past which go a long way in explaining *why* people feel and think as they do *now*. History is necessary for the *sociological imagination*.

This whole discussion really points to this: sociology can be distorted in two ways. It can move from reality by soaring flights into meaningless, abstract theorizing, or it can become a series of fragmented problems concerning social adjustment. Both courses are bereft of the historical dimension and comprehension of the interrelatedness of the whole and its parts. Both lack the sociological imagination.

---

[5] *Ibid.*, p. 6.
[5] Robert Merton, "Now the Case *for* Sociology," in the *New York Times Magazine*, July 16, 1961, pp. 19-20.

1. THE PROBLEMS OF A METHODOLOGY IN SOCIOLOGY

The purpose of knowledge in a general sense is for the "quickening of human life . . . the advancement of the human spirit *per se*."[7] The goal of scientific knowledge is fitted into this overarching purpose; it seeks to enable man to augment and order his experience. In the social sciences this vocation asks the dual questions of *why* and *whither* in human behaviour and tries to prepare the ground for their answers.

The problem can be put in a two-fold way. First, how does man get at the causal nexus which will provide some notion as to why this or that happened and is happening; and second, how does he overcome the basic fact that he is part and parcel of that causal nexus, part of that object?

The solution is not so simple as it once was. A clear-cut distinction could be made in the eighteenth and nineteenth centuries between the method (subject) and the object of study. This was a result of Newtonian, mechanistic physics which spilled over into the study of human behaviour. Then it was that primitive social sciences believed there were discoverable laws ruling man's behaviour in a deterministic and inexorable fashion. The so-called scientific method combined the inductive approach with deductive logic for internal consistency in hypothesizing. It was all based on empirical observation, giving the scientist a supposedly fool-proof method. Simply, get the facts and generalize from them. But a revolution occurred in the physical sciences which affected the social sciences. The universe no longer was viewed as a mechanistic thing. Darwin in biology had introduced the concept of change. Lyell had already begun this new way of thinking with his work in geology. The study of astronomy added to the final dissolution of a universe of iron-clad laws. Karl Marx picked up the challenge with his work in economics and social philosophy. Henri Poincaré in his little volume *La science et l'hypothèse* summed it up when he said a hypothesis was not a hard and fast law forever a part of the storehouse of scientific knowledge once it had been verified. No, it too is subject to constant scrutiny and has no continuing home, no sacred position. In science, he said, there are no abso-

---

[7] Huston Smith, *The Purposes of Higher Education* (New York: Harper and Brothers, 1955), p. 2.

lutes. Thus the relationship between the hypothesis and empirical research became reciprocal or circular. The scientific process entails collecting facts to verify hypotheses. These verified hypotheses then serve as guides to uncover, analyze and systematize facts. In the atomic physics based on the work of Max Planck, Rutherford, Albert Einstein and others, this new process becomes particularly acute. Rutherford's methods were recently described:

> He had a driving urge to know how nuclear phenomena worked in the sense in which one could speak of knowing what went on in the kitchen. I do not believe that he searched for an explanation in the classical manner of a theory using certain basic laws; as long as he knew what was happening he was content.[8]

The physical scientist has long ago abandoned the search for *laws*. This must also be for the social scientist.[9] Niels Bohr makes certain comments which lend support to this whole discussion:

> In every experiment on living organisms there must remain some uncertainty as regards the physical conditions to which they are subjected, and the idea suggests itself that the minimal freedom we must allow the organism will be just large enough to permit it, so to say, to hide its ultimate secrets from us. On this view, the very existence of life must in biology be considered as an elementary fact, just as in atomic physics the existence of the quantum of action has to be taken as a basic fact that cannot be derived from ordinary mechanical physics. Indeed, the essential *non-analyzability of atomic stability in mechanical terms presents a close analogy to the impossibility of a physical or chemical explanation of the peculiar functions characteristic of life.*[10]

This statement seems to rule out any simple reductionism as behaviourism in the social sciences or, for that matter,

---

[8] Sir Charles Ellis in *Trinity Review* (Cambridge, Lent Term, 1960), p. 14, quoted in E. H. Carr, *What Is History?*, p. 75.

[9] See above, Chapter Three, pp. 126-128.

[10] Niels Bohr, *Atomic Physics and Human Knowledge* (New York: John Wiley and Sons, 1958), p. 9.

the natural sciences. The central thrust of Bohr's statement is that the method of science has changed because the understanding of the object has changed. Moreover, this object, whether it be in the physical universe or in human behaviour, has become much more complex and fleeting. It is a kind of Proteus, says Gurvitch. Human experience "escapes us when we think we have caught it; we are dupes when we believe we have penetrated its secret; we are victims of it when we believe we are free of it, if only for a moment." [11]

What this discussion is leading to is the growing awareness on the part of both physical scientists and social scientists that there is a profound relationship between the subject and object, the method of observation and the object of observation, which is suggestive of a dialectical tension that cannot be neglected. This is to say the method is determined by the object; likewise, the object changes and is conceived in new ways by the method employed. The method of research is an operational tool in the hands of an observer. The observer in the social sciences in particular is also a part of what is observed. This makes his task particularly difficult and the old conceptions of "objectivity" come in for some hard scrutiny. Again, Niels Bohr does not limit this problem to the social sciences.

> The critical point is here the recognition that any attempt to analyze, in the customary way of classical physics, the "individuality" of atomic processes, as conditioned by the quantum of action, will be frustrated by the unavoidable interaction between the atomic objects concerned and the measuring instruments indispensable for that purpose.[12]

In another passage Bohr makes this much clearer. Though lengthy, it is worth quoting verbatim for purposes of illustration.

> You will surely all have heard about the riddles regarding the most elementary properties of light and matter which have puzzled physicists so much in recent years. The apparent contradictions which we have met in this respect are, in fact, as acute as

---

[11] Georges Gurvitch, *Dialectique et sociologie* (Paris: Flamearion, 1962), p. 8.

[12] Bohr, *Atomic Physics* . . . , p. 19.

those which gave rise to the development of the theory of relativity in the beginning of this century and have, just as the latter, only found their explanation by a closer examination of the limitation imposed by the new experiences themselves on the unambiguous use of the concepts entering into the description of the phenomena. While in relativity theory the decisive point was the recognition of the essentially different ways in which observers moving relatively to each other will describe the behaviour of given objects, the elucidation of the paradoxes of atomic physics has disclosed the fact that the unavoidable interaction between the objects and the measuring instruments sets an absolute limit to the possibility of speaking of a behaviour of atomic objects which is independent of the means of observation.[13]

This is a critical observation. Its meaning for the physical sciences still has not been fully realized. It serves to highlight even more the position of the social sciences. They are faced with this "moving relativity" plus the existential position of being part of the object itself. This at once sets them apart from the natural and physical sciences in that their problems are more acute and more complex when it comes to being a "science" in the full sense of the word.

In recent years the social sciences have become aware of a general malaise among many of their fraternity. The reason is that there is growing concern the brotherhood is failing to answer the really significant questions facing humanity. The *why* and *whither* have taken on a will-o'-the-wisp character. Tools for statistical research have been developing rapidly, but the solutions fail to come. The drilling has produced no moisture for an arid land. The research seems to be barren and fruitless. It is a vast desert of abstracted theory, or empiricism, or concern with trivia. The crucial question becomes one of discovering the method which will enable the social scientist to observe and describe human behaviour in as objective a fashion as possible. This leads to the basic contributions of Georges Gurvitch. In these introductory paragraphs basic problems which plague the social sciences were considered. It is the purpose of the description which follows to show that Gur-

[13] *Ibid.*, p. 25.

vitch is quite aware of these problems and has posed some solutions which should be carefully weighed. Up until now he has been treated with indifference and almost totally neglected. Thus far the catalogue of issues reads like this: 1) How can social science and history be mutually supportive? 2) What is the proper arrangement between theory and empirical research? 3) What is the relationship between method and object, subject and object, the observer and the observed? 4) How can the totality be grasped and its individual parts still studied? 5) How can the purposes of knowledge be served, answers provided to the questions of *why* and *whither* in an age of increasing intellectual and academic specialization? Obviously these issues are interrelated. They will serve as the criteria for analyzing Gurvitch's method and his understanding of the object of sociology.

2. METHOD AND OBJECT

It has long been an accepted axiom that a discipline in order to be a science must follow the scientific method. This is the only criterion. The object is not important. If the method is followed, this is sufficient. Now it has become patently true that this is too simple an explanation. It is readily agreed that the object and method are reciprocally interactive. The method is determined in large part by the object. The object may change, thereby requiring the method to change. They must be seen together: object and method, observer and observed. As indicated above, the very nature of the scientific method has evolved in response to the type of universe that has emerged before the persistent efforts of the scientists. The tools or the methods one uses as a scientist are no more absolutistic than the hypothesis mentioned previously. Moreover, as the quotations from Bohr so explicitly state, this method has become increasingly dialectical, in terms of the relationship of the instruments of observation (including the operator) and the material being observed. It is also dialectical in the sense of the term "complementarity", which means that seemingly contradictory hypotheses verified under separate and different conditions, are actually mutually supportive and contribute to the overall "storehouse" of factual material. One theory of light is applicable under certain given conditions. Another theory is equally *true* under other circumstances. It is in the face of this growing realization of dialectical quality to both the physical universe and social reality, that Gurvitch goes beyond the simple basis for a discipline's being called a science. He points out that all reality is dialectically interrelated by virtue of the human element, itself a dialectical tension between the individual and the collective. Even if the natural universe were not dialectic, the method for studying it involves the human factor. The choice of artificially derived frames of reference brings in this dialectical aspect and hence calls for operational processes which are applicable to such phenomena. In other words, every science, and more acutely sociology, constructs its object of study. It chooses, generalizes from the phenomena it observes, never encompassing all that universe. As knowledge expands, the periphery of mystery extends. Artificially conceived abstractions serve as the categories for systematizing and analyzing. Hence the method and the object are, in this sense, one.

> One sees therefore, that a whole dialectic already exists between the spheres of the real, the operational framework of the science and the object which it constructs from this method. But this dialectic is particularly intense in the social sciences by virtue of their "engaged" character where conscious and unconscious value judgments enter in and against which they must unceasingly struggle.[14]

The dialectical method is proposed by Gurvitch then as the solution for this problem of the relationships between the object and subject, the observer and the observed, summed up in the problem of objectivity. If a science is going to be a science, it will have to adopt a method which will deal realistically with this "engaged" character of the social disciplines. E. H. Carr, in a Cambridge lecture, delineates this notion.

> In the social sciences subject and object belong to the same category and interact reciprocally on each other. Human beings are not only the most complex and variable of natural entities, but they have to be studied by other human beings, not by independent observers of another species. Here man is no longer content, as in the biological sci-

---

[14] *Dialectique et sociologie*, p. 183.

ences, to study his own physical make-up and physical relations. The sociologist, the economist, or the historian needs to penetrate into forms of human behaviour in which the will is active, to ascertain why the human beings who are the object of his study willed to act as they did. This sets up a relation, which is peculiar to history and the social sciences, between the observer and the observed.[15]

Such differences in the domain of study require the social sciences to find a way of handling this quality of "engagement." The dialectic seen as a hyperempirical and radically relativistic method is the way to deal with this characteristic. Gurvitch, then, is meeting head on the problems of subjectivity and the nature of the material being studied. He notes the inextricable bond which dialectically links the proper domain of the discipline with the method for studying it. The true nature of the dialectic will be revealed in the character of this sphere of study which for sociology is social reality.

3. SOCIAL REALITY AS THE TOTAL SOCIAL PHENOMENA

Martin, in his study of Gurvitch, errs in stating that "sociology is defined [for Gurvitch] by its method rather than by its object." [16] He has failed to see how Gurvitch relates reciprocally the domain of study and the method. Martin is contradictory when in the next paragraph he asserts, "for Gurvitch social reality is its [sociology's] object of study or the total social phenomena." [17]

He is right in this statement. However, it is the object of concern which will determine the method for getting at these phenomena of social life. As that object changes, so does the method. There is no sacred scientific method which the scientist is obligated to follow. C. Wright Mills once more nails down the point:

> Polykarp Kusch, Nobel Prize-winning physicist, has declared that there is no "scientific method," and that what is called by that name can be outlined for only quite simple problems. Percy Bridg-

---

[15] Carr, *What is History?*, p. 89.
[16] Martin, *Depth Sociology* . . . , p. 7.
[17] *Ibid.*, p. 8.

man, another Nobel Prize-winning physicist, goes even further: "There is no scientific method as such, but the vital feature of the scientist's procedure has been merely to do his utmost with his mind, no holds barred." "The mechanics of discovery," William S. Beck remarks, "are not known . . . I think that the creative process is so closely tied in with the emotional structure of an individual . . . that . . . it is a poor subject for generalization . . ." [18]

The object of sociology will not only determine and relativize the character of the method, but this object will be the definition of the vocation of sociology.

First, to follow Gurvitch's lead, what is *not* the domain of sociology? It is well to remember that Gurvitch is convinced sociology must have a *specific* field of study. It must study a particular reality in a particular way. This is what sets it apart from other social sciences and from history. Hence, J. S. Mill's definition is unacceptable, since it is too general and ignores not only the specificity of social reality but its very existence.[19] Other authors see sociology as the integrative discipline of the particular social sciences. This throws it into the lap of epistemology, and refuses it status as a science itself. All discussion on method is fruitless; and moveover, the comparative method which is so much a part of sociology is eliminated by such an understanding of the domain of study. This agrees with C. Wright Mills's criticism of one sector of what he calls *abstracted empiricism* in American sociology. This "school" defines the function of sociology as that of being a pathfinder for the onrushing social scientists. Quoting Paul F. Lazarsfeld,

[The sociologist] is so to say the pathfinder. . . . When a new sector of human affairs is about to become an object of empirical scientific investigations, it is the sociologist who takes the first steps. He is the bridge between the social philosopher, the individual observer and commentator on the one hand and the organized team work of the empirical investigators on the other hand. . . ." [20]

[18] Mills, *The Sociological Imagination*, p. 58.
[19] *Traité* . . . , I, 4.
[20] "What is Sociology?," Universitets Studenkontor, Skirvemaskinstus, Oslo, September, 1948 (mimeo) in Mills, *op. cit.*, p. 59.

This really denies sociology a life of its own, a domain of study, a vision and a vocation.

Gurvitch next tackles the so-called formalists. These theorists, such as von Wiese and Georg Simmel of Germany, attempt to overcome the position of the former criticism by giving sociology a specific status. However, they choose the wrong method. Simmel says that "sociology studies the forms of interpersonal relations." Gurvitch comments that the great merit of this position is to indicate that sociology in its generalizing will necessarily have to look for distinct types of structures. But the great weakness of this theory is to see forms without contents. . . . This approach spins theories about forms but does not include the concrete expressions of groups and societies.[21] Furthermore, to reduce the essence of social reality to interpersonal relations is to fall hopelessly into a nominalism which also denies the existence of real groups and societies, or more generally social reality as a specific entity.

In general, Gurvitch reacts against all theories which deny the irreducibility of groups and of the society, which fail to see them as indecomposable realities.[22] Hence, the *culturalists* arose as a distinct school to combat this "formalism" and nominalism of von Wiese, Simmel, Dupréel, Bogardus, Park and Burgess, and Znaniecki, among others. The domain of sociology, however, is dissolved by the cultural anthropologists and abstract culturalists, as Alfred Weber (brother to Max), into the culture or civilization as such. The definition of sociology would be somewhat like the following for these cultural anthropologists:

> Groups and societies are only the executing instruments of a score which has been orchestrated in advance—this score is the "system" or "form" of a civilization. All that remains to the sociologist is to discover the different types. They are quite numerous for some (Toynbee saw about twenty); for others there are only a few discernable (Spengler recognized only four).[23]

Gurvitch does not make room for cultural anthropology as a separate discipline. For him this study is within the

---

[21] *Traité* . . . , I, 5. Cf. Durkheim and Fauconnet, "Sociologie et sciences sociales," *La revue philosophique*, 1903, p. 401 ff. Cited in a footnote, *Ibid.*

[22] *Ibid.*, p. 6.

[23] *Ibid.*, p. 7.

domain of sociology. Gurvitch feels more affinity between himself and the cultural anthropologists of the United States than he does with the sociologists. It is a point worth remembering. French sociology in general is closer to cultural anthropology than it is to sociology in America. More will be said about this observation in the critical section.

It was Marcel Mauss who cleared up the true relationship between society and civilization. Civilization, he says, is a social phenomenon of the second degree. Like all total social phenomena, it has its boundaries and its particular spirit. "The form of a civilization is the totality of its specific aspects which reveal the ideas, the practices and the common products, or more or less common ones, of a certain number of given societies, invented by and carriers of this civilization." [24] Mauss underlines the dependent character of societies and civilizations. There are as few civilizations without societies as societies without civilizations. This conception of the total social phenomenon, which will be scrutinized at length shortly, strikes at the roots of abstract culturalism in sociology. Culture is the content of society, the cement of groups and global totalities. To separate culture from the domain of society is to deny society once again specific, concrete content. Such abstraction is impossible. Current definitions of society in contemporary American text books suggest the difficulty of making this separation which Gurvitch is describing. For instance, one of the most popular college texts says a society has four characteristics: 1) it occupies a definite territory; 2) it provides for a means of reproduction; 3) it is an independent entity; and, 4) it includes a comprehensive culture.[25] If culture is necessary for a society, and society essential for a culture, how can the two be studied separately? This question will be considered at a later point in this study.

The fundamental roots for Gurvitch's view of social reality are found in works of the "founders" of sociology. He pays particular attention to Saint-Simon, Proudhon, Comte, Marx and Spencer. These thinkers are important precisely because they saw "the specificity of social reality." [26] Saint-Simon called sociology "social physiology." He saw society as a real entity in movement, in which the collective efforts,

[24] *Traité* . . . , I, 8.
[25] Henry M. Johnson, *Sociology: A Systematic Introduction,* (New York: Harcourt, Brace and Company, 1960), pp. 9-13.
[26] *Traité* . . . , I, 8.

both spiritual and material, were something different from the individual participants with whom they interacted and interpenetrated. For Auguste Comte, human society (Humanity with a capital "H") was a real totality. It imposed itself on its individual members as both subject and object, as the acquired and the effort, the speculative and the active, all in all, a totality which implied religion, education, and knowledge as regulative forces within it. Proudhon saw social reality as an immanent totality, the product of collective efforts, revealing several levels or dimensions. It was made up of collective power, reason, creativity and conscience or mind. Justice and the "ideal" were often in conflict. Other levels were law and similar agents of social control. Marx, the foremost prophet of social realism, viewed the social classes, society and man himself as real entities. These totalities were created by the interpenetration of social life illustrating a dialectical tension between the productive forces and the means of production (the social structures) ; the spiritual products or cultural works of religion, ideas, representations were all implied in the material production itself. Such groups as social classes in certain frameworks could be a productive force escaping the "ideological superstructures." [27] Finally, Spencer saw clearly that the domain of sociology consists in studying "institutions," the means of "social control," and "social structures." For him these were *real* entities.

The real precursors of Gurvitch's thought are Emile Durkheim and certain of his disciples. Looking at Durkheim first, Gurvitch discovers three separate definitions of sociology in his writings. The first two are explicit, the final one is implicit. Gurvitch has long been recognized as one of the foremost critics—in the finest sense of the word— of Durkheim. He says the first definition of sociology, according to Durkheim, is given in his *Règles de la methode sociologique* (first edition, 1894). Here the theorist states that sociology is an autonomous science; "a social fact can only be explained by another social fact" and "must be treated as a thing." Society thinks, feels, and acts completely differently from the members of it considered in isolation. The social fact for Durkheim is exterior to the individual and exercises such a constraint upon him. In the second edition of his book, Durkheim clears up some mis-

[27] *Ibid.*, pp. 8-9.

94

interpretations by adding that this external constraint may be seen as a kind of "social pressure." He suggests that the individual is affected by the "free social currents" of the collective mind. This world of the social facts cannot be known by introspection. It can only be known by its *collective representations*.[28] The second definition has Durkheim agreeing with Marcel Mauss and Fauconnet in what they wrote in *La grande encyclopedie française* of 1901. Here sociology is the science of institutions. "The institutions are the ensemble of acts and ideas which are incorporated as the contents of these structures. The individual finds himself before these acts and ideas which are more or less imposed upon him." [29] Durkheim himself wrote, "Sociology can be defined as the science of institutions, of their origins and function." [30]

Gurvitch criticizes this definition as being much wider and more relevant than the first, but the term "institution" has a rigid, almost cadaverous character. There is no room in this definition for the creative, the unexpected, the effervescent. Moreover, this was the phase in Durkheim's thought when he rejected the rights of any other social science to have a domain of its own to study. If this is the science of social institutions, would not economics study economic institutions, political science, political institutions, etc? He concluded that all the social sciences are really absorbed into that of sociology. However, Gurvitch points out that different methods can be used to study the same area. Sociology is typological in its method, the particular social sciences are systematizing and analytical, history and ethnography are singularizing. Moreover, the same domain may be studied at different levels. Social morphology looks at the ecological and the morphological superstructure; grammar studies the signs and symbols incorporated in language; the science of law examines the patterns and roles of law, etc.[31] In Durkheim's third definition he sees various levels, or depth sociology, also nascent in Proudhon (as previously mentioned), Marx, Bergson, and Hauriou, all preparers of the way for the real task of sociology and for its definition as well. Durkheim failed to see the plurality of methods which could be used to study this multi-dimensional

---

[28] *Essais* . . . , p. 5.
[29] *Ibid.*
[30] *Ibid.*, p. 6.
[31] *Traité* . . . , I, 10.

social reality.[32] This aspect will come from other sources in Gurvitch's background. Still, Durkheim, according to Gurvitch, had the great merit of seeing the need to view social reality from a double perspective: that of looking at it as a social whole and at the same time examining the characteristics within that whole. However, Durkheim tried to establish too tight a causal line. Thus, he forgot the functional correlations, the calculation of probabilities, tendencies towards regularity and the modes of integration within the totality. Moreover, he had not sufficiently distinguished between the different social types. He was of the belief that such clear-cut qualitative distinctions would fragment the total nature of social reality, and one would be unable to see the *continuous* line of their development. This necessity to see an evolutionary development from the archaic or primitive to the advanced and complex (quite obvious in his *Elementary Forms of Religious Life*) failed to include the great contribution of Max Weber, namely that of comprehension (*verstehen*) which enables the sociologist to establish these qualitatively distinct "ideal" types.[33] According to Gurvitch, Weber borrowed this conception of *verstehen* from the historian Dilthey (1833-1911) who really meant by this term, "the direct grasping" or intuition of the real concrete totalities and the human meanings which are a part of them. However, Weber could not accept this definition, since he was hamstrung by a conception of the human conscience which is closed and not open. This makes it impossible for an intuitive grasping of the ensemble, the real, the concrete in social life. Weber is the victim of a radical nominalism and individualism which characterizes his conception of social reality. He rejects straightway the direct apprehension of social groupings or societies; he knows only fragmented particles, a mere collection of individual behaviours. Weber defines sociology in the following way:

> Sociology is a science which attempts the interpretative understanding of social action in order thereby to arrive at a causal explanation of its cause and effects. In action is included all human behaviour when and in so far as the acting individual attaches a subjective meaning to it. Action is

[32] *Ibid.*
[33] *Traité* . . . , I, 12, and *C. I. S.*, XXVIII, 9-10.

social in so far as, by virtue of the subjective meaning attached to it by the acting individual (or individuals), it takes account of the behaviour of others and is thereby oriented in its course.[34]

Elsewhere, Weber makes this statement which underlines the nonrealist position of this great thinker and the place where Gurvitch finds his greatest difficulty in accepting what he has to say:

> . . . For the subjective interpretation of action in sociological work all collectivities such as states, associations, foundations, must be treated as *solely* the resultants and modes of organization of the particular acts of individual persons, since these alone can be treated as agents in a course of subjectively understandable action . . . for sociological purposes there is no such thing as a collective personality which "acts". When reference is made in a sociological context to a "state" or a "nation" or a corporation or a "family," or "army corps," or to similar collectivities, what is meant is, on the contrary, only a certain kind of development of actual or possible social actions of individual persons.[35]

Gurvitch asks if Weber doesn't fall into a kind of psychologism which is a result of his "interpretative comprehension" limited to the individual participant. He also points out this psychologism is limited by his "culturalism." Here Weber reduces all the social sciences to *sciences of culture (Kulturwissenschaften)*.[36] Weber goes on to attribute roles, symbols, patterns and values, the role of a "predominant factor," depending upon the subject being treated. This is particularly spelled out in his sociology of religion writings, i.e., *The Protestant Ethic and the Spirit of Capitalism*.[37] However, this culturalism did lead to his formulation of the typological method which has been an invaluable contribution to sociology. This method grew out of Weber's polemic against Rickert. The latter denied the possibility of sociology's becoming a science of culture, since it

[34] Max Weber, *The Theory of Social and Economic Organization* (Glencoe, Illinois: The Free Press, 1947), p. 83.

[35] *Ibid.*, pp. 101-102.

[36] *Traité* . . . , I, 13.

[37] Max Weber, *The Protestant Ethic and the Spirit of Capitalism* (New York: Charles Scribner's Sons, 1958).

wanted to generalize in an area where generalizations are impossible. Weber discovered his typological method in response to this criticism. Types in sociology are considered to be "founded on the interpretative comprehension (understanding) of the meaning of behaviours, first of all, a subjective meaning, but which includes the cultural significations as well. These types are intermediary between generalization and individualization. . . ." [38] By generality Weber does not mean an average or mean point; nor does he mean by individuality the sense of uniqueness. "The ideal type as Weber used it is both abstract and general. It does not describe a concrete course of action, but a normatively ideal course, assuming certain ends and modes of normative orientation as 'binding' on the actors." [39] It then described a *typical* action, not a real concrete one. It is a methodological tool, not an absolute concept. "The ideal types of social action which for instance are used in economic theory are thus 'unrealistic' or abstract in that they always ask what course of action would take place if it were purely rational and oriented to economic ends alone." [40]

These types then are irreducible to any other types. They are qualitative and discontinuous types. "They are conscious stylizations . . . coherent images which are original or unique and serve as operational references for empirical research." [41] In this sense Weber always emphasized the pragmatic aspect of this concept. "Only the movement from the 'subjective sense' to the 'cultural meaning' furnished, according to Weber, by the particular social sciences, seemed to him to limit the hypothetical and somewhat utopian character of his typology." [42] This typology of Weber was minutely broken down into various categories: social relationships, types of groups, types of global societies, types of power, procedures, types of charisms, types of struggles, types of religions, and various other types, including types of whole civilizations. Gurvitch suggests this taxonomy has a close affinity with George Simmel and his *social forms*. Whether this is so or not, the relationship between Weber and Simmel is in their mutual nominalism which denies the

[38] *Traité* . . . , I, 14.
[39] Weber, *The Theory of Social.* . . . , p. 13 (Introductory remarks by Talcott Parsons, the translator and editor.
[40] *Ibid.*, p. 111.
[41] *Traité* . . . , I, 14.
[42] *Ibid.*

specificity and realness of collectivities or social reality. "Weber reduced the social facts to 'chances' of individual behaviours and to meanings, ignoring thereby all other levels of social reality: the morphological base, the organizational level, symbols, roles, attitudes, and the collective mind." [43] Weber, like Simmel, von Wiese, and the majority of the American sociologists, sees the social as a web of interpersonal relationships whose unity is a "probability." "Weber ignored totally the problem of social structures; he did not grasp the conception of the total social phenomena at any of their levels; he impoverished social reality to the point of denying it altogether." [44]

In summary, Weber made two great contributions: a) he developed a typology which was both discontinuous and qualitative; b) he did not fall into the trap of linking comprehension to explanation. However, he is at fault in the following ways, according to Gurvitch's view:

1) He made an arbitrary liaison between comprehension and subjective interpretation.

2) It is impossible to justify the passage from subjective meanings to social and cultural meanings.

3) He failed to leave any room for objective criteria in the establishment of types.

4) The types which he did establish were linked to a spiritualized culturalism.

5) The unfortunate fragmentation of types made it impossible to apply them to the various levels of the total social phenomena.

6) The destruction of the social reality was caused by his radical nominalism. This made it impossible for Weber to grasp the reality of groups, classes, and the "We," as well as their cultural works.

7) He tried to combine culturalism, psychologism, and formalism, but failed to do so. They remained quite heterogeneous and resembled globules of oil on the sea of social reality.

8) Finally, the total absence of a dialectical spirit made it impossible for Weber to see the total social phenomena or to grasp the collective wholes as real totalities.[45]

Moreover, he failed to see that comprehension and explanation are only passing moments of one and the same

---

[43] *Ibid.*
[44] *Ibid.*, pp. 14-15.
[45] *Traité* . . . , I, 15.

process. This would become clear only in espousing the dialectical approach which clarifies this relationship and all others that go to explain the dynamic quality of social reality.

Marcel Mauss is the terminal point of any discussion for Gurvitch on the definition of the method and object of sociology. This disciple of Durkheim defined sociology as a science which "applies the wholistic method to the study of the 'total social phenomena.' " [46] Mauss, in his efforts to understand the phenomenon of "potlatch" among the Kwakiutl Indians of North America in particular, developed the notion of the total social facts, "that is to say, these phenomena such as "potlatch" set in motion . . . the whole of society and its institutions . . . all these phenomena are at once juridical, economic, religious, even aesthetic and morphological." [47] "These are 'wholes' or entire social systems which we have described according to their functioning . . . they are dynamic . . . as opposed to a rigid or cadaverous condition . . . while considering these as wholes we perceived their essential quality, a movement of the total, a living aspect . . ." [48] Mauss gives this definition to sociology: "The principle and the end of sociology is to apperceive the group as a whole, and its behaviour as a whole." [49] "The view of the total social phenomena can meet the arguments of the historians who say sociologists are too abstract by separating society into bits and pieces." [50] It can also aid psychology, since sociology sees "the whole man or the complete man in which the body, soul, and society are interrelated and where the total social phenomenon and the total man tend to mean the same thing." [51]

Gurvitch gleans five lessons from the sociology of Marcel Mauss:

1) His conception of the total social phenomena was a reaction against the hyper-spiritualism of Durkheim's last period. Mauss substituted a relativistic realism and empiricism.

2) Mauss reacted against the rigid, fixed notions of Durk-

---

[46] *Ibid.*, p. 18.
[47] *Sociologie et anthropologie* (Paris: Presses Universitaires de France, 1950), p. 274.
[48] *Ibid.*, p. 275.
[49] *Ibid.*, p. 276.
[50] *Ibid.*
[51] *Ibid.*, pp. 276, 304-305.

heim's institutionalism and saw social reality as dynamic, in movement, exhibiting tendencies of revolution and explosion within the most tradition-bound groups or societies.

3) He reacted as well against the separation of comprehension and explanation as two different processes. He could not accept the Weberian reduction of comprehension to an interpretation of the internal or subjective meaning of individual behaviours.

4) He was opposed to every kind of abstract culturalism.

5) Finally, he found unacceptable the separation of sociology and history according to objects of study. Both deal with the total social phenomena. Only their methods differ.[52]

Marcel Mauss, then, occupies the most important place in Gurvitch's immediate background. It is his heuristic conception of the total social phenomena which serves as the symbol to explain the multi-faceted, complex dynamic unity of social reality. This is not to say that Gurvitch accepted everything Mauss had to say concerning this notion. In fact, he makes it clear where he feels the sociologist failed. First, Mauss hesitated to accept or rather did not spell out his qualitative typology to the extent that it clearly distinguished sociology from history. The reason for this is that Mauss identified the total social phenomena with the global societies and with them only. In other words, he was unable to see how these phenomena could also be incorporated into the microsociological elements and the lesser macrosociological groupings. "But, to establish types of global societies along the lines of the total social phenomena, it is necessary to type their structures." [53] The total social phenomena would have no body, no form, no handle by which to generalize. It is essential then, to type their structures whether they are complete or partial. (A structure is complete when it is a global society.) Secondly, Mauss failed to provide the points of reference for seizing these phenomena and their movements.

There is an absence of sufficient accentuation of the depth levels whose multi-dimensionality provokes a perpetual coming and going of mutual implications and polarizations; insufficient attention is paid to the tension between the astructur-

---

[52] *Traité* . . . , I, 18-19.
[53] *Ibid.*, p. 19.

CARL A. RUDISILL LIBRARY
LENOIR RHYNE COLLEGE

able, structurable and structured elements which are juxtaposed in the social macrocosms.[54]

The total social phenomena can only be seen in dynamic wholes moving from structuration, to destructuration and on again to restructuration. In the last analysis, it is the dialectical movement among the microsociological aspects, the groupal and class macrocosms and the global societies, each with its own manifestations of the total social phenomena, which escapes the otherwise sharp perception of Marcel Mauss. This will be Gurvitch's own contribution to this notion.[55]

In sum, Mauss lacked the proper method to view this object of sociology. His typology was imprecise; he also failed to understand the place of the dialectic as the *modus operandi* for grasping these total social phenomena in their totality. The dialectic is the only assurance the sociologist possesses that every philosophical pretension will be eliminated; moreover, it is the only method which can possibly grasp the full impact of a social reality so susceptible to change, to movement, to upheaval, to volcanic eruptions, to the unexpected; it is the only method which can at one and the same time provide a way of understanding both the centripetal and centrifugal forces which are operative in the social whole.

Thus Gurvitch comes to this conclusion: "One cannot define the specificity of sociology without stipulating precisely at once its domain and method whose interpenetration give birth to its object." [56] This then, is the more concise and explicit statement of the relationship between object and method. The domain of sociology is social reality. Social reality is the total social phenomena.

There is no doubt in the minds of laymen as well as professional sociologists that a quality of life exists which is called social. It is obvious to the practiced eye as well as to the untrained one that man is a social creature. Aristotle's dictum, "man is by nature a political animal," still holds when taken in its generic sense. Yet the notion of social life, social reality, groupal living, and society is ephemeral. It is elusive and difficult to grasp. Its content escapes categorization and neat conceptualization. Still, there is this

[54] *Ibid.*
[55] *Ibid.*, p. 19.
[56] *Ibid.*

aspect of life which calls for disciplined attention and study. Scholars, writers, artists, musicians, historians, and social scientists have been trying to describe it. Mass movements, social classes, Western civilization, the Muslim world, political parties, the primitive cultures, the family and clan units, and economic groupings are some of the names given to group phenomena. These are far from precise terms. Others are even more vague. Still social reality has an irreducible quality for those who follow the findings of Emile Durkheim. It is something more than the sum of its individual members. This social reality is a real totality; it is far from static. It is moving, creating, changing, threatened from below, from without, and from within by all kinds of conflicts and tensions. It is never at rest. Even the most tradition-bound global societies have within them the latent seeds of radical change. This era is one of rapid social change. Increased technology, communications, globe-encompassing means of transportation have brought once isolated peoples into relationships with persons of divergent backgrounds and outlooks on life. The process of change is constant and swifter than in yesteryear. A group or a class, a society moves from this hierarchy of relationships to the next hierarchy in a matter of years, or even months. At the center are those classes or groups in conflict which vie for power and through revolution upset the former arrangements instituting their own notions, their own hierarchy of ideas, symbols, roles, attitudes, organizations and creative endeavors. Social reality is caught in a tug-of-war between the centripetal forces which unify and the centrifugal forces which threaten to tear it apart. If such disintegration occurs, the new forces soon right the ship or rebuild it and put it on a tentative even keel.

Unilinear, unidimensional, single views of this social reality which would fix and arrange, systematize and absolutize, are outmoded. New conceptions, new methods, new visions must be found to describe a social reality which has changed so much from that which the first social scientists began to look at in the beginning years of their disciplines.

Social reality is more than its surface manifestations. One can count noses, houses, cars, trucks, schoolrooms, acres of land being farmed, tenements, playgrounds, the number of votes for a candidate, ascertain age, sex, length of residence, and increases in population density, but this will not explain social reality. One can add up the number of times one person speaks to this or that individual in a small group, the number of times this individual is chosen for leadership, the number of times this process is followed to make a certain decision, but this will not describe the profound qualities of social reality. The question of *why* asserts itself at each juncture. For instance, *why*, asked M. Mauss, do these North American Indians practice "potlatch?" Is it for juridical reasons? Do the economic motives answer this question? Are the religious aspects sufficient to explain this phenomenon? No, none will do alone. The solution only comes in seeing this as a total social phenomenon.[57]

But how are these total social phenomena arranged? What exactly are they? Again, looking at "potlatch" it is readily discernible by external observation that certain material factors are involved, certain artifacts can be catalogued, certain numbers of people located in certain ways, involving this amount of foodstuffs and banquet tables, etc.; all this can be added up and tabulated. But this is only the surface manifestation of "potlatch." It tells the observer something, but it fails to answer the total question of *why*. Beneath, one can see certain social organizations at play. The arrangements of the families, the ceremonies that accompany this practice, the ritual, the specific ways of social organization, in sum, make possible the practice of "potlatch." These tools of social life are discernible no longer by external observation, but are only comprehended by getting at their various meanings. In other words, this stratum of social life is less accessible to the sociologist. He must dig more deeply, and when he does, he discovers this is not all. The organizations are insufficient to explain everything.

Obviously social reality is more than what can be observed by the external tools of the physical senses. These fail to explain. The sociologist must explore in depth the more profound levels of social reality to capture even a partial understanding of its life. Hence, taking a lead from the work in psychology, Gurvitch has developed what he calls a "depth sociology." The total social phenomena are arranged not only horizontally but vertically. It is this vertical view of social reality that commands a closer inspection.

---

[57] *Sociology of Law*, pp. 263-264.

THE TOTAL SOCIAL PHENOMENA

I. THE VERTICAL VIEW OF SOCIAL REALITY.

The origins of this notion in Gurvitch's thought are easily traceable to his work in social law theory. The chapter on his background spelled this out in some detail. There are two levels, generally speaking, to social life: the organized and the spontaneous. Or in Marxian terminology, the super-structure and the infrastructure. There are various degrees to these two levels. These degrees are discernible on a vertical line moving from the hardened crust of the mor-phological manifestations through the levels of the super-structure, becoming more supple as the descent is made, finally crossing over into the realm of the spontaneous.

It is essential to see this conception of depth sociology as a symbolic image or tool for grasping the whole idea of so-cial reality. This is a device and not an absolute. The pro-cedure for describing this fundamental conception of Gur-vitch will be first, to show the development of his thought, second, the method for distinguishing between these stages, and third, the description of the ten depth levels.

Briefly, the development of Gurvitch's notion of depth sociology followed his studies in legal sociology which grad-ually moved into general sociology. As indicated above, he saw social life divided between the two general levels of superstructure and infrastructure. This thought came from his concentrated studies in social law, especially as he sought to work out the notion of obedience and the source of the law's authority. Why do people abide by the law? He an-swered that beneath any type of coercive power was the social force, the infrastructure of lawabidingness built into the warp and woof of social life. If one explored this notion deeply enough he came to the *normative fact* which is the ground for all authority in law. This normative fact was a creature of the social collectivity and in turn changed and affected it. It was at once the creature and the creator of social life. This normative fact existed at the spontaneous level beneath the crusted surface of the organized social life. Going back further into Gurvitch's life it is well to recall that the notion he had of social law and the general outlines of his sociology came from the direct experience of the Rus-sian revolutions. These two levels to social reality were crystal clear to the young student. In times of relative peace and quiet these levels are less discernible, but still they pro-vide a method for understanding and explaining social life.

Gurvitch says he is not the only one who had had such

notions about social reality. He includes in the list of the precursors of depth sociology, Proudhon and Marx, Durkheim and Hauriou, and Bergson and the phenomenologists (who proceed by inversion and reduction towards the "immediate"). The basic ideas which have been underlined by Gurvitch have been mentioned previously. It is sufficient to say that Gurvitch feels each one of these thinkers, though he had the notion of depth levels as descriptive of social reality, nevertheless could not escape creating a hierarchy of values. Proudhon as a rationalist gave the most important place to collective reason. Marx placed greatest emphasis on the material forces of production. Durkheim, who rejected in his early career every temptation to give the primary position to morphological factors, gradually placed the collective mind in a superior rank which he identified as Logos or Spirit. Bergson finally reached the conclusion that the social spontaneity incarnating the *élan vital* in society is of primary importance. Hauriou, influenced by his Thomism, affirmed without hesitation the superiority of the spiritual in the drama taking place among the various levels of social reality.[58] In sum,

> It would no longer be possible to consign depth sociology to a particular philosophical thesis. Depth sociology would have to renounce every tendency towards supporting one type of method such as "inversion" or "phenomenological reduction," since as a science it could have no particular philosophical orientation whatsoever.[59]

This last statement is of particular importance in the development of Gurvitch's thought on the vertical view of social reality. In a footnote to this passage just cited, he recognizes that he erred in both his *Essais de sociologie* of 1938 and *L'expérience juridique* of 1935, by proclaiming the special value of phenomenological reduction or inversion for the depth analysis of social reality. He does the same thing in his *Sociology of Law*, 1940. One passage from these works will be sufficient to illustrate his allegience to this philosophical position. In *L'expérience juridique,* he asserts that in order to grasp the "immediate juridical experience" it is necessary to proceed by an effort of "reduction and inversion (which . . . goes downward by stages),

---

[58] *La vocation* . . . , p. 65.
[59] *Ibid.*

moving from daily experience of juridical life to the pure experience of the immediate." [60]

His *Essais de sociologie* produced this statement:

> There remains only one way to find the objective criteria which will enable making the distinction between the different forms of sociability: it is the method of inversion or phenomenological reduction (Husserl), which is the immanent decomposition of the domain by digging deeper to the superimposed levels of social reality.[61]

He goes on to say that this descending process, which moves from one depth level to another until one arrives at the most profound source of social experience, is the method of depth sociology and reveals a vertical social pluralism.

Finally, in his *Sociology of Law*, he states that:

> The best approach to problems of the sociology of the noetic mind (or of the human spirit) and to the determination of its exact place among the various sociological disciplines, would seem to be via the levels—or depth—analysis of social reality. This type of analysis is inspired by the "method of inversion" (Bergson) or "phenomenological reduction" (Husserl), i.e., an immanent downward reduction through successive stages towards whatever is most directly experienced in social reality.[62]

What method does he use to get at these depth levels? Martin, in his study, suggests that though Gurvitch denies any allegiance to the phenomenological method of reduction or to Bergsonian inversion, he still unconsciously maintains this as the way to move from one level to another until the deepest point is reached, the ground of being, the ontological fact which is before everything else. Gurvitch in recent publications admits that he tended to favor a particular philosophical method in order to grasp the depth levels. He feels now he has succeeded in divesting himself of every tendency in this direction because he has developed his dialectical method. The radical "hyper-empiricism" of this new approach militates against any philosophical "reductionism" and makes it possible for him to utilize several

---

[60] *L'expérience juridique*, p. 63.
[61] *Essais* . . . , pp. 20-21.
[62] *Sociology of Law*, p. 42.

means to get at the vertical pluralism of social reality. The different depth levels interact in varying ways. They are hierarchized differently according to the types of societies and their global structures, as well as partial structures. This requires constant surveillance and study of each of these depth levels as they function within the various frameworks of social reality. There is no general scheme for social reality. It can only be determined by examining the various discontinuous and qualitatively different types of social frameworks.

There are three methodological rules to remember when applying this vertical view to social reality:

1) To say that one level is more profound or a deeper position than another is not to imply a value judgment. This merely means that a level is more accessible or less accessible to direct external observation. Hence, the most "superficial" layer is that of the morphological and ecological factors. This signifies that these factors are more readily observable. "The stages below in social reality are, therefore, simply those which require a greater effort in order to grasp them and study them scientifically." [63]

To talk in terms of depth is really to talk of the degree of difficulty involved in grasping the "data" or the phenomena which exist beneath the obvious in social reality. In this sense, sociology follows the goal of any science, namely, to "find the hidden." [64]

2) This second rule concerns the total view of these phenomena. All of these depth levels are indissolubly linked together and interpenetrate. If they were isolated from one another, they would cease to exist. Each is a moment of the total social phenomenon. Each is united irreducibly and indivisibly within this total complex. Gurvitch makes it plain that there can be no system of continuity developed between these different levels. In reality the more valid characteristic is that of discontinuity. There is never a time when a society is totally cohesive or completely disruptive. The two forces of cohesion and disunity or divisiveness are at work. It can be described only in terms of degrees of cohesion or diversity. There are moments, fleeting moments, when conflicts are overcome and a complete sense of unity is realized, but they soon pass. Witness the Algerian in-

---

[63] *La vocation* . . . , p. 66.
[64] *Sociologie et dialectique*, p. 7.

dependence. Moments of unity existed perhaps when such independence was proclaimed after so many years of torment and conflict, but this unity was short-lived. The conflicts, the tensions and the divisions returned in short order. The degrees of disunity must be plotted. This is the way in which to see these total social phenomena.

These tensions between the phenomena are not only observable within the global societies where the task of discerning them is much easier, but within the various groupings, social classes, and even the microsociological elements. "To limit the conception of the total social phenomenon to global societies would be committing a grave methodological error. Each group and even each form of sociability can and must be equally conceived as total phenomena, that is, envisaged in the whole of their depth levels." [65] This means that the approach of analysis remains the same in every aspect of sociology. It does not change. It must also be kept in mind that the three sociological planes or types are only distinguished pragmatically and methodologically. Their divisions are always relative and they, too, form a whole. They are inextricably bound together. The types of societies, the types of groupings, and the forms of sociability presuppose each other and are dialectically related. They, then, make up what is known as the *complete total social phenomena.*[66] In a summary statement, the total social phenomena are the points of reference for carrying on sociological study. They suggest at once the necessary unity of the task as well as the various levels or domains of research which are available and which must be undertaken. They unify the effort, while at the same time breaking down the task in order that the work is scientifically *respectable.*

Finally, the nature of social reality reveals a constant compromise being formed between continuity and discontinuity. In sociology discontinuity is stressed over continuity. The reverse is so in history. Nevertheless, in order to eliminate any errors and overburdening of the facts concerning this facet of sociological analysis, it is essential to realize that the degress of continuity and discontinuity vary even according to the different types of social frameworks. This stresses once again the necessity of turning to the dia-

---

[65] *La vocation* . . . , p. 68. Cf. also *The Spectrum of Social Time,* p. 7.

[66] *Ibid.*

lectical method and to a super-empiricism coupled with a radical relativism.

3) The number of depth levels is not fixed. These are merely operational tools for studying social reality from one viewpoint, the vertical. It is not an *a priori* conception. "The validity of these sociological frameworks can only be verified from a practical standpoint." [67] It is possible to have N ≠ 1 number of depth levels. Clearly there is no room for absolute boundaries or partitions in science. Sociology is looking for some conceptual tools which help in getting at the analysis of social reality, to the end of explaining *why* and *whither*. Every scientific step is a partial understanding. It is based on applied rational procedures situated mid-way between the "instrumental" and the "dialectic" and the "coherent." "Depth sociology constructs and delimits social reality in more or less artificial levels in order to arrive at some effective operational frameworks which can serve as points of rapport for empirical research." [68] If these frameworks are going to do their job they must remain flexible, supple, and subject to change as the need arises. It may be they will have to be added to or some levels deleted. "The *dialectization of the simple,* which Gaston Bachelard considers as the vocation of contemporary science, finds in sociology a particularly singular and complete application." [69]

II. THE DEPTH LEVELS OF SOCIAL REALITY

Gurvitch proposes depth sociology as one way to look at social reality (the total social phenomena). If the sociologist follows from the most superficial layer down to the less accessible levels until he reaches the least accessible, he will have *one* way of describing the strange, exciting, continually changing and deceptively appearing social reality in which he and every human being live. The techniques for getting at these various levels will change as the process downward continues. The more simple methods or tools will be sufficient for the more superficial layers; the more complicated tools will be required to arrive at a sufficient description of the lower depth levels. The following approach in depth can be traversed:

(1) *The surface level of morphology and ecology.* This

[67] *Ibid.*
[68] *Ibid.*
[69] *Ibid.*

layer is viewed from outside. It is the most superficial and the easiest to observe. Here the observer notes the perceptible persons and things; he is looking at the "geographic and demographic basis of society." [70] He notes the density of population, its distribution in relationship to the soil, its mobility in the urban centers; he marks the number and kinds of churches, monuments, buildings, prisons, residences, stores, factories, means of communication, various means of transportation, the types of products, both farm and industrial, tools, machinery, and workshops. These are all part of "social morphology." [71] It is at this level that one notes the interpenetration of the natural milieu with the social attitudes and influences. Even the geographical factors have been transformed by the social activity, by the human element. The very reason for the desire to "control" the natural environment is socially derived. It is out of this process of socializing the material milieu that the conception of property arose. Property, then, has a social meaning implicit even in the most individualistic notion of private ownership. "The property consists in an intense participation of the things of society; all that is, in one way or another, appropriated, is penetrated by social fluids." [72] This suggests the reality of social layers beneath the notion of property which sustain the whole system of property. This was the basis for Marcel Mauss' discovery of the "total social phenomenon" as he observed it in the whole practice of *Le Don, forme archaique de l'echange*, 1923.[73]

(2) *Social organization.* Probing more deeply into social reality, one soon encounters the organized aspect of social life. A meeting is held at the local union hall to decide what the decision will be concerning the latest offer from the board of directors of the local steel plant; a marriage ceremony is held in a church where at a particular moment in the service both the religious organization and the state are represented. The Congress defeats a bill for medical care; the Supreme Court decides the states must reapportion their legislatures. These are all illustrative of the "organized" side of collective life. "The organizations are those preestablished collective behaviours which are managed, hier-

---

[70] *Sociology of Law*, p. 43.

[71] *La vocation* . . . , p. 70.

[72] *La vocation* . . . , p. 71.

[73] Cf. his *Sociologie et anthropologie*, pp. 145-284. This monograph is reprinted in these pages.

archized, and centralized according to certain derived patterns and which fix in advance the expected behaviour in a more or less rigid manner." [74]

These organizations exercise considerable constraint or social pressure. They are one of the ways in which social control is applied. There is always a certain distance present between the organizations and the spontaneous social life characterized by the sense of "We." This distance is always plotted in terms of degrees. This also points to the "real" social life which can never be captured in an organization. The organization is only partially successful in reflecting or containing this spontaneous level beneath. Here is Gurvitch's early work in sociology of law being applied. In fact, his discussion of the differences between authoritarian regimes and democratic systems clearly delineates this notion of the interpenetration of the superstructure by the infrastructure.

Gurvitch makes it especially clear that the organization is not to be confused with a social structure. He is particularly short with the American sociologists who have not seen this organized aspect as being only one level of social reality. They have been impeded by their nominalism to such an extent in order to bring these atomistic elements into some kind of unity, they have had to rely on the notion of organization. They have tried to distinguish between formal and informal organization in order to take care of the nonstructurable elements (astructurable in Gurvitch's terminology), but this is to confuse the two separate categories of organizations and structures. The organizations form an important part of the structures, but they are only one layer of social reality, one aspect of the total social phenomena which are partially revealed (*in toto*) in each structure. The organizations can never express a global society even if that society is rigidly and completely organized. ". . . The importance, the efficacy, role, characteristics, weight and number of organizations, vary functionally according to the social structures which make them possible and in which they are integrated." [75] Elsewhere Gurvitch makes this point even clearer when he states:

> The structures represent a precarious balance of
> multiple hierarchies; as such they constitute a phe-

---

[74] *Op. cit.*, p. 71.
[75] *La vocation* . . . , p. 407.

nomenon which is much more complex than the organizations. The structures have a considerably richer content than the organizations and this makes the notion of structure more complex as a concept. If the structures never succeed in expressing entirely the total social phenomena, the organizations, taken separately in their whole, never succeed in representing entirely the structures.[76]

More will be said about these relationships when the discussion centers on the "horizontal" aspects of social reality. Suffice it to say at this juncture that Gurvitch is making every effort to define very carefully the conceptions of *organization, structure* and *total social phenomenon*. Care must be taken in showing how he personally defines these terms, in order that his theoretical position is understood.

If the organizations are only partial expressions of social structures which are themselves partial expressions of the total social phenomena, then one must push further into the interior, or below the surface, to discover the next level of social life which is revealed to the sociologist as he makes this effort to probe beyond the mere surface of things.

(3) *The stratum of social patterns.* In Gurvitch's original expression of these depth levels, he did not include the role of social patterns. He went further to the layer of symbols. His *Sociology of Law,* published in 1946 in the United States, did contain this level. Why did he decide to include this stratum? Has he complicated the study of social reality from this perspective of depth analysis by adding this stratum of social patterns or models? He will also add the levels of social roles and attitudes. The same question can be asked.

This level containing signs and signals and rules lends a certain regularity to social life, whether this be in the form of a set of expectations one can make concerning a certain behaviour or as an overriding influence which leads to a specific pattern of behaviour. These models or patterns cover a vast domain of traditional clichés, slogans, social signals and signs which are formulated in advance, plus very temporary fads, modes and fancies. They are a particular level of social reality because they go beyond the sphere of organizations where, indeed they play a prominent

---

[76] *Ibid.,* p. 439.

role. In fact, these latter could not exist without them. They also influence the collective behaviours which take place outside the organizations. In other words, these patterns affect the two levels on either side of them, and are distinctly different. How? Certain illustrations will help to indicate this. This will also show how many factors are included in this substratum: national and regional dishes, fashions in clothes, industrial and agricultural techniques, manners, etiquette, protocol, are all examples. What is more, national and local festivals, education, political life, juridical life, and even moral and religious life are permeated by these patterns. "The social patterns guide and direct not only behavior but also mental life itself, whether it be collective or individual." [77] This would include both intellectual colorations such as the mental "states" of representations, perceptions, memories and opinions and mental "acts" of judgments and intuition, and emotional and voluntaristic colorations, encompassing the irrational or affective side of human nature.

Patterns are both traditional customs and routines and the passing fashions and modes of any era. Hence, patterns are neither simply rigid normative rules by which groups are ordered, nor are they fleeting fads of a given society, but they are in some sense both. Currently, there is a distinction made between cultural patterns and technical patterns. Gurvitch feels this somewhat valid, though relative. They once again interact. The cultural models would relate to the spiritual or value-oriented side of social life. These would reveal the character of religion, knowledge, art and education, plus morality and law. Technical models would refer to those aspects of daily life such as the recipes for preparing a certain dish, or the methods to carry out economic transactions. However, it is clearly seen that the way in which economic life is organized and regulated affects the cultural patterns, since no segment of social life is totally made up of either ideational or technical processes. Perhaps the most dramatic example of this basic interaction to which Gurvitch is pointing is the description of the impact of technical change on cultural patterns given in the UNESCO study edited by Margaret Mead and entitled *Cultural Patterns and Technical Change*.

[77] *La vocation* . . . , I, 73-74.

> Technical change is . . . as old as civilization and since time immemorial the ways of life of whole peoples have been transformed by the introduction of new tools and new technical procedures, as inventions like the plough, the domestication of animals, writing, the use of steam, the factory assembly line, and the internal combustion engine, have been diffused from one country to another. Relationships or relative dominance between two peoples, population balances, dynasties, and whole religious systems have been upset by some change in technology, just as the inventions which underlie technological change have themselves arisen from changing conceptions of nature and of man.[78]

Gurvitch finds it necessary at this level of social reality to distinguish clearly between signs, signals and symbols. He points out that the American behaviorists so often identify signs with symbols. Signals as such do not have a symbolic character. They merely act to remind, to transmit an order of society or group which in turn prescribes a certain behavior on the part of the members. Hence, when the whistle blows in a factory at 8:00 a.m. it is a signal that work is to begin officially. The signals are closer to technical patterns than cultural ones.

Social signs are certain expressions "which are substituted for a particular meaning and fulfill the role of an intermediary between this meaning and the collective or individual subjects who are called to comprehend or to grasp it." [79] An example would be an arrow pointing the way to Paris. This arrow says simply, this is the shortest way to Paris and it is by this route. These signs are not symbols. They express very completely what significations they wish to convey. This is not so for symbols. The reason why will become clear when that level of social reality is discussed.[80]

In answer to why Gurvitch decided to add this stratum to the seven original depth levels, the reason probably lies in his discussions and readings and experiences in the United States, particularly with cultural anthropology just

[78] Margaret Mead, ed., *Cultural Patterns and Technical Change* (New York: UNESCO, 1953), p. 9.
[79] *La vocation* . . . , pp. 75-76.
[80] Class notes, the University of Paris, November 26, 1956.

coming of age early in the 1940's. As has been maintained up to this point, Gurvitch is more closely allied with the whole school of cultural anthropology in the United States than he is with the work here in sociology. The comparisons will be made in the subsequent chapters. It is enough to say at this juncture that his whole discussion of cultural and technical patterns subsumed under the heading of social models shows his coming to grips with this "new" area of study in the United States. It was only after World War II, as Clyde Kluckhohn points out in his *Mirror for Man,* that cultural anthropology began to be studied seriously in many of the colleges and universities.[81]

It is also clear that Gurvitch tries to show there is a distinctive difference among the levels of organization, social patterns and collective behaviors. This latter considers those more or less regular collective behaviors which are not linked to an organization, and thus have a distinctive quality of their own.

(4) *Unorganized collective behavior.* The social patterns imply this level. It is this unorganized collective behavior that fulfills the social models. There is often a separation or inconsistency between the expected behavior and that which is observed. This gulf varies of course. It is only on rare occasions that the behavior does not follow the expected patterns of the more superficial level. The study of these more or less regular behaviors reveals a hierarchy based on the criterion of spontaneity. One moves from the more rigid and regular to the more unpredictable and dynamic. The following will serve as an illustration of the scale:

a) Rituals and traditional ceremonies founded on rigorously defined traditions, which are followed to the letter. Religious ritual, juridical and administrative processes are particularly clear-cut examples.

b) Then come the collective behaviors such as practices, morals, routines, or "kinds of life" which are much more supple than the ritualistic and traditional type. Perhaps the term folkloric would be acceptable to describe this style and behavior.

c) Fashions and fads are fluid and changing behaviors. They are not linked to custom or habit, but are constantly renewed and subject to revision. One observes these in

---

[81] New York: McGraw-Hill, 1949, pp. 168 ff.

fashions, be they literary, artistic, philosophical or millinery.

d) Finally comes the "level of collective behaviors" which reject the accepted patterns and promote the unexpected. These are the nonconformist, the insubordinate, and the "highly irregular." [82]

These distinctions recall once again Gurvitch's previous work in social law and the sociology of law. It is enough to recount from his *Sociology of Law* that two vertical classifications were given: "jural reality corresponding exactly to the two superimposed strata of active sociality: spontaneous sociality and reflected sociality." [83] In other words, these were the two levels of the organized and unorganized law which correspond to the distinction between the organized behavior and the unorganized behavior or the vertical degrees which are obvious at this particular level of social reality and help exceedingly in the scientific description of what is.

Gurvitch goes on to state that if this level of regular collective behavior were recognized and so defined, it would eliminate the confusions which have arisen over the term *institution*. Especially these confusions are obvious in the Durkheimian school, the work of Hauriou and above all with the Americans such as MacIver, Sorokin and Parsons. Of late the term has been linked with social structure, which has only added to the confusion. A discussion of this problem will follow in the section on social structure. It is adequate at this point to say that the real difficulty comes with trying to link patterns, organizations and regular collective behaviors together in the same concept. The term *institution* is either used in too broad a sense or one too narrow. It would be better to eliminate it from the sociological vocabulary and follow a procedure which would define these in more specific and specialized terms.[84]

[82] *La vocation* . . . , p. 79.

[83] *Sociology of Law*, p. 221.

[84] An example of the kind of definition against which Gurvitch is reacting is this one given in Harry N. Johnson's sociology text: "A social institution is . . . a recognized normative pattern. As such, it applies to a particular category of relationships. Thus the institution of marriage is a complex normative pattern that applies to all marriages in a particular system or a particular segment of a social system. These marriages (relationships) conform to the pattern in varying degrees, of course; but married partners all *know* the pattern itself, if it is truly institutional, and they regard it as morally valid and binding.", p. 22.

(5) *The web of social roles.* In describing the collective behavior of varying regularity it became obvious that there was a level beneath which there was another more spontaneous level, tending to be more innovating and creative, more unpredictable and more prone to do the unexpected. In this whole description of the total social phenomena it is becoming clear that the criterion for the separation and the discovery of depth levels lies with the element of spontaneity. "The combinations and interpenetrations of the social roles appear to us as representing a level in depth which is more spontaneous than that of unorganized behaviors of varying regularity." [85] The position of this depth level is exactly between the collective behaviors and the more profound level of collective attitudes. These webs of social roles, which can support the structured and even organized aspects of a society along with the spontaneous, effervescent and creative, are defined in the following way:

> Social roles are web-like springboards for possible collective and individual actions. They contribute to the structuration and destructuration of the macrosociological social frameworks, whether only in realizing the unexpected, in innovating or even modifying more or less profoundly, and, to a limited extent, contributing to the re-creation of the social frameworks and their structures. [86]

There are several kinds of social roles. 1) The *structural* social roles such as those of status, or belonging to organizations, imposed roles or the traditional and routinized roles of regular behaviors; 2) *symbolic* social roles which can be the same as the first, but they form bridges and junctures between the organized and the spontaneous; 3) *fluctuating* social roles which are clearly a part of the more spontaneous elements. They contain the rich possibilities of the unexpected, the modifying, the creative. 4) The *latent* social roles which are played by certain social classes; 5) the *aspired* social roles also belonging to certain groups and social classes as well as individuals; 6) finally, *imagined* social roles existing somewhat apart from this web of interlocking roles; this has to do with imaginary roles certain persons think they hold and must be associated with the psychopathological. [87]

[85] *Ibid.*, pp. 80-81.
[86] *Ibid.*
[87] *La vocation* . . . , p. 80.

Gurvitch is wont to point out that these webs and dramas of social roles are played by groups as well as individuals. He criticizes G. H. Mead for his reducing social reality to the interplay between roles and persons. This ignores the collective nature of groups as well as the specificity of social reality. Moreover, it ignores the other depth levels of social reality and overemphasizes one aspect, one stratum, one layer of the total social phenomena. On the other hand, he attacks Linton, Parsons and others for confusing the terms *status* and *role*, either in giving them too broad a connotation or too simple and banal an interpretation. He finds himself in agreement with J. L. Moreno when he points to the impossibility of roles being isolated. They always tend to form clusters. He cites Sorokin approvingly when he says "without an entire drama there can be no role, for a role is possible only in the context of all the roles of the drama. A role can become a social role only in the presence of a social matrix." [88]

However, Gurvitch finds certain deficiencies in Moreno's theory. These criticisms serve well to suggest what Gurvitch includes positively in his conception. He discovers a lack of clarity in Moreno's characterization of social reality in general, of groups and the microsociological elements in particular. Moreno still attributes the social roles solely to individuals. He fails to understand that these *trames et drames* (webs and dramas) of social roles form indissoluble wholes themselves which must be understood as a separate depth level. Moreno does not take into sufficient account the conflicts and struggles between the various roles being played by the same individual or group in different social situations. There is lastly a lack of adequate analysis of the relationship "between certain roles and the processes of structuration plus a negligence of the variations or roles which are present in the different types of structure." [89]

Gurvitch uses certain examples to illustrate this theory. He points to the obvious fact that each individual participates in several different groups at the same time. Hence, the individual plays a different role in each group. The type of person he is varies according to the group or the situation. He may be a militant member of his local union and

---

[88] *Ibid.*, p. 83.
[89] *Ibid.*

a docile husband. Another example cited by Gurvitch is the way in which the role of an individual or group varies according to the social juncture. A revolutionary may after a time become a conservative as the reins of change have been taken up by those who have gone beyond him. Karl Marx expressed this with special vigor when he described the changing roles of social classes. This generation's revolutionaries become the next generation's reactionaries. To wit, says Marx, look at the role of the bourgeoisie.

A final example deals with the conflicts and antinomies which spring up over the desire to get and maintain one's hold on the status positions. Here one can see the conflict between the "regular roles," the symbolic, aspired, latent, and modified roles. These conflicts exist as much for groups as for individuals. When they come between groups there is usually a change in the whole social structure; when they occur between individuals and within the individual, this often leads to neuroses and inferiority complexes.[90]

What is apparent here is that the roles played by the different groups and individuals are often in turmoil and in conflict. They are rarely in total harmony. These antinomies and tensions go a long way to explain these same factors in social reality as a whole. These conflicts can be followed on the horizontal plane as well as in this vertical description. "In effect, the social roles prescribed by an organization could easily be distinguished from the social roles which are much more spontaneous, less regular and which come from a direct common action." [91] These could then be distinguished from the desired roles, which are latently present and which the collective or individual subjects strive for and lay a claim to in the future. In other words, this depth analysis could select a faculty in a university or a labor union and follow this method of studying the different levels of social roles with a guarantee of some very interesting results.

In conclusion, these social roles are webs of social positions, both collective and individual. They cannot be separated from each other, from other social roles or from the social framework in which they are enacted. They are one stratum of the total social phenomena. They are a part of the whole. "To consider a social framework, a group, a

[90] *Ibid.*, pp. 84-85.
[91] *Ibid.*, p. 85.

THE TOTAL SOCIAL PHENOMENA

structure, or an organization as a simple assemblage of social roles is to fall once again into the nominalistic error of failing to see the whole." [92] These skeins of social roles, forming indissoluble wholes, serve as positions from which collective and individual action springs; this leads to the unexpected, to the creating and modifying of the social frameworks themselves. However, these webs of social roles never entirely express the whole. They imply something beneath them of a more spontaneous and dynamic quality. It is the level of collective attitudes, the first real level of the spontaneous or collective mind.

Why did Gurvitch add social roles to his original set of seven levels? This can only be a guess. During his stay in New York he had come into contact with the work of Moreno and the whole movement of sociometry. Moreover, he had been much impressed by the thought of G. H. Mead. He had long been an admirer of Mead's efforts to explain the relationship between the microsociological and the macrosociological. As Gurvitch worked through this material concerning social roles, he felt he had discovered the immediate bridge between the more spontaneous factors and the organized collective behaviour and social patterns. These webs of social roles are not as dynamic and effervescent as collective attitudes. They are the last semblances of superstructure. Perhaps the biggest reason is that Gurvitch did not feel he could neglect the enormous work which had been done in this whole area. It seemed to be a useful category for specifying this depth analysis, if kept in its proper perspective.

(6) *Collective attitudes.* This new level marks the advent of the spontaneous itself. The observer now enters the domain of the collective mind. These attitudes open up the more profound levels which represent the unorganized, the immediate, the spontaneous first enunciated in Gurvitch's social law theory. Many would reject this area of concern as being outside the realm of sociology. This, they would say, belongs to psychology or social psychology. Gurvitch reminds the student that it is difficult to separate the total psychological phenomena from the total social phenomena. This was explained in detail in Chapter Three. He specifies in an additional remark from *La vocation* that "for us the attitudes belong at once to the 'total social phenomena' and

[92] *Traité* . . . , I, 163.

the 'total psychological phenomena' which represent two intersecting circles sharing the same 'territory' concurrently." [93]

Now what is a collective attitude? To begin with, it is a kind of disposition which pushes a real collective unity to do this or that act. It is a very particular kind of social environment in which the "organized elements, models, signs and rules exist as much as the practices, social antagonisms, collective values and ideas." [94] These attitudes serve as a privileged climate for certain symbols, especially of the emotive type, by which collective values are expressed in a social framework. An attitude is an essential part of every social grouping. This will be one aspect of the definition of a social grouping which will be the particular concern of the next section of this chapter.

Social or collective attitudes represent the most paradoxical aspect of social reality. They can be persistent and fluctuating, predictable and totally unreliable, easily understood and grasped and veritable will-o-the-wisps. In sum Gurvitch offers this definition:

> They are wholes, social configurations (*Gestalt*) more often latent than actual, which imply at once a mentality, in particular of affective preferences and dislikes, of predispositions for certain types of behaviour and reactions, for certain tendencies to assume certain precise social roles. They possess a collective character and are contained a social framework where the social symbols are manifested and where the particular scales of values are accepted or repudiated.[95]

The attitudes cannot be detached from the total social phenomena. They are one aspect of the whole. "They are one aspect of the social *Gestalt*, expressing the environments whose importance for social reality cannot be overlooked." [96] It is an error to oppose the individual attitude with the collective one. This is the old story of the false conflict between the individual and society. They are related through the dialectical process of ambiguity, complementarity, mutual implication, polarization, and reciprocity

[93] *La vocation* . . . , p. 86. A footnote.
[94] *Traité* . . . , I, 164.
[95] *La vocation* . . . , p. 87.
[96] *Ibid.*

of perspectives. Moreover, persons change their attitudes in accordance with their roles and the groups in which they play out these roles. This is one of the reasons why public opinion polls so often fail to ascertain the true "public attitude." Pollsters confuse the somewhat hesitant responses of the so-called representative sample which are "stacked" and "directed" from outside, with the real attitude of the group and the person. If one is going to be successful in getting at what a person thinks or feels on a specific subject, he must bridge the gap between what he says and what his real attitude is.[97]

The American school of social psychology has reduced this element of attitude to strict psychological categories. In doing this, they have stripped it of its most important characteristics. This has led to some grave errors. The most apparent is in thinking that if one simply changes the attitudes of individuals, they will be able to ameliorate successfully a social condition. The best example is in the problem of the Negro's rights in the United States. All the education in the world, every attempt to change attitudes without at the same time attacking the very structure of the problem, will result in complete failure. An attitude is a part of the total social phenomena, and by virtue of this, it implies all the levels of social reality (organized and unorganized); it is a partial whole itself, a social configuration in which the mental is only one aspect. This is the important feature of the idea, so often overlooked by an approach which sees only the psychological factors. This partial approach is the common error of many persons of "good will" as well as individuals who would protect the status quo in the South. The proper view of the collective attitude is necessarily a sociological one. It is a collective Gestalt, one level in the whole of social reality. This level then contains more than the webs of social roles, the practices and styles of a particluar life, the flexible and organized activities of the participants and the groups of a given social reality. It is a support for all of these upper strata, and it affects them at every stage. Still, this is only the edge of the collective mind or the outer limit of the truly spontaneous levels. Probing more deeply the observer is confronted by the level of symbols, not signs or signals, but symbols, which are at once the products of the mind and

---

[97] *Ibid.*, p. 88.

the means through which the mind acts and expresses itself.

(7) *The social symbols.* The level of social symbols begins to strike at the heart of the spontaneous infrastructure. It is extremely vast and penetrates nearly every one of the total social phenomena. Expressing the very same role as the "normative facts" for social law, these symbols, being both the producers and the products of social reality serve as the cement which binds and gives unity to these multiple phenomena. It is through the level of symbols that the separations and fissures are healed or reunited. It is also significant to repeat that the very notion of the total social phenomena is a symbolic conception attempting to describe the nature of social reality. In this sense, it is illustrative of the apparent truth that this reality cannot be grasped in its completeness by one conception or a series of conceptions. It is beyond the adequacies of language. Yet, symbols are essential if a start is to be made towards any kind of comprehension.

In essence, the symbols urge or beckon the members of a society to participate directly in the "contents of that which is symbolized." [98] Gurvitch underlines his assertion that symbols cannot be reduced to signs or signals. Symbols can never express the full meaning of that which is being symbolized. The symbol is always an inadequate vehicle. This is the first principal characteristic of a symbol. The second characteristic is the way in which it pushes, cajoles, calls the subject to which it is addressed to participate in that which it signifies. This implies also that there is a close relationship between the symbol and the symbolized. They mutually interact. One might compare this to means and ends. They are never entirely separated. The ends affect the means and the means influence ultimately the ends, especially if means inconsistent with the nature of the end are employed to realize this end. Hence, this same kind of dialectical interaction is observable between the symbol and the symbolized.

Some examples of social symbols which Gurvitch uses are the statue of Joan of Arc calling forth certain collective values evoking national loyalty, the totem which symbolized the god of the clan, the cross which reveals a whole gamut of values and ideas as well as the actual memory of Calvary and the Resurrection, and the national flag which brings

---

[98] *La vocation* . . . , p. 90.

forth the responses of patriotism. The activities of the mind are necessarily dependent upon symbols which are socially derived. Hence, all mental activity is in a profound sense, a social process.

Every social symbol has two poles: first, it is a particular kind of "sign" and second, it is an instrument for participation.[99] Just because symbols may be more "rational" today is no reason to assume that they are becoming simple signs (meaning, they are expressing completely that which is symbolized). This is to overlook the volatile, changing, multifaceted character of social reality. Moreover, the symbols will always remain as means to participate in that which is symbolized, which is distinctly different from the role of signs as defined above.

"One of their essential characteristics is that they reveal while veiling and veil while revealing, and that while pushing towards participation, they also restrain it." [100] This points to the extremely ambiguous character of symbols, which is a way of underlining their "human and social quality." [101] Symbols can be either intellectual, meaning their dominant characteristic has to do with logical categories, or mathematical formulas or conceptual frameworks for particular sciences; they can be predominantly emotional as in the mass for the dead or the celebration of a wedding; finally, they can be primarily volitional, that is, they serve as devices for affecting radical change. As is often the case, they can be all three at the same time. It would be more accurate to emphasize this "functional pluralism" of symbols. This again illustrates the way in which the total social phenomena and the total psychological phenomena intersect. They are dramatically present in this level of social reality.

> One can say therefore, that the symbolic function is inseparable from man in his individual and collective life, since he is first of all a constructor of varied symbols, the mission of which is to master the obstacles which he faces or at least to manage them better.[102]

The symbols have a task of expressing that which is in-

[99] *Ibid.*, p. 92.
[100] *The Spectrum* . . . , p. 3.
[101] *La vocation* . . . , p. 93.
[102] *Ibid.*, p. 95.

expressible. The way in which they "succeed" at this job depends on numerous variables: 1) the subjects who create the symbols or who elaborate on them, 2) the subjects who are the objects of these "created" symbols, in other words the "receivers," 3) the types of partial or global social structures, 4) the historical circumstances, 5) the social frameworks such as types of societies, groupings or forms of sociability, 6) the relationship between the symbol and the symbolized, 7) the nature of the obstacles which the symbol faces and must either master or manage, 8) the particular characteristics of the symbol or the symbolic content, 9) the number and manner of illusionary elements or strictly straightforward material, 10) the degree of rigidity or suppleness to the symbols, and 11) the degree of intensity of each depth level and the conflicts between them.[103]

These variables go a long way to suggest the extreme relativity of this depth level. Also shown is the close affinity between the symbolic sphere and the total social phenomena. This reaffirms the symbolic character of the notion itself. The total social phenomena as a symbolic conception only very inadequately expresses what social reality happens to be. This is why these terms and these levels cannot be seen as absolutes or as *a priori* truths. These depth levels are inadequate, partial, and incomplete substitutes for social reality. The explanation of the universe is the obstacle confronting the sociologist. This is perhaps a partially successful attempt to manage the affair.

There is little doubt that these symbols seek to fill the gaps, fractures, and splits which are present in social reality. They are a fluid social cement. "In this fashion the social symbols are more attached to the non-technical products of civilization, such as language, education, knowledge, morality, art, literature, religion, law, etc." [104] Gurvitch here leans towards the common idea that religion and other similar cultural products integrate and unify societies.

Since symbols are incomplete signs, or substitutes, it is imperative to ask the obvious question. For what are they substituting? What is this content to which they point? There is a sense in which certain intuitive We feelings must exist prior to symbols, undergirding them and giving them validity. Why then do symbols become fatigued?

---

[103] *Ibid.*, pp. 95-96.
[104] *The Spectrum* . . . , p. 3.

These are questions which need to be faced and which point to deeper levels of social reality. Again, it is obvious that such questions arise from Gurvitch's analysis of social law and his experiences in the events of the two Russian revolutions.

(8) *Creative collective behavior.* The spontaneous elements are becoming more apparent. It is an easy thing to study social reality from the standpoint of supposed regularities and predictable orderliness. But this is too simple and overlooks one of the most important aspects of social reality. There are those who would say in order for any study to be made of society a clear-cut pattern of regularity must exist. Gurvitch asserts that this is not true. There are those who would say for the collective itself to be real such regularities are essential. This is likewise false. Gurvitch maintains that there are those critical moments in history when the existing structures, patterns, and symbols have been overturned. A new regime has been instituted; new patterns and symbols and organizations have been formed. These periods must be explained. Sociologists cannot afford to neglect these "revolutionary" factors present in the total social phenomena. Though they are dramatized at those decisive "moments of truth" when the issues are crystal clear and the "overthrow" is complete, this phenomenon is present during every epoch. Creative collective behaviour constitutes that special stage of social reality "where innovation, choice, invention, . . . in short, the degrees of human freedom, . . . are partially exposed to view." [105] Here, it becomes acutely apparent that Gurvitch's experience during the Russian revolutions, his trials during the war and his observations within French society, especially during these past years of the Indo-Chinese and Algerian colonial conflicts, have all played a part in his "discovery" of this level of social reality. This also illustrates his debt to both Fichte and Bergson.

Reasons for neglecting this depth level are numerous. As previously stated, it is easier to study a "static" society than one which tries to make room for the unexpected. The term "institution" has caused much difficulty in taking into account this factor of human freedom. The individualistic character of most notions about innovation and creativity readily denies that change, revolutions, and invention may

---

[105] *The Spectrum* . . . , p. 4.

be brought about by collectivities. In fact, the two are interrelated to such an extent that it is false to separate them categorically. Finally, it is false to juxtapose the dynamic and the static. This is an utterly simplistic notion of social reality. This is one of those residual problems of the nineteenth century and implies the philosophical idea of order versus progress.

It is far more in keeping with the nature of social reality as it is revealed to the historian and the sociologist to recognize that in "every society, in every group, every moment of their existence, an agonizing drama is being played between the conservative forces and the innovating forces." [106] These innovating forces are at work up and down the depth levels, provoking the reactions and the resistances to their creative impulses. It is only in particular circumstances that these forces of human freedom succeed completely. Still they are constantly at work.

What motivates these creative collective behaviours? What stimulates them to action? It is implied that beneath are certain values, ideas which serve to compel certain actions. This becomes the next depth level.

(9) *Collective ideas and values.* "Behind all types of collective behaviour and attitudes, behind all organizations, all patterns, signs, role and symbols, exists a whole world of collective ideas and values." [107] Before the sociologist is the question of the meaning of certain gestures, patterns, signs and symbols which are used by a particular group. Perhaps these have a religious function, or they are of juridical importance, or they have a certain economic significance. The sociologist is faced with the task of interpretation and comprehension. His only source of help is to get to the fundamental meanings, which means coming to grips with the values and ideas that are behind these gestures, signs, symbols and patterns.

This does not mean that the sociologist takes a particular philosophical position just because he is dealing with values. The reverse is true. To neglect the study of values implies certain preconceptions about the nature of social reality and human existence. Sociology is not concerned with the validity of this or that value. It is concerned with what values and ideas are important for this group or that society. It

---

[106] *La vocation* . . . , p. 100.
[107] *The Spectrum* . . . , p. 5.

is clear that values cannot be lived or grasped or created or affirmed without the intervention of certain *collective acts.* This makes it part of the domain of sociology.[108] Such sophisticated sociologists as Weber, Znaniecki and Sorokin have renounced the exploration of this depth level under the false modesty of saying this goes beyond the scope of sociology and belongs solely to philosophy. They do this, says Gurvitch, in curious ways. They assert that values sort of drop from the sky, that human behaviour is unilaterally dependent upon these miraculous elements which are to be studied and catalogued by theologians, philosophers and jurists. Sociologists, for the sake of scientific objectivity, must keep clear. This is once again to deny specific content to social reality. It is the old deficiency of the formalists, who would create the categories but siphon off the real content, leaving only empty shells.[109] The sociologist must see that there is a depth level of ideas and values which are not merely epiphenomena of material forces, as Marx would have it, but concrete phenomena, in and of themselves, which react with all the other levels of social reality in a dialectical fashion. However, these ideas and values are held by and are creatures of a collective mind, signifying another depth level. This becomes the deepest layer of social reality. It is that which undergirds all the other strata. It becomes the final step in the process of depth analysis.

(10) *The collective mind.* This final rung in the descending reductive process is the passkey to Gurvitch's vertical view of social reality as well as the basis for his sociological "realism." This depth level also shows his continuing allegiance to the Durkheimian tradition. It is at once his most provocative and most difficult idea. Hence, it will be necessary to dwell at some length on this conception of "collective consciousness" or the collective mind.

The collective consciousness is found at every level. It is the last level to be studied and since it interpenetrates all the strata of social reality, it has a distinctiveness of its own, meaning it has a proper domain, a certain "territory" along this vertical continuum. "From the sociological point of view, it does not possess priority, but constitutes one

[108] *La vocation* . . . , p. 104.
[109] *Ibid.,* p. 105.

among many of the levels of the total social phenomena, which ought to be taken into account." [110]

This level is distinctly separated from ideas and values. It can grasp them and hold them just as do individual minds. Moreover, it is the most profound level from the standpoint of spontaneity and immediacy. As was mentioned above, this level gives the element of "realism" to the whole of social reality. It is of course united with the other nine levels, but this collective mind gives the distinguishing specificity to the work of sociology. The collective mind or conscience is the great contribution of Durkheim. Gurvitch is following in his footsteps, but he does so only after rejecting what he finds impossible to accept in the Durkheimian scheme.

The reader will want to refer to an earlier section of the chapter for a brief description of Durkheim's development.[111] In general Gurvitch finds three points where Durkheim fails: First, he gives the collective mind a totally transcendent character. This is what Bidney calls cultural idealism as opposed to cultural realism.[112] Second, Gurvitch reproaches Durkheim for identifying the collective mind with the Logos or Spirit (idealism again), or an *a priori* reason which leads him to identify it with a Supreme Being, leading finally to the affirmation of its divinity. Third, he rejects Durkheim's employing of the term collective mind in a purely singular fashion. Gurvitch will maintain there is a plurality of "minds."

The collective mind is the foundation of Durkheim's thought. He finds in this conception the irreducibility of the social. It is the most important part of social reality. It gives society its specificity and posits the notion that such a "given" is more than the "sum of its parts."

Durkheim's notion of "institution" gives rise to his development of depth levels which lead irresistibly to the collective mind itself, the primordial quality and substantive factor which is beneath all of social reality. The term institution calls for the following appraisal: each institution can possess an external constraint which influences the lives of the individual members. More than likely this is a simple pressure which comes from outside as well as within

---

[110] *The Spectrum* . . . , p. 5.
[111] See above, pp. 94-96.
[112] David Bidney, *Theoretical Anthropology* (New York: Columbia University Press, 1953), pp. 23-53.

the social entity. In order to study these institutions it is necessary to understand their internal significations in their collective acts, and for that it is essential to go below the surface to find the symbols which lead to the values that consequently point to the direct mental life of the collective mind which is the source of such values.

All in all, Durkheim attempts to do battle with those thinkers who would reduce social reality to a simple exercise between individual minds, or "human relations" in the modern terminology. His special object of attack was Tarde. However, Gurvitch finds that Durkheim himself is subject to the same criticism. He reduces all communication to the interdependence of isolated individual minds. This he does through symbolic communication. The reason for this is that Durkheim held the currently outmoded conception of a closed conscience. Thus communion has to be founded on symbolic forms. In depending on this, however, Durkheim actually takes the very same position as Tarde. He sees the collective mind as an outcome of individual minds. Now comes the crucial question, as far as Gurvitch understands it. "How is communication possible between individuals, since the symbols must have the same meaning, and is this same meaning possible without a union, an interpenetration, a partial fusion of the minds, which underlie all symbolic communication?" [113]

Gurvitch goes further to ask why this contradiction exists in Durkheim. The answer has already been given. Durkheim is bound to the "classical" conception of the conscience or mind which understands it as being closed up within itself. It is as Martin suggests, a kind of Leibnitzian monad.[114]

> It is the negation of the latent aptitude of the conscience to be open, to become intuitive; it is a fundamental misconception which represents the conscience as a kind of circle or box and not as a *tension* towards that which is beyond it and which resists it, as a beam of light *intending* towards its larger essence.[115]

This idea of openness and the Husserlian notion of intentionality will be more and more important as this dis-

[113] *Essais de sociologie*, p. 123.
[114] Martin, *Depth Sociology* . . . , p. 114.
[115] *Essais de sociologie*, p. 123. (Italics supplied.)

cussion leads to Gurvitch's own definition of the collective mind. Obviously the problem here is that of the creation of the collective mind in such a way that it does not soar into a transcendent abstractionism and still retains an irreducible quality. Gurvitch's idea is much more than a simple interaction of individuals, the nominalistic error. Gurvitch finds the only way out is the "opening" provided by the intuitive dimension of every consciousness. This opening is always virtual and seldom totally actual. But nonetheless this is the way in which the fusion does take place and the collective mind becomes a reality *sui generis*, without necessarily floating into a transcendent abstraction that requires the valiant effort of sheer faith for its existence; this hopelessly involves the theorist in a philsophical position which is outside the realm of sociology *per se*. This non-symbolic interpenetration which is possible through the immediate and direct route of intuition makes the existence of the collective mind properly psychological. This means that the base for this collective psychology is an immediate mutual intuition by the minds. "Outside of this approach it is impossible . . . not only to distinguish clearly the symbols from the values and ideas, which are the immediately given, but also to support the irreducibility of the collective consciousness, from a psychological analysis." [116]

Durkheim so clearly indicated that the existence of the collective consciousness was necessary if sociology were to have its proper area of study. Since he made that assertion, and since he rejected the psychological notion of an open conscience, he had to go elsewhere for a justification of the collective mind. This was done through his appeal to a transcendent, "idealistic" abstraction. Now the only way to defend the transcendence of the collective consciousness is through metaphysical arguments. Gurvitch finds Durkheim was forced to turn to these arguments more and more as he progressed in his elaboration of this idea. His last important work, *Les formes elementaires de la vie religieuse,* is replete with such arguments. If the individual consciences are closed, then there is only one way to affirm the existence of this collective conscience; that is to assert it is above and beyond them. They are not juxtaposed against this collective mind. It is external to them, and not im-

[116] *Ibid.*

manent. Conversely, the collective mind, by virtue of the latently open conscience, becomes a partial fusion which is immanent to each conscience, and each individual conscience is immanently present within this partial fusion (the collective mind). This interpenetration or participation of consciences, individual and collective, is understandable by the dialectical method of "reciprocity of perspectives." This is Gurvitch's way of solving both the metaphysical and psychological problems. It is one of his most important contributions.

Durkheim runs into further difficulty, asserts Gurvitch, with his allegiance to the "closed" conscience, since it must also apply to the collective type as well. Hence, the levels of values, and ideals cannot be immediately grasped by the collectivity. "These ideals, etc., are its products, its subjective projections and in this collective subjectivism the autonomy of the ideal world is obscured." [117]

Gurvitch's debt to Fichte and Scheler and Husserl is apparent when he contends that the ideal world in Durkheim's presentation does not "resist" the collective mind, is not the *object* of the intuitive act, is "not affirmed as its immediate and irreducible datum, and therefore, heterogeneous to it; it [the ideal world] only becomes a result of this conscience." [118]

What this means is that Durkheim, because of this essential flaw in his thought, can only envisage the spiritual world as a mere epiphenomenon of the collective conscience. It has no existence in and of itself which would make possible its study by the particular branches of sociology such as religion, laws, morals and knowledge, as well as by general sociology. He tries valiantly to save the objectivity of this collective conscience, making possible the distinction between it and the level of ideas, values, and ideals, but he is forced to espouse a Supreme Being, a "Conscience of Consciences" who is seen as above and beyond.

Gurvitch declares that both a collective subjectivism and a dogmatic metaphysical position which proclaims the existence of a Logos, must be put aside if depth analysis is to go anywhere. In sum, the greatest contribution of Durkheim is his notion of the collective conscience. Gurvitch readily admits this and feels it is worth saving. He is of the

[117] *Essais de sociologie*, p. 124.
[118] *Ibid.*

opinion that Durkheim failed to probe the possible scope of this conception. This is because he did not see all the levels of social reality. These levels, in order to exist, must rely on the collective mind itself. For example, "the collective behaviours would lose immediately their unity and would be dissolved into a heap of dust composed of individual actions which have no liaison to hold them together." [119] The same is true of ideals, ideas and values. They would be devoid of the social dimension without this real collective mind.

What is necessary, Gurvitch concludes, is to study the collective mind in and for itself as a separate level of social reality (which is the domain of collective psychology), but also carefully relating it to the other levels with which it interpenetrates and fuses. Durkheim never really did this kind of study. He was too caught up in a collective subjectivism which was the creator of everything else, and a metaphysics of the Spirit, which was his way of justifying the existence of this collective conscience.

What then is the corrected version of the collective mind, according to Gurvitch? In answering this question Gurvitch must solve the basic problem which has come to light in the preceding discussion. How are the individual consciences and the collective conscience reciprocally and immanently related? Or, how are the individual consciences fused to produce the collective conscience? Gabriel Tarde, he says, saw the collective conscience immanent in the individual consciences; Durkheim was equally successful in understanding the immanence of the individual consciences in the collective conscience. Both were only half answers. [120]

First the components of the collective mind must be considered. The collective mind is consciousness. This leads back to Gurvitch's reliance on Husserl and the phenomenologists. What is consciousness but the intending of something, even if it is fictitious? One cannot be conscious of nothing. Hence the conscience goes beyond itself and becomes itself by focusing on that which is heterogeneous to it. It meets a resistance which gives it its reality. It apprehends, intends the objective phenomena (the real essences) which implies that they exist, they are real. [121] This is what Gurvitch means in the passage quoted above when

---

[119] *Ibid.*, pp. 126-127.
[120] *Ibid.*, pp. 142-143.
[121] *Les tendances actuelles* . . . , pp. 43-45.

he says there is the aptitude on the part of the conscience to utilize a *tension* towards "that which is beyond it and which resists it, as a beam of light intending upon its larger essence," the object that light finds on which to shine.

This intentionality is the way by which Gurvitch brings about the fusion of the individual consciences. This fusion creates the collective mind. The total result is a reciprocal immanence of the individual and collective consciences. Depth sociology "considers that the conscience is no less immanent to the society, the world, to being, than these are to the conscience." [122] The psychic and the conscious are imbedded in other realities. There are degrees to this immanence and to this intentionality. When these two factors are at a minimum, when the dominant feature is passive contemplation of the obstacles or objects encountered, these relations are called *mental states*. (Examples would be representations, memory suffering, satisfactions, stray impulses, etc.) When the intensity of immanence and intentionality are average, they are known as *opinions*. These are always hesitant and uncertain. The maximum intensity comes when the obstacles lead to an overwhelming desire to eliminate them and to create new situations. These are classified as *mental acts*. Examples would be intuitions with intellectual emotional or volitional tinges, and judgments. To be more precise, the distinction between *mental states* and *mental acts*—being these two elements are the end points of the immanent-intentional continuum—is that the former do not succeed in transcending themselves and "opening" up to the object of intentionality, whereas the latter do rise above themselves and grasp the content or participate in the content "proved or affirmed as heterogeneous to the acts themselves." [123]

There are intellectual mental states (e.g., collective representatives, collective memories, collective perceptions), emotional mental states (e.g., collective satisfactions, sufferings, repulsions, joys, griefs and aspirations), and volitional mental states (e.g., active tendencies, stray impulses and collective efforts). Likewise, these same three divisions obtain for mental acts: intellectual (e.g., intellectual intuitions, collective judgments), emotional (e.g., collective preferences and dislikes based on values, collective acts of

[122] *Traité* . . . , I, 169.
[123] *La vocation* . . . , p. 111.

sympathy, love and hate) and volitional (e.g., acts of decision, choice, and creation).[124]

In keeping with Gurvitch's schema in each social framework these various mental states and acts are arranged differently, and their mental "colorations" are also different for the same reason. It is the same for the collective opinions which hold the middle position on this continuum of mental life.

What Gurvitch is trying to do here is to set up some kind of criteria for distinguishing between the different manifestations of social life at its deepest and most elusive levels. He recognizes that it is only under very unusual circumstances that the fusion is complete, that the intentionality is realized to its fullest, that mental acts are performed. There must be a way of distinguishing these from the more passive and "quiet" periods in social life. (Bear in mind those Russian revolutions.) Hence, in certain social frameworks, during certain periods of history, the mental states (corresponding somewhat to Durkheim's use for symbols, values and ideas which serve to carry on the traditions of a society and its culture), rely on the more superficial levels of social reality. These become the more determining factors.

This dependency upon the types of social frameworks and the historical circumstances holds just as much for the relationships between "interpersonal and intergroupal collective mentality and the individual mentality." [125] These three mentalities explained in the terms *Ours* (We, group, class, global society), *Yours,* and *Mine,* make up the essential reality of that which is called the psychic or mental. This reality "is defined as the drama of an increasing or decreasing tension which is affirmed more and more as the *Ours,* the *Mine* or the *Yours* (singular) in the fundamental experience of life which means directed towards the spontaneous." [126]

To clarify the distinctions further, when passive contemplation of the obstacles encountered is the result of this *tension,* then one can call this an *intellectual* function of psychic life; when the tension leads to certain docile and yet efficient adaptations to these obstacles this may be called an *affective or emotional function;* finally, when the

---

[124] *Ibid.,* p. 112.
[125] *The Spectrum* . . . , p. 6.
[126] *La vocation* . . . , p. 106.

upshot of this tension is a real effort to destroy and go beyond these obstacles to the creation of new situations, then one is confronted by a function of the will or a *volitional function*.[127] These, again, are only descriptive terms. One may be dominant at a given time and in a certain framework, but like social life, this is a *total* phenomenon and all are latently present.

There is a patent relativity to the mental life. The tension or fusion depends on the particular circumstances. This also underlines the total nature of this psychical element. Neither the individual, the interpersonal nor the collective is predominant. They are all present, for this is a whole phenomenon.

> There is less reason to attribute to individuals (Egos) taken as isolated fragments or in their relationships with the Other, the exclusive capacity for mental states, opinions and psychic acts than to refuse this very thing to collectivities: the We, Groups, social Classes and Global Societies.[128]

These three mentalities, interpersonal, individual and collective, are three directions within the total psychic phenomenon. They are in tension with each other and therefore must be studied from the standpoint of the various dialectical processes, complementarity, ambiguity, polarity, mutual implication, and the reciprocity of perspectives. It is the last process which is of capital importance in the comprehension of the relationship between the collective and the individual minds. It is the way in which the fusion is completed, the collective conscience is created and the individual maintains an immanent role within it. This is Gurvitch's answer to the Durkheimian contradiction. In the *Essais de sociologie* he clearly outlines this idea. The collective conscience and the individual conscience are only abstractions from the same concrete totality of the psychic. The pressures towards conformity and obligation are at work both in the individual and the collective mind at the same time. The dialectical process of reciprocity of perspectives presupposes both the irreducibility of the collective conscience and the individual conscience and the mutual interpenetration or immanence of these two consciences.

[127] *Ibid.*, pp. 106-107.
[128] *Ibid.*, p. 107.

This immanence results from an intuition of the consciences which are *open* to each other.[129]

To go further, this is not the only process by which these relationships are to be viewed. The other processes of the dialectical method reveal in clearer fashion the immanence and the *tension* or indissoluble linkage between the collective and the individual, the interpersonal, intermental and collective, the *Me, Other and We*. The singular of *I, Your and Our* is too narrow. It denies these collective acts and states. This is a result of the conception of the closed conscience (self-contained and turned in on itself). It is a position which affirms the "pure I." This is purely speculative according to Gurvitch. All empirical and historical data suggest this is outmoded. The idea of the open conscience, ranging in degrees of openness, clears the way for the conception of the collective conscience as the creation of individual consciences of a given collectivity, but which remains immanent to them and they to it. This makes room for the fundamental basis of social reality, the necessary existence of a We. The only possible way for Me, You and Him to communicate is by virtue of an underlying We, which is in turn inscribed in a group which is also inscribed in a wider relationship. Recall here the whole discussion of the normative fact and its necessary implication of ever-wider, more encompassing social wholes which give the law efficacy and meaning. The same holds for the intuition of the Other by an I. This can only take place if *I* and *You* exist within a *We*, participate in such a *We*, and thus have a basis for communication through symbols and signs and signals but also for the mutual intuition of each other.

This then is the heart of the collective mind: there is an irreducible tension among the I, the Other and the We. They are inseparable in Gurvitch's thought. They are three poles of the same phenomenon. If one speaks of the individual conscience, he is speaking of a tendency in the direction of the I. If the collective conscience is the primary concern this means an emphasis on the We pole; each implies the other. The method for analyzing these three poles of the collective consciousness is necessarily dialectic. Those processes of complementarity, mutual implication and reciprocity of perspectives are most often used to describe and understand these liaisons. In reality this method joins to-

---

[129] *Essais* . . . , pp. 136-137.

gether the efforts of sociology, psychoanalysis, behaviourism, the psychological analysis of cultural works and sociometry to study the total social phenomena which are always collective, individual and interpersonal at the same time, as well as being at once intellectual, emotive and volitional.[130]

This dialectical method, especially the process of reciprocity, has been consciously or unconsciously employed by many scholars.[131] In keeping with the basic thesis that subject and object are falsely separated in scientific exploration, thereby making explicit the contention that the object of sociology determines the method and the method used will result in a certain type of data, depth sociology calls into service the dialectical method. This approach clarifies the relationship of the collective mind to the individual minds. It serves to explain the various ways in which the depth levels cohere and remain linked together in a dynamic whole.

This completes the vertical view of social reality. Such a view which has moved from the superficial, the obvious, the object and sense data of social life, down through the strata beneath that make up the whole of social reality, is only an image, a symbol itself, to help in the description, comprehension and explanation of this aspect of human endeavor. There may be too many, or not enough depth levels. This is a tool for analysis and the number of strata used as points of reference for this study is relative. It is a device and solely that. Such an approach is based on certain presuppositions which are explicitly denoted by Gurvitch.

1) All the social sciences study the collective and individual *efforts* of man to create a society. The emphasis, then, is on effort and not on result, as such. Act always predominates over artifact.

2) Illustrating his inheritance from the phenomenologists

---

[130] *La vocation* . . . , I, 15.

[131] Those authors particularly cited by Gurvitch begin with the "young" Marx, who espoused a dialectical sociology which saw the tension between the individual and society (his *Economie politique et philosophie*, 1842-1843, shows the "mutual implication" of "total man" and "total society"); this "liaison" is seen in the following: Charles Cooley, *Social Organization*, John Dewey, *The Public and Its Problems*, George H. Mead, *Mind, Self and Society*, A. Kardiner, *The Individual and His Society*, Scheler, *Wesen und Formen der Sympathie*, Mauss, *Sociologie et anthropologie*, and Halbwachs, *Les cadres sociaux de la memoire. La vocation* . . . , I, 110, lists others.

and Fichte, Gurvitch asserts that the "science of man" is the science of liberty and all the obstacles which it encounters. "There are as many branches of the science of man as there are directions man's efforts take and the kinds of obstacles which they overcome." [132] The social sciences are characterized by their common object of study: the *human condition.* Each considers this condition in its own way and hence works out a specific object and method of its own. The reciprocal relationship of object and method is explicitly noted.

3) The total effort takes precedence over the particular activities. This means the compartmentalization of the social sciences is always relative because man is a whole and social reality is one. It will not do to fragment either entity.

4) The total social phenomena have a primacy over all their particular levels. These various levels making up each total social phenomenon have not only a methodological primacy over the astructural, structural and structured sectors, but an *ontological* one. This is the fundamental starting point for Gurvitch. Ontology is the ultimate reference.

5) The various social phenomena are related dynamically and dialectically. Hence, all separations between them are relative. The existential fact is their wholeness; they are *total social phenomena,* united in a complex web which is social reality.[133]

This total social phenomenon is ontologically prior to everything else, namely, forms and structures; but it is impossible to conceive of this phenomenon existing in a vacuum. It is always contained in some type of framework, and the way in which the various levels of the phenomenon are arranged is dependent upon the particular social framework. Actually, frame means the type of social relationships. The total social phenomenon is a result of social involvements. But the frameworks are merely forms without content. They provide the context in which people relate. The total social phenomena speak of how people relate and the results of those relationships. It remains the task of this next chapter to describe these "horizontal" characteristics of social reality and to show how the vertical and horizontal views of social reality intersect and are mutually dependent upon each other.

---

[132] *La vocation* . . . , I, 15.
[133] *La vocation* . . . , I, 15-17.

CHAPTER V

THE HORIZONTAL VIEW OF SOCIAL REALITY

1. FROM SOCIAL BONDS TO SOCIAL GROUPS

Sociology studies the total social phenomena. It also looks at the way in which these phenomena arrange themselves in social frameworks and structures. Gurvitch contends that a typology of the ways in which the total social phenomena are hierarchized is one critical aspect of sociological analysis.

The typological approach is distinguished from the singularizing method of history and ethnography and the generalizing method of the natural sciences. Sociological types are discontinuous and qualitative. This does not rule out the possibility that they can be repeated. It does say the types are mid-way between generalization and radical relativism. This approach generalizes for purposes of showing there is indeed a real specificity to each type; it singularizes (as does history) in order to show by further comparison among them, which frameworks are repetitive. To be sure, sociology uses the data of history, but only to show the discontinuity of social types. It emphasizes the ruptures among them. Continuity is the particular aim of history. It seeks to bridge these ruptures to which sociology points.

Sociology's typological method presupposes that totalities can be understood and their meanings grasped. The method is only used in sociology to study these social wholes. Social types are not rigid constructions or fleeting images, nor are they the "ideal types" of Weber. "They represent certain *dynamic frameworks* of reference adapted to the total social phenomena and called on to promote explanation in sociology." [1]

Sociological types have then an intermediary character: they are between generalization and the systematic plans

---

[1] *The Spectrum* . . . , p. 13. (Italics added.)

devised for research projects; they take the middle ground between explanation and comprehension and are at the midpoint between continuity and discontinuity. The only method for maintaining the balancing act between the various positions is the dialectical.

I. MICROSOCIOLOGY: THE ANALYSIS OF SOCIAL ELECTRONS

The first type of social framework deals with the most basic and elemental forms of social life. These elements are the microphysical particles which make up a real collective group or global society. These are at once astructural, infinitely varied, dynamically related and the most abstract elements of social reality. Their interrelations are complex. Proudhon is right: "Reality is by nature complex; the simple does not come from the ideal nor take us to the concrete." [2] The existence of complexity must not deter the social scientist from making every effort to comprehend and explain.

Briefly, microsociology studies those "social electrons" which every group contains. They are "the modes of being bound into the whole and by the whole, 'forms of sociality' of which any real collective unit is composed . . . the microsociological types are the types of social bonds (the *We*, the 'relations with others')." [3] As indicated by this statement, there are two kinds of "social bonds." The first has to do with the partial fusion of persons resulting in the "*We* feeling"; the second involves the aspect of opposition. This is best described by the pronouns *me, you*, or *him*. The *We* concerns the degree of interpenetration of different selves to form the "collective mind." The "relations with others" has to do with those ties which are interactive and interdependent. This is the level of interpersonal relations in American parlance. Gurvitch takes L. von Wiese's categories of *rapprochment, repulsion* and *mixed* to describe such "relations with others." The polar relations are the first two; some social ties of this type are a mixture of both. The use of signs and symbols is more necessary for these social bonds of "relations with others." They are more or less *closed* individuals and must have a common ground of communication in some type of symbolism.

---

[2] *Du principe federatif*, Dentu Edition, 1853, p. 38, quoted in Gurvitch, *La vocation* . . . , I, 205.

[3] "Mass, Community, Communion," *The Journal of Philosophy*, XXXVIII, (August 28, 1941), 486.

When the symbols are the chief base of social connection, the minds as well as behaviours, though they converge by having the same signs, remain more or less closed to each other: they have only communication common to them. But when the union among minds as well as among behaviours outweighs the symbols, they interpenetrate to various degrees of depth and intensity, and thus constitute an immanent whole.[4]

Recalling the previous chapter, it is evident Gurvitch is underlining his conviction that the collective mind (the *We*) is prior to every other form of sociality, since the other forms must, in large part, depend upon symbolism. He has changed his statement of this position between his *Essais de sociologie* and the latest edition of *La vocation actuelle de la sociologie*.[5] This means that not all "relations with others" need go through the mediary of symbols or signs. The deepest "relations," such as those of friendship, love, and brotherhood, may be intuited directly. But the important thing which Gurvitch is saying here is that the persons remain distinctly individuals and are never entirely subsumed in the other. He goes on to say that "relations with others" usually means between two persons, whereas the *We* involves usually three or more (3 to n ϕ 1). However he would admit that the *We* feeling is possible for two individuals. These two types of social bonds are present in the social life of any person or group. Two individuals who are related as husband and wife, intuiting thereby these relations of interdependence, also play the role of *We parents* or other types of *We* in relationship to children and friends, etc.[6]

It is clear that the *We* is ontologically prior to every relation with the other, even though these "relations" are intuited. The most intimate relations concern two persons who find there a partial opposition, an "active obstacle or a shock." [7] This intuition is only virtual or latent and is ultimately expressed through signs and symbols which make it active and real. Such signs and symbols, gestures, words, declarations and words are dependent and "must be based

---

[4] *Ibid.*
[5] Cf. *Essais* . . . , pp. 49-67; *La vocation* . . . , I, 116-280; and *Traité* . . . , I, 172-184.
[6] *La vocation* . . , I, 138-139.
[7] *Ibid.*, p. 138.

on a prior union of minds, on a pre-existent *"We."* Language is not the basis of the partial fusion of the *We* because language presupposes it." [8]

In the schematic outline of the forms of sociality (see page 150 for diagrams) Gurvitch moves from these two basic types to show the different degrees of partial fusion and partial opposition which can result. In keeping with the theory of the collective mind, only the active forms of sociality would produce values, ideas and ideals; only this type would have common work to do, and hence serve either the general interest or the particular interest, depending on the historical situation or the type of social bond.

These social electrons must be viewed as total social phenomena. They are frameworks for these depth levels, these factors which as a totality are social reality. They are never capable of organizing the depth levels into a hierarchy. They include them all either in an actual or a latent fashion. For example, when husband and wife are manifestly in love with each other to the extent that they are wonderfully sensitive to the feelings and thoughts of each other, they are still living within their relationship all the depth levels, though unstructured and lacking a hierarchical arrangement. All the depth levels are present in every form of sociability.[9]

Finally, Gurvitch makes the "vertical" distinction once again, illustrating the intersecting of these two views of social reality. That is, there are spontaneous and organized expressions of the social bonds.

One of Gurvitch's most important and frankly exciting ideas is the explanation of the different degrees of fusion in the *We*. These degrees of intensity are succinctly outlined in this paragraph from Gurvitch's article in *The Journal of Philosophy.*

> Partial fusion among minds opening to each other, and among behaviours interpenetrated in a "we," may appear in different degrees of intensity and depth. When the fusion is very weak and only integrates superficial states of consciousness which open only at the surface and remain closed with regard to what is more or less profound and personal, sociality is *mass*. When minds fuse, open

---

[8] *The Journal of Philosophy*, XXXVIII, 487.
[9] *Traité* . . . , I, 172.

out, and interpenetrate on a deeper and more intimate plane, where an essential part of the aspirations and acts of personality is integrated in the "we" without, however, attaining the maximum of intensity in this integration, sociality is *community*. When, finally, this most intense degree of union or of "we" is attained, that is, when the minds open out as widely as possible and the least accessible depths of the "I" are integrated in this fusion (which presupposes states of collective ecstasy), sociality is *communion*.[10]

Gurvitch first relates this to the problem of social pressure. He notes that contrary to what one might suppose, the more superficial the intensity of fusion, the more closed the individual consciences are to each other; the least amount of fusion brings about the most pressure. Where the mass-phenomenon is strongest, the pressure of "the collective mentality on the individual 'I' is strongest." [11] It follows then, that the greater the fusion, the less pressure is exerted. Hence, community represents the mean or average, and the communion phenomenon illustrates the least pressure being exerted on the individual ego. In sum, the stronger this social factor is present in the "ego" the less feeling of pressure is sensed. "For then it penetrates the depth and intimacy of the 'I' which finds itself internally joined to the other egos." [12] This means essentially that the dialectic of the reciprocity of perspectives make itself felt once again. The *I* and the Social are not enemies at war, but are fused into the same substance. Only the intensity of that fusion varies; this can be plotted on the Mass-Community-Communion continuum.

Obviously this conception of mass has nothing to do with numbers or such popular notions as crowds, masses, nations, races and classes. Mass as a partial degree of fusion is based, as are the other two, on collective intuitions. Thereby the Mass can be distinguished from herds or gatherings or crowds.

Gurvitch makes a second observation concerning these degrees of fusion. The intensity of interpenertation and the size or numbers involved are in inverse proportion. In

---

[10] *The Journal of Philosophy*, XXXVIII, 487.

[11] *Ibid.*, p. 488.

[12] *Ibid.*

general, the larger the aggregate or group, the more superficial are the social fusions. In other words, the smaller
groups have a greater chance of realizing the intense cohesion of communion. "A 'We' which is restricted and intensified to the place of being a Communion, risks losing
size and ability to expand, while if it relaxes and allows itself to unbend to the point where it is a Mass, it is possible
to grow and expand." [13]

A third characteristic is that the intensity of the fusion
in the We and the force of attraction that it exercises on
its members corresponds precisely. In effect, the force of
attraction exercised by the We is felt so much more when
this We penetrates into the innermost depth of the self
creating a mutual participation of the most intense nature.
It follows that a Communion exercises on its members a
force of attraction much greater than the Community, and
the Community itself holds its participants with greater
force than the Mass. Conversely, the Mass repels its members with more force than the Community.

In order to clarify these degrees more precisely it is helpful to analyze one end-point of this continuum. Communion will serve very well for this purpose. First of all, this
form of sociability represents the maximum degree of attraction and depth fusion in the We. The members feel
only a minimum of pressure. It is the most profound We,
and its participants have the feeling of being exempted
from all social and individual pressure. The Communion
presupposes the full and total participation, without re-
serve, in the We. Therefore, in the Communion, all other
conditions set aside, the reciprocal immanence of the self,
others and the We is expressed most profoundly. This is
precisely the reason why this form of sociability, being the
most intense manifestation of the collectivity, exercises the
least pressure on its participants. It appears to them as
the incarnated collective aspiration in which their own intimate aspirations are found re-enforced. The participants
of a Communion feel they are part of a movement which
can destroy every obstacle, can free them from their own
self-imposed bonds, can lift them above every condition
which would harm or hinder.[14]

The situation changes completely if one is not a member

---

[13] *La vocation* . . . , I, 145.
[14] *Ibid.*, p. 165.

of such an "in-group." He is looked upon with scorn. He is the reluctant, or recalcitrant, the indifferent or the adverse. The charm is broken. The Communion seems to him to exercise not the minimum but the maximum of pressure: it appears not as a center of attraction but of menace and oppression, not as a source of freedom but of servitude.[15] This ambivalence of the Communion reveals the acute conflict between its internal and external aspects. This is accentuated by bearing in mind that certain Communions are based on emotional experiences with certain intellectual and voluntaristic colorations bordering on the pathological. However some Communions may, on the contrary, result from certain mental acts which are very attractive to non-participants as well as the members. This is illustrated by certain Communions which have succeeded in actualizing some collective intuitions and have been able to apprehend values and new ideas which have weight and attraction for those unable to participate in the Communion. They even come to represent a source of "freedom." Resistance groups give this appearance to those under extreme oppression.

Gurvitch criticizes roundly those theologians and philosophers who wish to define a Communion solely in terms of "spiritual intuition." This, he feels, is to exclude the Communion from real social life. "They (the theologians and philosophers) have considered it as a direct form of participation of the isolated individual in divine grace, spirit or the cosmic whole. Thus, according to a certain Christian tradition . . . human minds can commune with Christ only when in isolation, and only through Him as mediator amongst themselves." [16] Communion is not the special province of geniuses, or saints or mystics and heroes, as Bergson would have it, but is open to all kinds of persons and groups and involves all kinds of experience, not just the religious. Bergson also thought there was a universality to Communion, but again Gurvitch says it is just the opposite. This is because as the groups expand in size the degree of intensity decreases. Moreover, the protection of the Communion against "impurities" always results in schisms. This is particularly observable in the churches, religious sects, magical brotherhoods and even among those Communions which supposedly have a rational basis as "schools

---

[15] *Ibid.*, p. 166.
[16] *The Journal of Philosophy*, XXXVIII, 493. Kierkegaard is an excellent example.

of thought." The more intense Communions are more susceptible to schism than those which are more lax. This explains the movement from "church type" to "sect type" in Troeltsch's terminology. It holds that that Communions which are tightly fused because of a common danger or a highly desired goal, once that danger is past or that goal is realized, tend to relax, to change in the directions of Community and Mass.

It is possible for the Communion to be expressed in a global society. An intense participation in the We can be realized by a large group of people, such as during a revolution, or when Paris was liberated in August, 1944, or when the home team scores a winning touchdown. However, once the crisis has been passed, the Communions tend to dissolve into the Community and Mass types. Their duration at this extended level is very short.

Gurvitch ends his discussions of these degrees of partial fusion by making it explicit that Mass, Community and Communion cannot be placed on a scale of values. He states it is imperative to rid the sociological vocabulary of every pejorative connotation to Mass and likewise to desist from elevating Communion to the preferred position. "From the ethical viewpoint . . . a scale of Mass, Community and Communion is . . . impossible. . . . In each of these three kinds of union, . . . the latter may just as well be negative as positive." [17] A mob of gangsters may commune intensely together as they plot their next crime.

> In relation to the most positive values, such as international peace or love of humanity, collective intuitions of a very weak intensity may be manifested and realized in sociality as Mass. Furthermore, we may commune in regard to external events (common fright, danger, etc.) and form a Mass in regard to moral duties and even to positive values (which are experienced with slight intensity).[18]

One last comment must be made concerning the organized and spontaneous levels of these degrees of partial fusion. This "vertical" view is most clearly evident when examining the differences between pressure and constraint. As noted in the second chapter in Gurvitch's work on social

---

[17] *Ibid.*, p. 495.
[18] *Ibid.*, p. 496.

law, he makes the distinction between these two at the point of organized versus spontaneous levels of jural life. The organized level exercises the constraint on the individual members since they are removed from the spontaneous fusions which characterize Mass, Community and Communion. The degree of this constaint depends on how open this organized level is to the spontaneous fusions in the We, representing the notion of collaboration. Organized sociability is guided by the principle of domination. These two principles of domination and collaboration serve as the extremes of a continuum once again explaining the difference between the organized and the spontaneous.

The following diagram (Figure 1., page 150) will illustrate the foregoing discussions on the microsociological types.

In conclusion suffice it to say these interlacings of social bonds make up the content of real collective groups. The groups become microcosms of the forms of sociality. It is here one enters the realm of macrosociology where these astructural elements or social electrons aid in the structuration and the destructuration of these new social frameworks.

SCHEMA OF CLASSIFICATION

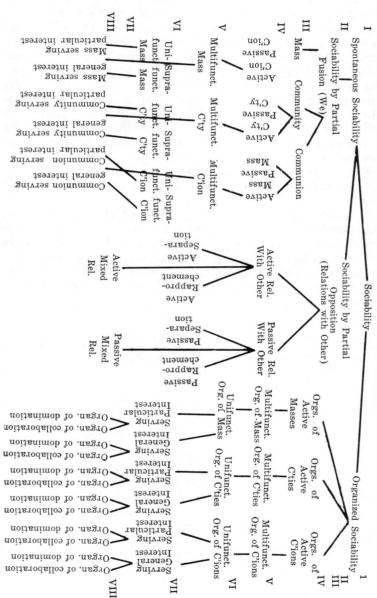

II. MACROSOCIOLOGY: AN OVERVIEW.

In his early work in social law, Gurvitch revealed how each realm of law called into existence a wider realm in order to give the former some point of reference as well as validity. So it is that the primary relationships or social bonds which were described in the previous section must depend on a larger whole, a group in this case, for basic concreteness. The group itself is partially inclusive and in turn must know the larger reality of the social class or global society for its existence and maintenance. Therefore, these three horizontal aspects of social reality mutually support each other and depend on each other. If one goes in the opposite direction, moving from the global society to the microsociological elements, this dialectical relationship is just as obvious. In this way the horizontal dimension must be studied in the same wholistic way as the vertical total social phenomena with which they intersect.

The microsocial electrons are held together in a cohesive fashion by real, collective units which Gurvitch calls particular groupings. A grouping is the first phase of macrosociology. In leaving the domain of microsociology one is now confronted with real collectivities which are externally observable. They have a qualitative aspect which can be empirically observed. There are certain material factors which are discernible, certain "crystallized" collective attitudes which can be marked, plus certain collective behaviours which can be recorded. Groupings "tend . . . to transform into patterns and clichés the symbols, values and particular ideas which they use." [19] Put another way, these groupings emphasize the more rigid, more organized and structured levels of social reality while the microsociological elements underscore the more spontaneous. This is only natural, since groupings tend to order, structure, and organize, which is quite different from the astructural social electrons. Indeed it is impossible to think of a group existing at all as a real collectivity unless this "ordering" did take place and certain equilibria be established among the different levels of social reality and the highly volatile social bonds. A relative cohesion takes place within this macrosociological framework which distinguishes it from the microsociological bonds.

---

[19] *La vocation* . . . , I, 281.

Furthermore, this collective unit is irreducible. It is irreducible to any of its forms of sociability which it organizes in hierarchies and arranges in certain configurations. "The group is more than n ϕ 1 of its forms of sociability, just as the global society is more than n ϕ 1 of the groupings which it includes within its framework." [20] The point is, the unity of the group cannot be reduced either to its forms of sociability or the depth levels at its interior. It is richer than the sum of these elements. It is a real collectivity. Gurvitch underscores this contention, all the while pointing to the particularity of the groupings. In other terms, he is saying the realism can be carried to the extreme of denying the difference between a social class, for example, and a grouping of locality, or the nominalism can be so emphasized that groups fail to be real but are merely collections of interacting participants. Therefore, a "differential typology" [21] is needed to escape either one of these pitfalls. This means that an intransigent pluralism is necessary in macrosociology as it was in microsociology. The tapestry of social life at the macrosociological level is no less complicated. It must also be kept in mind, warns Gurvitch, that a classification of any sort is only valuable when it leads to empirical research. It is always tentative and only attempts to guide. The theorist should take the lead in such activity. Only from the historical-empirical approach can an authentic scientific study be made. A classification is a rational or logical attempt to set down some categories for research. These come by way of the historical-empirical route. Gurvitch disagrees with the assertion that too many classifications lack a logical consistency and that when they possess it they are not applicable to empirical research. This kind of hopeless, circuitous reasoning Gurvitch combats with particular fervor.

III. THE ANALYSIS OF SOCIAL GROUPINGS.

There is a great interest in every country in the study of groups: "A million little bargains are transacted every day, and everywhere there are more 'small groups' than anyone could ever count." [22] It takes only a cursory glance at social science journals to indicate how wide is the interest in

---

[20] *Ibid.*, p. 283.

[21] This is the subtitle of the first volume of *La vocation actuelle de la sociologie* which is the best introduction and summary of Gurvitch's thought.

[22] Mills, *The Sociological Imagination*, p. 133.

studying groups of all varieties, including every phase of social life from factory to village to home to local political party to teen-age gangland. Gurvitch contends the working categories for such a study are spotty, vague and shoddy. He asks why this is so. He then shows that the reasons for this may be seen historically. He says in reaction to the organic nature of the middle ages and its subsequent destruction at the hands of the absolute monarchs who rose during the seventeenth and eighteenth centuries, that a special effort was made to see that every particular grouping was denied an existence which would interpose itself between the individual and the territorial state. Then in the nineteenth century when economic groupings began to arise, these were not recognized for their particularity but rather were subsumed under certain ideas about the future of society or the nature of the state. The particular groupings thus were ignored for what they were in and of themselves. This tendency was soon followed by the interpretation of society as the field of research and particular groupings were only appendages to this grand society with a capital "S." The groupings were attached to the notions of consensus, order and institution as well as to interindividual and intermental relations.[23]

Some denied the specificity and reality of groupings in reducing them to fictional unities, patterns or complexes of individual relations. This is the most radical type of nominalism against which Gurvitch wages constant battle. Here he finds the Americans firmly entrenched, at least those who place such an exorbitant importance on the face-to-face groups, the small groups which "serve as an example for the cohesion of society at large." This is ridiculous and impossible, Gurvitch contends. His reasons will become explicit.

The next error in the study of social groupings has come from the false dichotomy of culture and the social framework. This is impossible, as Gurvitch contended in Chapter Three where he reacted against a rigid formalism which would denude every social framework of any specific content. Culture is that content.

Finally, he states, the typology of social groupings is doomed to failure unless certain factors are remembered: 1) Social groupings are abstract-concrete by nature, fall-

---

[23] *Ibid.*, p. 289.

ing midway between the abstract microsocial elements and the concrete global societies. 2) Social groupings are no more reducible to their contents than global societies are to theirs. 3) The groupings are richer than any of their forms of sociability taken alone or as a whole. Each social grouping can be an autonomous center for the creation of patterns, signs, symbols, rules, values and ideas, particularly of social control. 4) A social grouping is a partial cohesion of its contents, which means that it in turn is part of a larger whole. 5) Neither the groupings, the forms of sociability nor global societies are wholly autonomous, but all presuppose each other and in fact are interdependent. Hence, a dialectical approach is required to study these relationships. 6) Any hierarchy of groupings or forms of sociability is relative. It is dependent upon the type of partial or global structure and the historical circumstances. A group's role will change according to its global structure and epoch. 7) The majority of groupings, it must be remembered, often include the same persons in their membership. That is, they interpenetrate and this mutual give and take, this overlapping of membership, will affect every kind of classification.[24] These factors must be kept in mind at all times. This has not been done in the past. Gurvitch hopes his schematic design will help clear up some of these misconceptions.

What then is a group?

> [It is] a concrete, but partial, collective unity. It can be observed directly and is based on collective attitudes and behaviour, continuous and active, having common works to accomplish. There is uniformity of attitudes, works and behaviour which constitute a structurable framework tending towards a relative cohesion of the manifestations of sociability.[25]

There are four essential parts to this definition. They have been touched upon previously. It should be sufficient to mention them only briefly before moving on to the classification of types.

1) This is a real collective unity. It is irreducible to any of its contents or to the total social phenomena. It is a

---

[24] *Ibid.*, pp. 289-291.
[25] *The Spectrum* . . . , p. 84.

unity because the centripetal forces are stronger than the centrifugal forces and hence a certain cohesion is maintained. This means then that such a unity is directly observable. There are regularities and patterns which are readily discernible.

2) A group is created out of certain shared attitudes. How could such diverse groups as the different publics or the unemployed or ethnic minorities or social classes be groups unless they held to a common and continuous attitude which was opposed to other collective attitudes? It takes only a superficial analysis of any group to discover there is this common attitude which unites the persons of a group into something more than interpersonal relations. This very same common attitude is the bridge to the more spontaneous levels of social reality as well as to the organized strata. However, the collective attitude is not sufficient to create a group. Many attitudes exist which are continuous and collective but fail to bring on the formation of a group. The collective attitude must be linked with a common task. Furthermore such a union needs to be translated into a structurable framework.[26]

3) An active *We* is essential before this common task can be carried out. A passive *We* is incapable of engendering the energy to do this job, or to realize the particular goal or goals. (Here once again Gurvitch's social law theory comes to the fore.) Such active and continuous collective attitudes with certain tasks to accomplish are attached closely to the centripetal forces which go to create a group, and this is in itself a beginning of structuration.[27]

4) The final characteristic of this definition has to do with the structurable nature of this framework. The tendency towards structuration comes from its efforts at cohesion leading to the formation of a unity. "All groupings are structurable, but not all groups are structured." Thus, the economic strata, the unemployed, the age groupings, publics, crowds, producers and consumers can constitute groups. . . . They are only very rarely structured."[28]

To be structurable means there is a tendency to hierarchize the multiple elements at the heart of the group. If a precarious equilibrium is established, the group is said to be structured but *not* organized. Social classes, certain

---

[26] *Traité* . . . , I, 187-188.
[27] *Ibid.*, p. 188.
[28] *La vocation* . . . , I, 305.

professions, crafts, and families are structured; however, the different publics, ethnic groups, producers and consumers are *structurable* groups, but as yet unstructured. Obviously then every organized group is also a structured group. A group, however, may be structurable or structured but resist all efforts at organization. A social class is a good example of this. Keep in mind that the organized aspect of social life is only one of the depth levels which make up social reality in Gurvitch's scheme of things.

It is now time to look at the general classification of groups as Gurvitch outlines it. This classification has an essentially pragmatic character. The question to be put before any classification is whether it will be useful for empirical research, as a guideline for experiments and sociohistorical descriptions which lead to an explanation of this aspect of social reality.[29]

Gurvitch suggests fifteen criteria to distinguish these groupings. They overlap, to be sure, so that particular individuals are participants in several different groups. This is a relative number, meaning that it can be augmented or reduced as the need arises. Not every grouping has the same importance in each study. It all depends on the approach being made. Some groups will be important for the sociology of law while less significant for the sociology of knowledge. A selection of the relevant groupings is then essential according to the type of study undertaken.

The schema of classification follows:[30]

1) Content
   a) uni-functional groupings
   b) multi-functional groupings
   c) supra-functional groupings
2) Size
   a) small groupings
   b) medium groupings
   c) large or extended groupings
3) Duration
   a) temporary groupings
   b) stable groupings
   c) permanent groupings

---

[29] *The Spectrum* . . . , p. 87.
[30] Cf. *La vocation* . . . , I, 306-308; *Traité* . . . , 190-191; *The Spectrum* . . . , pp. 87-90.

4) Rhythm
   a) groupings of slow cadence
   b) groupings of medium cadence
   c) groupings of rapid cadence
5) Degree of dispersion
   a) groupings at a distance (non-assembled groups or aggregates)
   b) groupings of artificial contact
   c) groupings assembled periodically
   d) groupings in permanent meeting
6) Basis of formation
   a) groupings *de fait*
   b) voluntary groupings
   c) enforced groupings
7) Ease of admission
   a) open groupings
   b) groupings of conditional admission
   c) closed groupings
8) Degree of externalization
   a) unorganized, non-structured groupings
   b) unorganized, structured groupings
   c) partially organized groupings
   d) completely organized groupings

(Categories c and d above involve organization as an element of their structure.)

9) Function
   a) kinship groupings
   b) fraternal groupings
   c) locality groupings
   d) groupings of economic activity
   e) groupings midway between fraternal and economic activity
   f) non-profit groupings (activities without remuneration)
   g) mystic-ecstatic groupings
10) Orientation
    a) divisive groupings
    b) unifying groupings
11) Degree of penetration by the global society
    a) groupings resisting penetration by the global society
    b) groupings more or less submissive to penetration by the global society

     c) groupings completely submissive to penetration by the global society

12) Degree of compatibility between groupings
     a) complete compatibility between groupings of the same type
     b) partial compatibility between groupings of the same type
     c) incompatibility between groupings of the same type
     d) exclusive groupings

13) Mode of constraint
     a) groupings commanding conditional constraint
     b) groupings commanding unconditional constraint

14) Principles governing organization
     a) groupings of domination
     b) groupings of collaboration

15) Degree of unity
     a) unitary groupings
     b) federal groupings
     c) confederate groupings

The explanation of each of these types of groupings should clarify features already mentioned. First, it will show the pluralism of group life; second, it will illustrate the particularity of different groups, at the same time giving evidence of their irreducibility and concreteness; finally, it will show how these are abstractions from social reality. They mutually interpenetrate and complement, as well as require the existence of the larger totality, the global society, in order that the centripetal forces of the society dominate over the forces which would alienate and divide. In other words, the groups would destroy each other in unmitigated conflict if this larger whole were non-existent.

1) *Content:* A group may have one unique function (a common task to accomplish), several functions or a totality (perhaps quasi-total) of functions. Examples of a unifunctional type of grouping are an orchestra, an athletic team, a business enterprise, or a cooperative. The multifunctional grouping would include those of locality (municipalities, counties, regions and the state as a "block of local groupings" [31]), kinship groupings, age groupings (youth, etc.) and political parties. Certain ethnic minorities, mystical groups of the Middle Ages, and social classes

---

[31] *Traité* . . . , I, 192.

would represent the supra-functional type. The question might be raised as to why the state is included in the second category and not in the last one. The state cannot be identified with the global society, nor does it have suprafunctionality because of the inclusive nature of the society itself. This error of considering the state as being more than a multi-functional grouping of locality is due to the historically determined way in which certain global societies so classify the groupings that the state is placed in a privileged position. The impression is given that *"l'état, c'est la société,"* to change somewhat the famous assertion of Louis XIV.

Gurvitch also has changed his thinking between the first and second editions of his *La vocation. . . .* Prior to this latest edition he failed to find any group which possessed a suprafunctional role. He conceded this role only to the global society. (Either a nation or an international society would be such a global society.) However, a closer analysis of the social classes and certain national ethnic groups persuaded him that such entities have either a suprafunctional or a quasi-suprafunctional role. A good example of a quasi-suprafunctional ethnic group would be the Black Muslim movement in the United States.[32]

2) *Scope:* These three criteria of small, middle-sized, and large are, again, relative terms. They are important for the reason that size significantly influences the very nature of the group. At present the social classes are the most extensive; the family is the smallest and in between fall the other groupings such as states, economic organizations, professional groupings and churches. When describing a group as to size, it is necessary to correlate this size with the historical circumstances and the structures of the society in which it is included. They make an important difference.[33]

3) *Duration:* The descriptive terms are temporary, stable, and permanent. The temporary groupings are those which are dissolved as soon as their task to accomplish has been completed. Examples would be a crowd, a conspiracy or a plot a band of explorers, partisan groups of World War II, demonstrations and play groups.[34]

A stable type would be dissolved only under certain con-

---

[32] Cf. C. Eric Lincoln, *The Black Muslims in America* (Boston: Beacon Press, 1961).

[33] *La vocation . . .* , I, 311-312.

[34] *The Spectrum . . .* , p. 72.

ditions such as death, voluntary agreement, a decision by the majority of the members or a decree from the outside. "The majority of groupings from the household family . . . to labor unions and political parties . . . are stable groupings, but their duration varies according to their character and circumstance." [35]

The permanent variety of group is one whose dissolution is not foreseen. Such groups would be castes, churches, states, international organizations, professional associations and similar examples. These groupings are less dependent upon the members for their continuation and life, since they emphasize those depth levels of organization, patterns and regulations which give them a structured character. Gurvitch is quick to point out no higher value is placed on the permanent grouping. In fact, a stable grouping can last considerably longer than a permanent one. It all depends on the historical situation and the structures themselves.

4) *Rhythm:* The cadence can be slow, moderate or rapid. Each group has its own metrical time. Gurvitch has taken this notion from Maurice Halbwachs, especially from the work he did on *The Collective Memory*.[36] Evidently there are different rhythms to life as lived in the home or a factory, in an office or a high school, in a church or a labor union. The divergence is especially acute when comparing a village with a city. In certain groupings the rhythm is very rapid, while in others the cadence is slow and deliberate. Gurvitch finds the American term, social mobility, very helpful to describe a group's change in goods, tools, patterns, and symbols taken together as a whole.[37]

Locality groupings, such as kinship, move in a slower rhythm than economic or adolescent groupings. Political parties tend to be more rapid in their rhythm than states, which in turn have a quicker pace than churches. Churches tend to move more slowly than sects or religious orders.

These are generalizations of course and serve only as indicators for further study of groupings' movements within a particular global structure at a particular moment in history.

The classification of groupings according to their rhythm is very difficult. It is a delicate operation but a necessary one if a valid description is to be made of a real group. This

---

[35] *Ibid.*, p. 93.
[36] Paris: Presses Universitaires de France, 1950.
[37] *The Spectrum* . . . , p. 98.

means that such a study must take into account the conflict which arises between the times lived, the times which are conceptualized and the metrical rhythms of the groupings. These distinctions by Gurvitch come from his study of social time in which he makes a systematic effort to define the different types of time which correspond to the various types of social frameworks. A social time is not the same thing as rhythm. It is more inclusive and concrete. For instance a grouping with a rapid cadence such as the economic types at the interior of a social class, or businesses which change personnel seasonally or large cities, favor a social time that alternates between advance on the one hand and delay on the other. The time of long duration fits such groupings with a slow rhythm as churches and villages isolated from large cities.[38]

5) *The Measure of Dispersion:* The measuring terms are non-assembled groupings, those artificially assembled, groupings which meet regularly, and those in a continuous assembly. The first kind would be represented by non-structured collective units, e.g., the unemployed, producers, and the different publics, but also professional associations and social classes would be included. The church and state as permanent groupings would fit in between the non-assembled and those which meet with regularity. The mass element is especially emphasized through these non-assembled types; there are occasions when this does not hold however. Artificially assembled groupings are those which utilized the depth level of signs and symbols to bring the members together, e.g., political party members who never attend the meetings or members of a committee that never meets.[39]

Groupings which meet with some regularity would be illustrated by the annual meeting of a corporation or a cooperative as well as factories, business offices, high school classes, theatrical companies and grade schools.

Permanently convened, intimate groupings would include the domestic family, small hamlets, boarding houses, schools and convents. Certain observations pertain to this configuration of groupings characterized in general by their degree of dispersion:

> The permanent groupings tend to be non-assembled
> groupings or at least groupings which assemble

[38] *Ibid.*, p. 75.
[39] *Ibid.*, p. 75-76.

very rarely; conversely, certain temporary groupings tend to remain assembled during the entire
length of their duration, such as a rescue team in
a mountain climbing accident. At the same time
non-assembled groupings often appear (at present
above all) as more effective and intense social
frameworks for knowledge, language, art, ethics
and religion than groupings which are more closely
assembled.[40]

This statement goes a long way towards depicting the
relativism and changeability of these categories. Observation and description must be doubly careful.

6) *The Basis of Formation:* The categories once again
are groupings *de fait,* voluntary ones, and those imposed.
These distinctions are necessary since a good number of
sociologists try to reduce all groupings to "associations."
However, "association" implies a voluntary group, and one
must take into consideration those groupings imposed on individuals either by force or circumstances. Hence, *de fait*
means the type of grouping where the members participate
without their particularly desiring to or without obeying the
directives of a precise organization. In other words, there
are groups to which one belongs without even realizing it.
Examples would be social classes, ethnic groupings, consumer groups, the unemployed and different publics. A
social class would fit the last description when the "consciousness of class" is at a particularly low ebb. There are,
of course, intermediary groupings between *de fait* and voluntary types such as professional groupings and worker
groups in factories.[41] The conjugal family and religious
sects also would belong in this intermediary capacity.[42]

Voluntary groupings are those "in which the members
participate by their own free will, that is, they adhere to
the group's rules and have joined on their own." [43] Such
would be professional unions, cooperatives, mutual associations, political parties, trusts, cartels, and philanthropic
societies. It is noteworthy that entry into some groups is
considerably easier than disassociation from them. This
factor is intertwined with the various forms of constraint.

[40] *La vocation* . . . , I, 318.
[41] Cf. *Le temps present et l'idée du droit social* (Paris: J. Vrin,
1931), pp. 18-19.
[42] *Traité* . . . , I, 193; *La vocation* . . . , I, 319-320.
[43] *Ibid.,* p. 320.

To say that voluntary groupings are always democratic or based on collaboration is to commit a grave error. Many voluntary types are thoroughly autocratic, while some *de fait* and obligatory groupings are democratic. The democratic republic is a prime example.

The household is a good example of an intermediary among all three types. It is voluntary in that the husband and wife decided to establish a home; it is imposed in that the state regulates rights and duties of family members; it is *de fait* for the children who are born into the home. In different societies the role of the family varies, a factor which must be taken into consideration at all times.[44]

An obligatory or imposed grouping can be either one which forces its members to participate or the type that obliges its beneficiaries to submit to its "rule." Some groupings are one or the other, while there are those which are both at the same time, such as the state or an established church. To clarify, there are two aspects of this definition; an imposed grouping is a corporation when it addresses itself to its members, and it is a foundation when it addresses itself to its beneficiaries. An example of an obligatory corporation would be the craft guilds during the Middle Ages; the foundation would be illustrated by the state as a performer of public services such as hospitals, schools, universities, and courts. It is obvious that the state fulfills both these roles. It is likewise so for an established religion or one which is predominant in a society. The promise of salvation is coupled with certain obligations imposed upon the adherent. During the Middle Ages, or in certain "primitive" societies where a unique religion is in force, this dual role is particularly clear to see. The separation of church and state introduces the voluntaristic element. However, to deny salvation to individuals carries a force which must be reckoned with.

Other examples of obligatory groupings are the *gens, phratries,* and *curies, eupatrides* and *demes,* and *patricians* and *plebians* in ancient Greece and Rome; the castes of India; the guilds, *jurandes* and *etats* of the Middle Ages. Some of these are corporations, others are foundations plus an element of *de fait.* One general observation can be made. The voluntary and *de fait* groupings are more spontaneous than the tradition-bound obligatory types. The state may at

---

[44] *Ibid.,* p. 34.

times be the exception to this statement. Above all, every effort must be made to get away from giving a priority to any one of these types. This is the error Gurvitch is seeking to combat in making these distinctions.[45]

7) *Mode of Access:* Open, conditional and closed are the descriptive terms. These groupings are distinguished by their "admissions policy". Open groups have no special requirements for membership. Often they are both *de fait* and voluntary. Rescue teams, philanthropic associations, public meetings, primary schools, muncipalities and certain publicly created groups which involve no barriers would be in this number.

Closed or exclusive types are impossible to enter. They were more prevalent in societies before our time, e.g., the *gens, phratries, patricians* and *eupatrides,* the *curia,* and the clans of ancient and primitive cultures; castes in India would also be examples. Some voluntary groupings are included. The trade guilds in the Middle Ages, secret societies, conspiracies and plots organized against admitting anyone would fit into this category. Our own day has few of these types. Perhaps the famous New York Social Register or certain trusts and cartels or the *haute bourgeoisie* which recruit solely by birth and heritage might be listed.

Most other groupings would fit into the conditional type. These conditions, obviously, will be extremely varied. Some will be exacting, others lenient.[46]

These criteria can be important. A group which has difficult membership requirements tends to be intolerant and/or oligarchic; a group which is extremely open may lack consistency. The first type favors patterns, regulations and rigid traditions; the second places the emphasis on the more flexible depth levels.

8) *The Degree of Externalization:* The criteria are unorganized, non-structured, and partially or completely organized groupings.

Gurvitch reiterates a favorite theme. "One has at times been tempted to distinguish groupings according to their 'degree of existence' or their more or less 'explicit' or 'implicit' character." [47] This is a dangerous practice counsels the sociologist. Such distinctions presuppose the existence of a grouping is dependent upon its organization or struc-

---

[45] *The Spectrum* . . . , pp. 77-78.
[46] *Traité* . . . , I, 194.
[47] *La vocation* . . . , I, 326.

ture. This is far from the truth. There are unorganized groups; but even if they become structured and organized, such forms can never totally encompass the social phenomena of the group in all its depth levels. In fact, often conflicts develop between the group as a total social phenomenon and its structure and organization. Always the total base of a group predominates over its *partial structures*. In sum, "the degree of externalization of a group in an organization or even in a structure, is not necessarily linked to the degree of its existence." [48]

By way of illustration, certain groupings are not only unorganized but unstructured, e.g., the different publics, the unemployed, producers, consumers, industries, segments of the economic society. Moreover the "patterns, symbols, values and ideas which are grafted onto the collective attitudes remain indeterminate. This affects their role in the global society. They possess only a latent structure, if any at all." [49] Keep in mind that such unorganized and unstructured groups can become rigidly structured in certain situations. This is especially so in the economic society.

Other groups are structured but unorganized. Such would be the social classes, teen-age groups or the "golden age" groupings, ethnic and national types, and certain crafts. Most of these can be organized. Others cannot be organized into one organization, e.g., the social class. This distinction of structuration is helpful when analyzing the social class from the standpoint of the subjective factor introduced by Karl Marx, the consciousness of class. One could measure this by accenting the tendency towards structure which is at work in the heart of each class. How fluid the middle class really is and how great the tendency is for the emergence of a techno-bureaucratic class could be measured by looking at the degree of structuration, especially relating this to the organizations which supposedly represent them. [50]

These groupings may become organized but usually only in a rudimentary fashion. The variables are important. For instance temporary groupings are less likely to be organized than those which have a longer life; fraternal and kinship groupings are more difficult to organize than locality types and activity groupings of different kinds. Hence, families, age groups, sects and religious brotherhoods have a difficult

---

[48] *Ibid.*, p. 327.
[49] *Ibid.*
[50] *Ibid.*, p. 328.

time being organized and yet they are just as much a grouping as those which successfully meet the requirements. The explicit or external factors fail to tell the whole story.[51]

Those groupings which are completely organized depend upon the happy conjunctions between their total social phenomena, structures and organizations for the maintenance of their force and the development of their character. An organization can be stultifying or aid in the growth and expansion of a grouping. It all depends on the usual variables of global society and historical circumstance. This is another very good reason why one must steer away from the criterion of "organization" for the existence of a group. Over-organization can kill the group as quickly as anything.

9) *Function:* Gurvitch lists seven functions by which to distinguish groupings. These may be unique or multiple. *Function* in his terminology is concerned with the specific work(s) the group has to accomplish.

a) Kinship—These can be founded on blood relationships or mystical origins. The domestic family is a present-day example.

b) Fraternal—The affinity may be derived from the situation (the economic strata within the social classes) or from belief, tastes and interests (groupings of age, sex, puberty rites, those possessing the same income or the different publics, cooperatives and fraternities).

c) Locality—These have a territorial character. The members are tied to a particular neighborhood and must maintain a certain order in this place where they live. Cities, villages and hamlets are examples.

d) Economic activity—"All groupings whose principal function consists in participation in production, exchange, the distribution of wealth or in the planning of consumption," [52] would be included here. Thus, occupations, professions, farms, workshops, factories, stores, offices, trade societies, trusts, cartels, and cooperatives would be examples of this type.

e) Intermediary between fraternal and economic activity—Certain groupings originally were based on family relationships, but also were economically oriented. Certain syndicates, shops, and crafts have had this mixed character. Good examples would be the old Knights of Labor and the Brotherhood of Railroad Engineers.

[51] *Ibid.*, p. 329.
[52] *The Spectrum* . . . , p. 80.

f) Non-profit—Those groupings which would fit this category are political parties, learned societies, art groups, civic associations, athletic unions and literary clubs.

g) Mystical-ecstatic—Churches, congregations, religious orders, convents, sects, magical brotherhoods, Masonic lodges, all would be examples of this type.

It is readily apparent that these seven types of groupings distinguished by their functions overlap with the majority of the other distinctions already mentioned. Churches and states are particularly clear-cut examples. This intersecting of various distinctions calls for a special type of study.

> They must be studied as to the repercussions which the diverse functions they possess have on the actualization and the equilibrium, in their framework, of the forms of sociability, on the character that their structure takes, on their capacity to include in this structure an organized element, on the expressions they give to knowledge, ethics, law, aesthetics, religion and education.[53]

The way in which this study is carried out is equally important. Gurvitch would say the sole approach which can adequately take all of these factors into consideration is a dialectical one, about which more will be said later.

10) *Orientation:* There are two distinctions, divisive and unifying. Divisive groupings tend to create conflict; unifying ones seek to reconcile. Two types do not fit this distinction. The social class is always divisive, while the locality groupings such as the state are always in principle groupings of unity. The remaining groups only exhibit a *tendency* to move in one direction or the other. This trend can be reversed under certain conditions. Hence, divisive groupings would include political parties, crafts, professional associations, labor unions, employer alliances, industrial associations, consumer unions, magical cults, sects and religious orders. "In contrast, factories, business enterprises, industries, managerial organizations, economic planning associations, social insurance bodies and universal churches are habitually groupings of union." [1]

One error must be eliminated straightway. This distinction cannot be linked with serving the "general interest" over against the "private or special interest." Gurvitch

---

[53] *La vocation* . . . , I, 332.
[54] *The Spectrum* . . . , p. 84-85.

means by general interest, as was pointed out in the discussion on his social law, the balance which is struck between the various opposing interests. This general interest can be helped or hindered by either one of these groupings, divisive or unifying.

11) *The Mode of Penetration by the Global Society:* This is described by these distinguishing terms: refractory, partial submission and total penetration.

The reason for this distinction is that on first glance unifying and open groupings would appear to be especially susceptible to penetration by the global society. However, on closer analysis this is not always the case, hence the reason for this more precise definition. This becomes plain when one considers the social class, certain social strata, age groups and publics, all open groupings; likewise, unifying groupings such as churches, families, factories and business enterprises and totalitarian states, together are refractory towards any penetration by the global society. On the other hand, divisive groupings such as crafts, professions, and the consumers (when they are groups) can be very easily influenced by the global society. This then shows that the problem of penetration by the global society is separate from the other distinctions and must be considered in its own right.

Refractory groupings may consciously or unconsciously resist this penetration. Their motives and means are varied. Maybe they feel excluded from the hierarchy of groupings ordered by society; or they consider themselves deprived of a rank or position they formerly held; or they are convinced they have a unique mission which sets them apart from the global society; or finally they are dedicated to the overthrow of the existing arrangement of groupings by the global society, meaning the destruction of the society's structure.[55] Groups which would fit the first of these possibilities are national minorities who speak a different language, racial minorities, the hard-core unemployed, slaves, serfs, or any other groups in modern society which are excluded from full participation in the whole range of functional groupings.

Those groupings which feel deprived of position are the estates general in France, kinship groups in areas of rapid social change, professions and craft guilds. All have been

---

[55] *La vocation* . . . , I, 336.

dispossessed in a certain respect. They are now separated from the mainstream of events and of life in the global society.

Among those groupings which claim to possess a unique mission would be the Catholic Church, which at various periods in history has tried to replace the framework of the global society with its own.

The revolutionary impetus as a refractory influence is evidenced in certain youth groupings and revolutionary social classes. The historical circumstance determines to a great extent the type of group this will be.

Most of the groupings fit the middle category on this continuum of global society penetration. Most of the kinship groupings, locality types, economic groupings, non-economic types, and even the mystic-ecstatic groups accept the patterns, ideas and symbols of the global society in which they exist. Of course they are selective, giving their particular interpretations to these depth levels. This is the side which refuses to be influenced totally by this external entity; but neverthless they remain in a kind of tension vis-à-vis the global society.

The groupings which become completely submissive to the global society are usually purely cultural or philanthropic, e.g., scientific, learned, literary, and artistic societies, universities, high schools, professional schools, foundations, public and private centers for research and academies. These are then groupings which are involved in social control in the broadest sense and in furthering the continuation of the global society.[56]

12) *The Degree of Compatibility between the Groupings:* The continuum runs along a line from those groupings which are compatible through those which are partially so, to the incompatible and exclusive. The latter category is set apart as a separate distinction. Gurvitch says it is possible to make one or two generalizations. First, in general, compatibility exists between dissimilar groupings. Cannot one participate quite easily simultaneously in a family, locality groupings, economic, non-economic, and religious types? Second, the incompatibility generally arises between groups of the same order. There are exceptions. Some groups are exclusive; these then will be considered separately.

The end points of the continuum are clearly understood.

---

[56] *La vocation* . . . , I, 338-339.

It is necessary to develop the mid-point, partial compatibility and the exclusive type of grouping.[57]

Partially compatible groups would mean that at certain times these like groupings would be incompatible; at other moments they would be able to co-exist. Professional groups, crafts, labor unions, industries, communes, municipalities, counties, regions, kinship groups, play groups, civic associations, certain religious associations and lodges would be compatible but at times develop situations where communication breaks down. There is nothing which says a person can't belong to several professional associations or be a member of several crafts or labor unions. But there may be moments when it is impossible to play all these "roles" consistently, when it is impossible to be a compatible member of all these groups simultaneously.

The weight may be in the other direction. One can be a member of basically incompatible groupings but find through tolerance and sheer will a modicum of compatibility can be developed. Examples would be political parties in Congress, national minority groups, and various confessional bodies comprising the World Council of Churches.[58]

The exclusive types on first glance would be fairly easy to designate: totalitarian states which would deny membership in any other group, certain religious sects and orders, prisons and slaves, plus ethnic minority groups with religious overtones, such as the Black Muslim movement in the United States. However, these are relative. Though the desire is to be exclusive, it rarely is realized completely. The same holds for total incompatibility or compatibility. These are abstractions once again, ways to describe and define. They are relative and limited. They must be viewed in this light and this fact constantly remembered.[59]

13) *The Mode of Constraint:* Conditional and unconditional are the modes. This is a new distinction. It has nothing whatsoever to do with a grouping being closed or imposed. Both conditional and unconditional can be used in these two types. The only exception is the exclusive grouping such as the totalitarian state.

The discussions on social law should be recalled to clarify conditional and unconditional constraint. Constraint has to do with the totality or unity of the grouping itself. The

---

[57] *Ibid.,* pp. 339-340.
[58] *Traité* . . . , I, 196-197.
[59] *Ibid.,* p. 197.

force of the constraint, the type itself, will depend upon the kind of grouping. Every group must depend upon some constraint for cohesion. Conditional constraint for Gurvitch means that a person can remove himself from it, get around it in some fashion. Unconditional means the opposite. Obviously if a group is closed, making it impossible to leave, unconditional constraint would obtain in that situation. This does not rule out the possibility that the conditional constraint can be of a violent nature. It can. If one chooses to remain in certain groups and the penalties for certain actions have to do with corporeal punishment, then this will be the case. The practices of universities of the Middle Ages, or modern-day fraternities in colleges, or any kind of hazing such as goes on at the military academies are all prime illustrations.

A family may exercise unconditional restraint on a minor child. Other groupings of locality can exercise the unconditional type. The point is that the state does not hold a monopoly unless one separates it from the other groupings of locality which also exercise a certain kind of unconditional constraint. Then, perhaps one can legitimately define the state as holding a monopoly on this unconditional variety of constraint.[60]

14) *The Governing Principle of Structures and Organizations:* Groupings of domination are distinguished from groupings of collaboration. Again, this refers back to the whole section on social law (Chapter II). Recall also the section on microsociology. The way in which the *We* can vary within different structures is shown. For example the authoritarian and autocratic *We* can exist and be quite strong within officially democratic structures. The reverse is also true. "The intensity of authoritarianism or democracy in a grouping cannot be established exactly if one looks only at their structure and organization. It is often a question of nuance and must be studied microsociologically." [61]

There are basically two factors which need to be remembered in terms of whether a grouping is democratic or authoritarian. First, the degree to which a superstructure (or the organized level) remains open to the infrastructure (the spontaneous level) is the degree to which it will be democratic or not. The more open and responsive it is to

---

[60] *La vocation* . . . , I, 348.
[61] *Ibid.*, p. 349.

this spontaneous level, the more democratic the grouping is. The tighter it is closed, the more autocratic it becomes.

Second, independent of whether a group is organized or not, another variable is "the rational or mystical character of the power which emanates from the group." [62] This means that if a group depends on a charismatic formula, a mystical or supernatural force, or a justification of power based on emotional factors, the authoritarian type will obtain.

It is also obvious that the type of grouping, democratic or autocratic, will depend on the kind of structure and regime which exists in the global society. Also how well do the various groupings interpenetrate with this structure and regime? Finally, no global society with either a democratic or authoritarian political structure is able to influence every aspect of the macrocosm. There will be many differences within the whole. This is why it is essential to study each one of these concrete groupings as to their democratic or autocratic character.[63]

15) *The Degree of Unity:* There are unitary, federationist and confederationist types. This continuum is very close to that given by most political scientists. Unitary refers to that grouping which orders its microsociological elements in a unique and direct fashion or its subgroups in such a way that it has central authority and they play only a subordinate role. Great Britain is a good example of the unitary type. The federalist type means that a synthesis is worked out between the grouping and its subgroupings to effect a unity where the balance of power is in the hands of the central group. The confederationist type is just the reverse of the latter. The subgroupings have the balance of power. The United States of America follows the federalist principle, the United Nations the confederalist one.

Gurvitch's sociological definition is especially significant.

Being given that every grouping whose structure and organization are sufficiently rooted in its total social phenomenon, that is each group which approaches more nearly the "corporation" type than the "foundation" type, can be, in its internal functioning, characterized as a "complex collective personality," as an equilibrium between the central personality and the partial personalities, as a syn-

---

[62] *Ibid.,* p. 350.
[63] *Ibid.*

thesis between a unique subject and a relation between certain multiple persons, the definitions which follow can thus be formulated: in the unitary group, the equilibrium between the central personality and the partial personalities is established in the complex collective person to the profit of the central person; in the federalist group, the same equilibrium is established in favor of an equality between the central person and the partial persons; finally in the confederalist group, this equilibrium is established in favor of the partial persons over the central person.[64]

This distinction is applicable to all types of groupings, the state and economic groupings included.

In conclusion several observations apply to the foregoing complete classification of particular groupings made by Gurvitch. First, these various distinctions intersect and overlap. This is deliberate and necessary. This complex result really stands for the various stances or positions one can take in looking at a grouping. There is an effort here to be systematic and yet open.

Second, this classification is relative. It is "unfinished" and always will be. It is a tool by which to analyze concrete groupings. Third, for Gurvitch, groups are real. They cannot be reduced to the sum of their parts. If they are real, just as any other phenomenon, they must be classified to facilitate their being studied analytically and logically. Fourth, this tapestry of groupings has a design, but that design changes according to the historical circumstances and the particular global society being studied.

This typology is worthwhile only if it can lead to empirical research. Such research has already been done in terms of the sociology of knowledge and morals. Gurvitch discovered it was much more useful to study these problems from the standpoint of groupings than that of microsociology (which is too unstable) or global society (which is too extensive). He has also found that sociometry can be used to test these hypotheses along with sociodramas involving *groups* and the use of the theater as a way of studying a control group.[65]

---

[64] *La vocation* . . . , I, 351.
[65] Cf. his article entitled "La sociologie du théâtre," *Les Lettres Nouvelles*, February, 1956, pp. 206 ff., cited in *La vocation* . . . , I, 353. Also, *Ibid.*, pp. 246 ff.

Finally, the usefulness of this typology becomes apparent when trying to get hold of such a difficult grouping as that which is known as the social class. This classification helps to define this collectivity more precisely.

2. SOCIAL CLASS

Social classes are social groupings, yet they are such a different type that Gurvitch analyzes them separately from global societies and particular groupings. One feels as if he enters a whole new world when he begins to think within the framework of social class. Once again, these are real groups and this assertion in itself sets Gurvitch apart from other social theorists. The analysis of this definition by Gurvitch will serve two purposes: first, it will help greatly in understanding his whole conception of macrosociology, and second, it will serve to show where he differs from and how he criticizes certain contemporary theories in social stratification.[66]

"A social class constitutes a universe, a collective whole which is so vast and rich that it is capable of rivaling even the global society."[67] The notion of social class is so confusing that one never quite knows where he is when reading in sociological literature. "The term 'social class' is used in different ways by different writers. It would be difficult to incorporate in a single sentence all the qualifications that should be made in any short definition."[68] This statement is characteristic. The sociologist in this case goes on to define what he means by social class, with the stipulation that the rest of the chapter will be spent in qualifying what he has said. This is all right but by the time one has worked his way through the maze of qualification he feels no closer to a concrete definition than when he started. Gurvitch has the merit of defining social class in a straightforward and unambiguous way. This is possible for him since he affirms right off that a social class is a real group. He finds considerable merit in the theories of Marx, M. Kalbwachs and Sorokin. He notes that Marx had the insight to see that social classes do indeed exist and are real collec-

---

[66] The sources for this analysis come from the following works of Gurvitch: *Traité* . . . , I, 198-203; *La vocation* . . . , I, 354-399; *The Spectrum* . . . , pp. 115-140; *Déterminismes* . . . , 176-190; and *Le concept de classes sociales de Marx à nos jours* (Paris: Centre de Documentation Universitaire, 1954).

[67] *The Spectrum* . . . , p. 115.

[68] Harry Johnson, *Sociology* . . . , p. 469.

tivities; moreover, they are special products of industrial society and have their birth with modern capitalism. Sorokin and Halbwachs saw the necessity of combining several criteria in order to get hold of the extremely rich content of social class, and they, too, realized the fundamental notion for a theory of social class is to affirm that it is a real collectivity, a true group, or "more, an irreducible macrocosm of groupings, an indissoluble social phenomenon." [69]

What, then, is Gurvitch's definition? A definition will have to distinguish a social class from particular groupings in general and will have to provide the framework for studying the social classes as they relate to the groupings which are found within them in certain rankings of their own, and in relation to the groupings which are outside their framework. The definition must account for their interaction with the global societies in which they exist, act and struggle (sometimes against the global structure), and for their dealings with the forms of sociability which make up their microsociological content.

There are six parts to Gurvitch's definition. Each will be discussed briefly. He counsels at the beginning of his presentation in *La vocation* that two misunderstandings must be cleared up immediately. First, contrary to some critics' evaluations, he includes in his definition the importance of both the cultural works of the classes and the existence of a "consciousness of class." In fact they are necessary to each other. The push towards a structure on the part of a class is actually its consciousness, and such a structure finds its cement, its cohesiveness in the cultural works produced to make this structure, i.e. patterns, signs, symbols, social roles, and specific ideas and values. It is because of this basic *esprit de corps* which produces these cultural factors that one can declare a social class exists, has a reality of its own which can be described. More will be said about this first response Gurvitch makes to his critics. On the second matter, there is little doubt that the economic aspect of social classes is a dominant one, responds Gurvitch to those who feel he has failed to take this into account, but one must not separate this factor from the total social phenomena. This is a persistent theme and is consistent with his whole theory. This will become clearer as the definition unfolds. [70]

---

[69] *La vocation* . . . , I, 357.
[70] *La vocation* . . . , I, 385-386.

1) The social classes are groupings *de fait*. Bearing in mind Gurvitch's central aim to illustrate how this classification of groupings is at once verified and empirically useful to delimit the notion of class, this first characteristic is readily seen. One does not choose to enter a social class. He belongs. It is an imposition of fact. This does not say that juridical regulations are imposed at the same time (unless the class is that one which is in political power). One makes a grave error about social class if he confuses it with the orders or castes of ancient history and modern India. "Social classes exist outside the *official* divisions . . ."[71]

2) Social classes are *non-assembled* groupings. They are not intimate groupings or permanent, or even periodical ones. They are particularly explicit examples of non-assembled groupings. "Isn't this what Marx meant by 'Workers of the world, unite!'?"[72] There is a strong impulse towards structuration (class consciousness) which is manifested in several different types of organizations which can enter into groupings that have an artificial basis for contact, but this in no way detracts from this characteristic of being a non-assembled grouping.

The social classes are the richest in content of all groupings and their production of cultural works is greater than any other type, especially the intimate and permanently assembled "small groups" which fascinate the American sociologists so much. This seems to undercut much of what they say about the *value* of small groups.[73]

3) Social classes are super-functional, *par excellence*. This means they even challenge the global structure, such as that of the nation, and it is this competition with their global structure which produces the drive towards superfunctionality. The way in which a social class expresses itself is in direct relation to whether it has gained the position of power, is ascending in power, or declining in power.

Obviously a multitude of organizations are required to express this collective superfunctionality of the social classes. Not one organization is sufficient to express this complex of functions. This is why the social class, though structured, remains unorganized. A dual conflict takes place with a social class. It struggles with the other social

[71] *Le concept de classes* . . . , p. 118.
[72] *Ibid.*, p. 119.
[73] *La vocation* . . . , I, 388.

classes within a global structure and with the global structure itself. "Each class is a whole world in itself and would like to be the unique totality, either by identifying with the existing global society from which the other social classes would be excluded or relegated to an inferior status; or by joining with the global society of the future where there would no longer be any social classes." [74] Two other things need to be said about this characteristic of superfunctionality. First, social classes are macrocosms of groupings. This means that within them are to be found many different types of groups and these too are in conflict to gain the top rung on the hierarchy; also there is competition between the different sub-strata of a class. This internal conflict is in inverse proportion to the intensity of the struggle between the classes for ascendency in the global structure. Second, it is patently clear by now that if one attempted to reduce the social classes to functional groupings (if this were the method of classification), the social classes would have to be left out. The picture is like this: certain functional groupings are so arranged that they form competing social classes. Other functional groupings make up the hierarchy of the global structure. These two hierarchies are in competition with each other. Add to this the hierarchy of groupings within each class which compete for the always relative equilibrium there (which can have grave repercussions on the whole global structure) and one begins to get an idea of the macrosociological tensions of social reality.[75]

4) This fourth characteristic has already been implied: there is a radical incompatibility between the social classes. Though social classes are *open,* they incorporate within them a spontaneous and radical element of dislike for the other classes. One cannot participate at the same time in two different social classes. This is so since there is a thrust towards structuration which implies a consciousness of class mixed with the "cultural cement" in the form of values, ideals, symbols, ideologies and outlook on life, including very definite political ideas.[76]

5) Constant resistance to penetration by the global society is the fifth characteristic of social classes. This resistance is based on the three factors of suprafunctionality,

[74] *Le concept de classes* . . . , p. 121.
[75] *Le concept de classes* . . . , pp. 120-122.
[76] *Ibid.*, pp. 123-124.

class antagonism and the drive towards structuration. There are other groups which resist this penetration such as the Catholic Church, certain youth groupings, and outmoded political parties. But none are as successful as the social classes. "Where the social classes exist and are effectively structured they are at once more refractory than all the other groupings to penetration by the global society and they are in competition with the hierarchy of characteristic functional groupings of the global society in which they live." [77] Each social class considers itself the unique center for the global society and seeks constantly to fashion that society in accordance with its cultural values, its form of consciousness. The ascending classes and those classes which have been dispossessed of power are the most impervious to the global structure. The class in power is most open to this penetration, all the while believing it is dominating the structure. If destructuration is threatened, a battle will ensue between the *status quo* class and the ascending class. Such is the time of revolution.

6) The social classes have an impulse towards intense structuration. This does *not* mean *organized,* to reiterate a point already repeatedly emphasized. A social class is a unified structure, but because of its superfunctionality it cannot be organized. Structuration is the clue to whether a stratum is a class or is becoming one. This really means class consciousness or "collective mentality." Marx was unclear about this term consciousness. He confused it with ideology.[78] Gurvitch feels one should leave to ideology the doctrinal political justifications of the social classes and show these functionally related to their cultural expressions. As to class consciousness, this is really returning to the conception of the collective conscience. "The collective conscience is a partial interpenetration of the individual consciences, an interpenetration which admits a scale of degrees." [79] Neither the individual nor the collective consciences can be reduced to each other. They are reciprocally related through the phenomenological conception of intentionality by which, to a certain degree, they are "open," they *intend* towards each other. These different directions make up the total psychical phenomenon: the collective conscience moves towards the *We,* the group, the global society; the in-

---

[77] *Traité* . . . , I, 201-202.
[78] *Déterminismes* . . . , p. 136, footnote number 1.
[79] *La vocation* . . . , I, 395.

dividual intends towards the *I* and the interpersonal conscience moves towards the *other*. This *troika* of intentionality is always present in the psychical life, in every conscience. The collective conscience exists just as much as the individual and it has a certain priority over the interpersonal since communication is necessary here, implying some sort of symbolic language.[80]

The complexity comes at the point of realizing that there are many collective consciences in a struggle constantly, and the most powerful, the most intense within the global society (the nation as a collective conscience) are those of the social classes. They dominate their groupings' collective consciences as well as those of the other groupings within the global society. This means that the social classes penetrate the other groupings and the *We's* within them as well as those at their interiors, but they repel the advances of the nation to a large extent. This class consciousness, then, is the basis for the unity of the class. This is the collective mentality which is combined with the cultural works and the ideology of the class to give each class cohesiveness and structure.[81]

There are other characteristics which could be mentioned to fill in this definition of class. It is an extended social grouping, permanent and open. The movement (vertical) between classes is possible, but difficult, since what is required is a change of mentality (consciousness) and kind and level of life. Gurvitch admits the place of external factors in evaluating social classes as to rank.

The final two characteristics of social classes are dependency upon conditional constraint and the natural divisiveness of social classes as implied by their radical incompatibility and their conflict with the global structure.

This definition then can be formulated:

> The social classes are particular groupings of great breadth and scope, containing macrocosms of sub-groupings, partial macrocosms whose unity is dependent upon their superfunctionality, their resistance to the penetration of the global society, their radical incompatibility with one another, their thrust towards structuration, implying a predominant collective consciousness and their spe-

---

[80] *Ibid.*, pp. 395-396.
[81] *Ibid.*

cial cultural works. These super-groupings only appear in industrial societies where the technical means and economic functions are particularly accentuated. They have the following traits: they are groupings *de fait,* open rather than closed; they are non-assembled, divisive, permanent, remain unorganized and possess only conditional constraint.[82]

Finally, social classes are relative in number. Their force, strength, and the intensity of their conflict must be ascertained in terms of the particular global social structures in which they live, and the historical circumstances of the moment. This requires a method which can take into consideration all of these factors simultaneously. Such a method will be dialectical. Before the method can be fully explained, two tasks remain: to define social structure and to define global society. These will be the central concerns of the next chapter.

The crucial difference between Gurvitch and many sociologists who have theorized on social class is his basic affirmation that classes are *real* groups. He does not hesitate to assert this claim. It is crystal clear in his thought. This is so different from much of the literature one must get through in American sociology in order to make an "educated" guess about the writers' conception of social class. As one writer puts it, "The *raison d'être* for the majority of the empirical studies has been primarily descriptive, merely to note the facts of social inequality." [83] Other studies have sought to measure the impact of social stratification upon the personalities of individuals and groups within a given society without looking at the society as a whole. The author concludes, "Few empirical efforts aim at validating a theory of social stratification in the sense either of relating the phenomenon to social systems generally or of explaining the development, maintenance, and modification of structures *per se.*" [84] Jean Floud, quoted in the above article, makes this observation: there has been largely "an attempt to separate the study of stratification in contemporary society from its historical context in Marxian notions of the class

---

[82] *The Spectrum . . . ,* p. 116.
[83] Harold W. Pfautz, "The Current Literature on Social Stratification, Critique and Bibliography," *American Journal of Sociology,* LVII, (January, 1953), 406.
[84] *Ibid.*

structure." [85] There is an amazing degree of agreement between these statements and the whole critical work of Gurvitch in this area. Theory is necessary in order to know where one is going, what is to be tested, how this social inequality is to be explained. The historical development is important. The type of global structure in which classes exist is important. Is there a difference between caste and class? Is it just a prestige factor or are there important correlations to be made between prestige, power, and political ideology plus social change itself? Is social class a substantive conception or merely a heuristic device? Gurvitch makes it clear where he stands. This is for him a substantive conception. Social classes are real. They have certain characteristics. These can be directly observed and measured. There are objective and subjective factors, but for Gurvitch they cannot be separated. They are a total social phenomenon. These groups embody a consciousness which varies in intensity. Such a consciousness alone can engender cultural manifestations. It is impossible to talk of cultural works apart from the collective mind, mentality or consciousness. Perhaps the popular term *esprit de corps* captures what he means. Gurvitch, though he does not mention this explicitly, would utilize the statistical methods for the morphological characteristics of social classes; he would depend upon sociometric devices, sociodramas and other depth testing means to get at the deeper levels of social class reality. He would urge the study of these classes within their own global social structures, taking into account their historical development and their present situation. The ways in which the various groupings are in conflict within the social classes, the tensions of the groups outside the social classes, the struggles among the classes and their drive for power within the global structure are all part of these total phenomena.

If one affirms a realist position, then every attempt to reduce social classes to "certain social categories, nominalistic aggregates, simple collections of individuals, the results of statistical procedures or assemblages of positions, statuses, ranks, roles and monopolies of power must be rejected." [86] They have an irreducible character which must be described and then explained.

---

[85] *Ibid.*

[86] *Traité* . . . , I, 199.

It becomes increasingly evident that if one is to study the social class, he must affirm there is a certain reality to the class as a group. Otherwise he is hopelessly lost in a maze of contradictions. These have already been mentioned. Nominalism, in essence, eliminates the whole problem of social class. Whether Gurvitch's realism solves the problem in advance is the question remaining. The most perceptive critic of Gurvitch's position is Raymond Aron. (American sociologists generally have not read Gurvitch and hence have had to remain silent.)

Aron, in his course given at the Sorbonne in 1956-1957, points to the essential issue. Nominalism knows the reality of the individual; realism, the reality of the collective. Both lead to a philosophical antinomy, he asserts. They are also in conflict with one another as concepts.

> The realist accuses the nominalist of letting escape an essential notion, the collective phenomenon; the nominalist reproaches the realist for inventing a collective reality which does not exist, or scarcely so, or unequally if at all.[87]

Aron believes it impossible to define once and for all such factors as class. Social reality is so complex and amibiguous. Hence, this ambiguity is necessarily a part of sociology, since it exists in social reality itself.

This means no single definition is sufficient even to specify different groups in a complex society. This ambiguity of social reality is illustrated by several examples: 1) the agricultural worker, artificially designated by the sociologist, has no consciousness of being a part of a group or class; 2) the organized proletariat of Paris are individuals who have the same work, similar wages and thought patterns, and have a consciousness of thinking in the same way. Moreover, they have a consciousness of their difference from other groups and their opposition to them.

Aron finds the majority of the groups situated between these two extreme cases. Most groups are never completely artificial, never completely internally unified.

This ambiguity of the social reality is the basic point of departure for all research on the social classes. One is able to define the reality of groups by the similarity in the ways

---

[87] Raymond Aron, *Le développement de la société industrielle et la stratification sociale*, (Paris: Centre de Documentation Universitaire, 1957), II, 38.

of living and thinking by the individual or by the consciousness of unity. However, a necessary connection between the degree of similarity among the members of a group and the degree of class consciousness is lacking. Some individuals are very different in their style of living and yet can feel themselves members of the same class. Some men who live and think the same can lack totally a consciousness of their unity. Indeed, the two phenomena are separable.[88]

Objective studies on social class are determined by the personal inclinations of the observer; his philosophical or political preferences enter in. Also the diversity of the reality itself influences empirical studies.

Aron considers the studies of Warner, Halbwachs and a national survey group in France. He observes that:

> The limitation of research projects of this order is that they neglect that which should be a part of the object of research as they study social classes. What is the decisive problem of the reality of social class? To what extent does the individual as a member of a complex society consider himself essentially a member of a class, and of a class which is opposed to other classes? [89]

Aron distinguishes three basic problems in the notion of class: 1) What is each class's relation to the economic and social conditions of its individual members? 2) Are the objective differences between persons psychologically real? 3) Is there a sense of class consciousness coupled with a feeling of opposition to other classes?

It is very difficult to define the lines between classes on an objective scale. Moreover, even if the French proletariat are different psychologically, still they are French, with the characteristics of the collectivity of France. Add to this the fact that *prise de conscience* of class is never present in the whole totality. Aron feels it is unnecessary to accept either the nominalistic or realist definitions. It is important, furthermore, to distinguish between class consciousness and class conflict. A very definite sense of class can exist without feeling the distinction will lead to a death struggle.

Keeping in mind the ambiguity of social reality, Aron declares there are only certain distinctions which can be noted about the concept of class. Class incorporates per-

[88] *Ibid.*
[89] *Ibid.*, p. 44.

sons who are never gathered together in one place. A social class is unorganized and has no legal status. One can enter and leave a class without knowing it. It is difficult to establish with certainty the class to which a person belongs. His manner of thinking is only one of the things a sociologist has to go on. An *ideal type* of class would look like the following: an ensemble of individuals found in a similar social and economic situation, utilizing the same thought forms and possessing a consciousness of being a group. Therefore, the three factors of this *ideal type* are: a) similarity of socio-economic condition; b) *prise de conscience* of this socio-economic condition, and c) the will for common action.[90]

Aron reproaches Gurvitch for his inclusion of two characterstics: resistance to penetration by the global society and the radical incompatibility of the classes due to an intense class consciousness. Aron feels these are not descriptive terms, though the previous characteristics are. These are part of a theory based on a certain philosophical position. It is not "evident that . . . the class is a *real* totality which has a consciousness of itself as a totality." [91]

In defense, Gurvitch points out that he recognizes the ambiguity of social reality. He constantly underlines its complexity and the "hidden quality" of social life. Now, as to the dichotomy between nominalism and realism, considerable ambiguity is present in Aron's position. On the one hand, Aron asserts that nominalism eliminates the problem of social class; on the other hand, he seems to say there are times when nominalism is the only way of explaining certain collective behaviours which appear to lack cohesiveness sufficient to warrant their being called a real group. In terms of an old adage, is there such a thing as being just a little pregnant? Is there such a thing as a class being only partially real? Gurvitch says no. Gurvitch explains there are both active and passive consciousnesses, latent or virtual manifestations of which can give the appearance of "nominalism." This comes from his whole discussion of the existence of "middle classes," meaning in this sense the tendency on the part of some non-assembled groupings to move in the direction of structuration (class consciousness among other things) which would give them a "class

---

[90] *Ibid.*, pp. 45-46.
[91] *Ibid.*, p. 31. (Italics supplied.)

status." These groupings appear to be between certain established classes. An example would be the newly constituted techno-bureaucratic elements. In another context, Gurvitch describes the relative strength of the *We*. The type of global structure and the historical situation will determine how strong this collective conscience (*We*) will be. It is unnecessary to deny the existence of the collective conscience. Also, certain criteria exist by which the agricultural workers can be tested to see if they meet the requirements for being a social class. They may simply be a non-assembled grouping *de fait* without a social class status.

As to the resistance to penetration by the global society and the incompatibility between classes, Gurvitch makes it clear these are relative. The resistance increases as the struggle for power with the global society develops. The sense of antagonism increases as the historical circumstances call for a class conflict. If the class is in power, as the middle class seems to be in the United States, then there is more penetration and less a feeling of consciousness to be expressed in political terms. Only when that position is threatened, as it was in the 1930's during the dark days of the depression, did the middle class take on a more "political character" and resist the thrust of the class(es) from below. Only then was the antagonism acute. As Howard K. Smith has said, the Roosevelt era was a conservative era in which the values, ideas, symbols and ideals of the ascendant middle class were protected and solidified. Roosevelt took certain measures to maintain the position of the middle class.

Probably Gurvitch would, in the final analysis, agree with Aron's three factors for his ideal type. These would fairly well fit the theoretical outline Gurvitch has given. The point is that Aron has failed to define what he means by class consciousness. Gurvitch goes beyond Durkheim, Aron and others who are willing to accept the Marxian assertion about class consciousness but fail to explore the reasons for the existence of this class consciousness. Though the morphological level is important, the will for common action is more deeply rooted in class consciousness and the existence of cultural works must somehow be explained. A mere description of these artifacts is inadequate.

Gurvitch asserts that sociology, if it is to exist as an independent discipline, must have its own realm of study. Such a realm is social reality. Social reality is the total social phenomena expressed through social frameworks which are more than mere mental constructions or heuristic devices, indeed real collectivities, irreducible to the sum of their parts and each one encompassing in a partial way the total social phenomena at all its depth levels. Social classes as social frameworks are macrocosms of social groups. They vary in number, intensity, power and structuration (*prise de conscience*) depending on the various tensions which occur among the depth levels, among the forms of sociability and among the various groupings. Such tensions depend upon the concrete historical situation.

CHAPTER VI

THE HORIZONTAL VIEW OF
SOCIAL REALITY CONTINUED

1. SOCIAL STRUCTURE

Social structure is different from organization. It is a unifying factor having a reality like that of groupings and social classes. There are characteristics to a social structure which distinguish it from groupings and classes. In Gurvitch's thought an understanding of social structure is essential before one can establish a typology of global societies.

Gurvitch is interested in a precision of language. Such precision is required if sociology is to reach the status of a science. Esoteric, obtuse and obscure definitions are unacceptable. Moreover, why muddy the waters with any more usages of a term? Try rather to reach some agreement. Make every effort to stay with a word and use it consistently. Gurvitch deplores such statements as these taken from a popular textbook:

> Such are the vagaries of sociological terms, "status" is sometimes used to refer to an individual's total standing in society. In that sense, it embraces all his particular statuses and all the prestige he may have for his personal qualities and attainments. The apprentice sociologist must learn to expect some *inconsistency* in the use of sociological terms, especially from one writer to another. The context usually helps to make it clear what sense is intended.[1]

Just as international meetings are held in the physical sciences to discuss terminology and definitions, so Gurvitch would urge that this kind of work be done in the social sciences. If no agreement can be reached, then the next

[1] Johnson, *Sociology: A Systematic Introduction* . . . , p. 19.

decades will resemble the recent ones in which would-be sociologists have felt impelled to spin new concepts, give new definitions, appropriate different words from the world of the physical sciences or psychology, couch them in an impossible "clarifying" language and publish them as original, veritable "breakthrough" in scientific thought. Such forays into the forest of verbiage deprive sociology of real value. As expressed by an ancient letter writer: "Some people have gone astray into a wilderness of words. They set out to be teacher . . . without understanding either the words they use or the subjects about which they are so dogmatic." [2]

Some have said that Gurvitch is also guilty of this shortcoming. Chapter VIII will deal with this criticism. Now comes the consideration of the problem of social structure.

The term social structure has a history going back to Karl Marx with his notions of infrastructure and superstructure. Gurvitch has appropriated these notions to distinguish between the organized and the spontaneous levels of social reality. Durkheim, of course, had considerable to say about "morphological structures." In politics and economics, in various areas of common life, the term is used, e.g., certain significant actions require changes in the *political structure*. In recent years the term has been used increasingly by sociologists and ethnologists in diversified ways which have resulted in the confusion described above. Gurvitch mentions in particular Radcliffe-Brown, Malinowski, Wirth, Murdock, Parsons, Shils, Merton, Levy and C. Levi-Strauss.[3]

He sees their use of this term, social structure, as a convenient way of escaping the inherent nominalism of their theories.[4] Since they have reduced social reality to interpersonal relations, to communications, or a network of roles, statuses and patterns, then structure seems to be a way of tying the loose ends together.[5] The result of such a usage of social structure is, in Gurvitch's view, to escape the obvious irreducibility of groups and global societies. Radcliffe-Brown, for example, makes a distinction between structural form and concrete structures (or the network of

---

[2] I Timothy 1:6-7. *The New English Bible* (New York: Oxford University Press, 1961).

[3] *La vocation* . . . , I, 401.

[4] *Ibid.*

[5] *Ibid.*

social relations). This distinction serves to show the difference between the static and the dynamic. The former has a staying quality while the latter provides for the change that occurs within a culture. According to Gurvitch this escapes the profound dialectic which takes place between "a real collective totality, its constituent elements and its participants; it also eludes the dialectical study of the relationships between the spontaneous flexibility of creative acts and the collectivity's precarious equilibria, cohesions, crystallizations and degrees of intensity."[6] All these are the component parts of a structure. In other words, Gurvitch asserts that such a use of structure denies the *total social phenomenon* of Marcel Mauss. So many contemporary sociologists refuse to recognize the concrete reality of the whole, which is irreducible to its constitutive elements. Such an affirmation of the whole leads irresistibly to the idea of structuration, destructuration and restructuration, a central plank in Gurvitch's conception of structure. It fits his whole theory of society being *en acte,* according to the term of St. Simon.[7] This is the dynamic element. As opposed to Radcliffe-Brown, it is collective as well as individual. Social relations are not alone in being creative and subject to modification. The concrete collectivity too, is in constant change; it has an observable cadence of structuration, destructuration and restructuration. Very evidently Gurvitch's experiences of the Russian revolutions come to the fore here. His preceding work in social law and the place of the spontaneous level of law are clearly present in this discussion.

Gurvitch finds little improvement in Radcliffe-Brown's disciple, Fortes. Fortes says in essence that the social structure is an abstraction serving as a point of reference for analyzing social situations. To Gurvitch this adds nothing to the definition. In Gurvitch's own terminology, the social structure is concrete and real while the types of social structures are abstractions to aid in the study of social reality.[8]

Both sociology and ethnology need the concept of social structure. This term will eliminate those propensities towards trying to establish a sociology of order or one of

---

[6] *Ibid.*, p. 402.
[7] *Les fondateurs français de la sociologie contemporaine: St. Simon et P.-J. Proudhon* (Paris: Centre de Documentation Universitaire, 1955), I, 12 ff.
[8] *La vocation* . . . , I, 403.

progress. Both tendencies are replete with value judgments. A real collectivity *en acte* eliminates such definitions. The notion of structure serves as a corrective to those conceptions which would juxtapose the dynamic and static. Such a juxtaposition is impossible if the idea of structure is viewed dialectically. Gurvitch claims his definition of social structure does away with all cultural abstractionism. This theoretical tendency tries to separate culture and society for purposes of study. Gurvitch contends such a separation is impossible and undesirable, methodologically and theoretically, if one holds to the idea that social reality is the total social phenomena.

Social structure is a way of clarifying the term *organization*. This is especially needed in sociology where the conception has been bandied about to such an extent it is devoid of precise meaning. Organization and social structure are not the same thing. Certain social structures provide the milieu for more and more organization. This seems to be the case in the present century. Other structures are less propitious. At no time can an organization express either the social structure in all its richness or the total social phenomena. This is likewise so for the social structure. It cannot capture the total social phenomena in their entirety. There is always that which spills over, which erupts, which creates the unexpected. This illustrates the *intermediary* aspect to structure.

Just as psychology needs some way to express the wholeness of personality, so sociology and ethnology require such a unifying principle. *Gestalt* theory does this for psychology; social structure plays a similar role in sociology and ethnology.

> Social structures are certain configurations, certain environments, certain ensembles *en marche,* put in relief and made concrete; in other words, they are concrete cohesions which are dynamic, and which give certain empirical points of reference to the thesis that the whole in sociology is irreducible to its component elements and its participants; at the same time the whole cannot exist without these several members; the two factors are dialectically related.[9]

This is the *Gestalt* feature of social structure. The struc-

---

[9] *Ibid.,* p. 407.

ture, though distinct from the total social phenomenon, does give these phenomena, when they are structured, greater concreteness and thereby greater distinctiveness. They come into sharper focus, especially as a global society. The social structure makes it possible to study global societies. A comparative typology is only realized when these concrete structures are visible and described, and then abstracted into types for empirical study.

Finally, a distinction is necessary between social conjuncture and social structure. By bearing down on the definition of structure, one sees how these two are different. Conjuncture as a conception comes from political economy. It is inevitably tied to history. When certain factors intersect or coalesce, the time is ripe for a certain type of functional grouping or social class or form of sociability. However, these conjunctures take place within a particular social structure and the impact is reciprocal. Their interrelationships are indeed much more complex than one would first think.[10]

These then are the reasons why the term *social structure* is essential to sociology and ethnology. Gurvitch's conception of this notion is diametrically opposed to certain contemporary movements in sociology, specifically the institutional theory of Talcott Parsons and his followers and the structural-functionalist movement under the leadership of Robert K. Merton. As Lipset and Smelser so clearly indicate[11] the new generation of sociologists in the United States have in large part come under the influence of either one or both of these schools which have their home bases at Harvard and Columbia respectively. The successor to Durkheim at the Sorbonne is critical of these two positions. His arguments are concrete. Basically they center in this notion of social structure as it relates to the total social phenomena.

I. THE INSTITUTIONALISTS.

Gurvitch centers his attack on the fuzziness of the definitions he finds in the work of Talcott Parsons. Three terms which lack precision are: *social structure, the social system,* and *institution.* They are often linked tautologically in

---

[10] *Traité* . . . , I, 208-209.
[11] Seymour M. Lipset and Neil J. Smelser, editors, *Sociology, the Progress of a Decade* (Englewood Cliffs, New Jersey, Prentice-Hall, Inc., 1961), pp. 1-14.

Parsons' writings, which explains nothing and only succeeds in making the task of sociological theory more difficult. Gurvitch laments that after such a long dearth of serious work in sociological theory, it is unfortunate the silence should be broken with the imprecise formulas of the *don* from Harvard. He finds Parsons' conception of institution to have so much breadth and ambiguity it has all but eliminated the idea of structure. He is caught in a vicious circle: "Social structure is comprised of a totality of institutions and the institutions are certain manifestations of structure." [12] This predicament is an outcome of Parsons' inability to grasp the full meaning of social wholes. He has attempted to do it by seeing them as collections of social relations, roles, positions, strata, values or rigid organizations. Parsons' ultimate goal is acceptable, but his aim is poor. There seem to be social collectivities, all right, and they have a certain concreteness in their appearance, but how exactly does one put his finger on the organizing principle, on that which gives the collectivity cohesion, unity, wholeness or reality. Parsons tries the modern formula. He takes the atomized individual and puts him in relation with another individual; they interact in some sort of ordered fashion (to do otherwise is to return to the Hobbesian fear of anarchy). Why this order? The basis for that interaction is a common set of values which when internalized are at once *institutionalized*. Perhaps the finest translation of Parsons is that of C. Wright Mills in his *The Sociological Imagination*: "People often share standards and expect one another to stick to them. In so far as they do, their society may be orderly." [13]

Social structure, according to Parsons, has to do with the more complex ways in which people are differentiated in their roles and positions so as to bring about this order. Such an arrangement of various roles based on expectations, obligations and correlative rights, is the social structure. [14] The whole thing is called a social system. "It is a system of interactions which is developed in a milieu, between certain motivated actors who communicate by a common culture." [15]

---

[12] *La vocation* . . . , I, 419.

[13] *Op. cit.*, p. 27.

[14] *La vocation* . . . , I, 419.

[15] Talcott Parsons, *Elements pour une sociologie de l'action*, translated by M. F. Bourricand (Paris: Presses Universitaires de France, 1955), p. 53, cited in *La vocation* . . . , I, 419.

This raises an immediate question. Is there in the thought of Parsons a difference between *social system* and *social structure?* The social system also seems to be identical with the idea of social action, e.g., in his book title, *Toward a General Theory of Action.* Gurvitch suggests that action in Parsons' usage is more closely allied to conduct or behaviour than it is to creative, raw, or vital action. In French there is a subtle difference between *action* and *acte.* This becomes important to Gurvitch. The place of Fichte's philosophy helps to suggest why. Moreover, *social action* and *social system* are identical with social reality in the Parsonian sense. Gurvitch notes that when Parsons talks of the role structure, this identification between action and system seems to be more clearly reinforced. Finally, Parsons himself declares he is seeking a "general theory of action" for purposes of discovering a common basis for psychology, sociology, ethnology and political economy. However, the distinctions are hazy.[16]

Parsons tries his best to extricate himself from such a lack of precision. He does this by continuously employing the phrase, "the structure of the social systems."[17] The analysis of this social structure is carried out on two levels: first, there is a description of the dominant value system, and second, the social differentiation which is arranged according to these values.

A stable system of interaction . . . invests its participants in terms of mutual expectations, which have the dual significance of expressing normative evaluations and stating contingent prediction of overt behavior. This mutuality of expectations implies that the *evaluative* meanings of acts are shared by the interacting units in two ways: what a member does can be categorized in terms meaningful to both; also, they share criteria of behavior, so that there are common standards of evaluation for particular acts.[18]

A person participates in these relationships according to socially designated roles. These are normatively regulated. Structurally, a "role component is the normative component

---

[16] "La structure sociale," *CIS,* XIX, 22.

[17] Talcott Parsons, *The Social System* (Glencoe, Illinois: The Free Press, 1951), p. 68.

[18] Talcott Parsons, et. al., eds., *Theories of Society* (Glencoe, Illinois: The Free Press, 1961), I, 42.

which governs the participation of individual persons in collectivities." [19] The social structure seems to be the normative pattern, that is, regularities of behaviour based on what is expected. Apparently the social structure is distinguished from the social system in that it refines the dominant scales of values and social norms, "thereby utilizing this sublimation as justification of the stratifications which characterize a given social system." [20] Social structure would be the *ideal types* of social systems which are constructed in accordance with the hierarchy of values dominant in the social systems. Gurvitch sees a close affinity with Max Weber's typological theory. [21] It is not surprising since Parsons has been greatly influenced by the German sociologist. Ideal types are abstractions from concrete social reality so formulated for purposes of analysis. To Gurvitch, this identification of social structure and ideal types has not helped to clarify the two concepts. Social structure in this definition has lost its concreteness, its reality. There can be *types* of social structure, but this is different.

Such an identification results in something else. Parsons is caught in the tangled web of confusing the method of study with the component element of social reality, which he himself says is social structure. To get out of this impasse he decides to make a liaison between social structure and the term *institution*. He attempts to define social structure by the word *institution* which is so vague and so abused that the outcome only serves to militate against any sort of precision.

Parsons and company define structure in this new sense as an institutional integration. Structure is a combination and a differentiation of institutions. "Sociological theory, then, is for us that aspect of the theory of social systems which is concerned with the phenomena of the institutionalization of patterns of value-orientation in the social system . . ." [22] Some of the Parsonian theorists go so far as to identify social structure and institution. What is institution or institutionalization? Social position of an individual, as stated above, is dependent upon certain norms and values. When the position is accepted, or when the norm is both widely accepted in a group and deeply imbedded in the

---

[19] *Ibid.*, p. 44.
[20] *Ibid.*
[21] *La vocation* . . . , I, 420.
[22] Parsons, *The Social System*, p. 552.

lives of the individual participants, a norm is said to be institutionalized. A cluster of institutionalized norms is usually referred to as a social institution. Another word for it is *normative pattern*. Already it is becoming apparent that social structure and institution are similar, if not the same. Gurvitch is of the opinion that the word institution is an unhappy choice. It is both too broad and too narrow. This is so if one takes the Durkheimian definition. Durkheim said institution meant the ensemble of acts and ideas which confronted the individual in society. However, it is obvious that all pre-established beliefs, ideas, values, and collective behaviours cannot be the same. Durkheim failed to make certain distinctions in his conception of institution. The concept is too narrow in that it overlooks certain elements of social reality which are a part of the social structure. These are the nonconformist, revolutionary, creative, free currents of the collective mind, which make up the forms of sociability.

Briefly speaking, the term institution is too vague. It has been prostituted to such an extent that little delimitation is possible, and few boundary lines can be established. It fails as a scientifically useful term for this reason.

Parsons, in his use of the term, tries to incorporate so many other popular definitions that the difficulty is intensified. He includes the idea of sanction, the cultural institution of Malinowski, the recognized and systematized morals of Sumner, official and quasi-official groupings, rites and procedure of MacIver, and above all the statuses, roles and rules of Ralph Linton. Such a mélange lacks coherence, unity and the quality of totality. Parsons attempts to synthesize these disparate elements under the rubric of common values and orientation towards values. He even claims, says Gurvitch, that such a common preference can be found in a global society.[23]

In essence, Gurvitch sees Parsons forced to create an artificial unity resulting in an artificial system whose keynote is integration. This does social reality a grave injustice. It totally neglects the spontaneous and unexpected, the effervescent and explosive facets of global societies and their components. The emphasis upon action as the basic element for analysis, instead of action in the creative sense, finds equilibrium and integration as the key terms. In contrast, Gurvitch sees social reality as dynamic, subject to

---

[23] *Cahiers Internationaux de Sociologie*, XIX, 27.

constant change; society is *en acte*. This is a result of both collective and individual effort, choice, invention, decision and creativity. There is an effervescence and freedom within social reality which must be considered. Parsons fails to go beyond "the expected, the sanctioned, the regular; he does not see the conflicts among classes, groups, scales of values, the different social times, the different determinisms and among the different depth levels themselves." [24]

In conclusion, Parsons' concepts and terms are fuzzy; he confuses the social system with the structure and institution as well as with social action. They are often used tautologically. The whole pattern reveals an incapacity on the part of Parsons to get beyond his spiritualism, ideal types) and nominalism (groups are not real) in order to seize social reality as a totality "and to explain the basis for the unity of these various collectivities." [25]

II. FUNCTIONALISM.

The foregoing discussion leads into Gurvitch's critique of functional-structural theory. Robert Merton is the important figure here. Gurvitch views Merton as more critical and astute a scholar than Parsons. However, he finds in his theory a plethora of confusions which complicate the task of sociology. These are confusions and difficulties which Merton himself has pointed to in evaluating functional theory:

a) First is the confusion resulting from a view of the interdependence of all the elements of social reality on the one hand and their constant movement on the other. In other words, there is no real understanding of "society *en acte*".

b) There is a lack of precision in distinguishing between motives behind certain behaviour and the observed consequences of such behaviour.

c) A confusion reigns among the functional "services" given to the whole and those meant only for a part of the whole.

d) A problem arises in declaring such and such a function indispensable and the admission of behaviours which are functionally alternative or equivalent.

e) A difficulty develops from juxtaposing the conformist

---

[24] *La vocation* . . . , I, 426.
[25] *Cahiers Internationaux de Sociologie*, XIX, 29.

patterns (adherence to the integrating functions) and the dysfunctions, which Merton refers to as "those observed consequences which lessen the adaptation or adjustment of the system." [26]

f) There is confusion between those functions which are indispensable and the functions which have no real role to perform.

Gurvitch observes that despite this set of valid questions facing functional theory, Merton and his colleagues go merrily on their way developing the *structural-functional* theory. The manner of their attempt to bring order out of chaos is by asserting that "structure affects function and function affects structure." [27] Furthermore, "functional analysis, all in clarifying the practices which appear irrational, accents the dynamic element of structure and aids in 'social engineering.' " [28] Gurvitch declares that when one is finished dealing with functional theory, he must reach the conclusion there is a patent lack of clarity in the terms *structure* and *function* and the way in which they interrelate.

To reiterate, Gurvitch defines *function* as a work to accomplish. Hence, he says a grouping is either uni-functional, multi-functional or suprafunctional. In social reality these functions (or works to accomplish) are also found outside the social structures. The active forms of sociability can have certain functions, the same holding true for certain unstructured social groupings. At the heart of partial and global structures, whole societies perform functions along with particular groupings, social classes, organizations, public services, *ad infinitum*. These functions can be negative or positive. They have a wide variety of purposes and take diverse directions. These functions are related in Gurvitch's theory as symbolic functions are related in mathematics. Merton's work includes a very clear definition of this symbolic function in mathematics: "[Function] refers to a variable considered in relation to one or more other variables in terms of which it may be expressed or on the value on which its own value depends." [29] This is essentially what Gurvitch means.

---

[26] Robert K. Merton, *Social Theory and Social Structure* (Glencoe, Illinois,: The Free Press, 1957, p. 51.

[27] *Ibid.*, p. 82.

[28] *CIS*, XIX, 30.

[29] *Op. cit.*, p. 21.

The heart of Gurvitch's criticism of Merton comes at the point where he finds the functionalists abstracting the concrete function of a particular *We*. These *We's* are totalities *en marche*. In other words they have something to do; they function.[30] There is a sense in which function for Gurvitch somewhat parallels the notion of role (in the collective sense) of George Herbert Mead and his followers.

Gurvitch returns to a previous criticism when he points out that social structures are dynamic elements. They are in the continual process of structuration, destructuration and restructuration. Such a dynamic interpretation poses all kinds of problems for the structural-functionalists who admittedly place the emphasis on "the statics of social structure and neglect the study of structural change." [31] When they do, it is in terms of the confusing distinction, *dysfunction*.

Finally, Gurvitch asserts that a separate *functional* analysis is unnecessary for the very reason that a hierarchy of *functional* groupings is observable in each global social structure and is studied from this standpoint. The conflict between this hierarchy and that of the social classes can upset the established stratification; or the particular groupings can take up those functions which were not theirs previously or abandon their original *works to accomplish*. The study of these calls for a certain type of functional analysis. Merton's method adds little to the understanding of these phenomena.

III. GURVITCH'S DEFINITION OF SOCIAL STRUCTURE.

What precisions does Gurvitch try to give to this concept of social structure? For his discussion of the term he goes back to an early notion, the total social phenomenon. Obviously, the social structure is an integral part of this total social phenomenon. Ontologically and methodologically there is before everything else a social whole. The structure comes afterwards. The total social phenomena always are more than their structure, either partial or global. To repeat something said earlier, these phenomena in their totality can be expressed a-structurally through the microsociological frameworks whether they be the relations with the other (inter-individual and inter-groupal)—this is the level of social interaction and social relations in American

---

[30] *La vocation* . . . , I, 429.
[31] Merton, *Social Theory* . . . , p. 53.

sociology—or the *We* and their different degrees of intensity (Mass, community and communion). The structural frame of reference only comes into the picture at the macrosociological level. It does not always obtain in every grouping. There is the possibility of structuration only in certain groupings; the tendency towards structuration is particularly intense with social classes. The global society as the most concrete macrosociological framework is always structured. This social macrocosm can never be reduced to its structure for the simple reason there are always a-structural elements at play plus the changing historical circumstances and the presence of non-structured groupings which can act in such a way as to upset the tenuous hierarchy that is the essence of its social structure. What is the difference between a non-structured group and a structured one? The former lacks this specific hierarchy of the forms of sociability, the depth levels, the means of social control, the different "social times," and social determinisms. The unstructured group would want for a clear sense of group consciousness and suffer from a deficiency in a cohesive culture.

Other elements are present in a global society. Each includes a hierarchy of functional groupings, competing social classes, patterns for the division of social labor and for the accumulation of goods; finally, each embraces its own precise civilization which it has created and from which it benefits. This comprehensive culture cements together these various factors.

In sum, the following elements make up a social structure:

a) Certain multiple hierarchies, most often in tension with each other and sometimes in competition.

b) Their manifest but precarious equilibrium requires constant effort at renewal and reaffirmation.

c) A certain *cultural cement* is created to combat this precarious existence and give it stability.

d) There is a clear group consciousness of these particular hierarchies and their tenuous character.

e) The constant movement of structuration, destructuration and restructuration links the structure with the society *en acte*.[32]

---

[32] *Traité* . . . , I, 213.

Earlier a distinction was made between an organization and a structure. The structure serves as a kind of "third man" moving in surreptitiously during the struggle between the organized and spontaneous levels. Seeking to profit from this conflict, it organizes these two levels according to its own goals. However, it doesn't always succeed. Evidently, organizations which exist within the structure would help in the structuration process. In these cases they are absorbed by the social structure. The contrary is never possible. The structure is impervious to the designs of organizations so far as they attempt to absorb it into their own life. However, certain social structures are greatly influenced by the organizations and must give them priority in the hierarchy of depth levels. This is true of the present era.

The function of structure as a concept is the same in the social sciences as it is in the physical sciences. It is an intermediary element, thereby illustrating its dialectical nature, its suppleness and its relativism. It is equally impossible to link it with the static elements or to assign it the dynamic role in social life. Gurvitch maintains over and over again a rigid separation between the static and dynamic factors of social reality is *passé*. Such a separation fails to meet the empirical data of the present world. So often social structure is confused with the types or with patterns. These difficulties can be overcome by seeing social structure as an intermediary element functioning between the total social phenomena and their expressions in the means of social control, or in the manifestations which one calls institutions. They are intermediary between these same total social phenomena and the organized aspects of social life, the various human meanings which are grafted onto the total social phenomenon. They serve an intermediary role between the *testings by fire* (fundamental creative initiatives) and the forces of stability; in other words, between the basic acts, both collective and individual, and their subsequent works. Finally, they are intermediary between a certain expression of a total social phenomenon and the way in which it is seen and expressed. Structure has a dialectical function, then. The tension which Gurvitch observes throughout calls for a dialectical analysis.[33]

At this juncture Gurvitch differs radically from other

[33] *Traité* . . . , I, 205.

social theorists, especially those in America. Rather than pointing to a stable social structure, a *fait accompli*, he places the emphasis upon the tension between stability and the creative act, between the factors which unite what Americans call "cultural norms and patterns" with those tendencies towards conflict, competition and destructuration. The structuration process is never complete. There is a constant effort to renew on the part of the existing structure; there is an equal pressure from the various stratifications within to tear down. If there has been a successful overthrow of the system, then the process of restructuration is going on. Obviously Gurvitch has been influenced by his testings by fire in the Russian revolutions. He was a keen observer. The experience was unforgettable. If one compares his experience with the placid, stable and easy frame of reference operative for most American and British sociologists, it is no wonder that the emphasis has been placed on the static elements of social reality for them. No wonder integration has been the key phrase and structural-functionalism the means by which one sees a society hold together. Neither is it surprising that the problem of change enters into the back door through the imprecise concept of *dysfunction*. Even the latent functions are still integrative functions giving support to those groups and individuals who otherwise are left out of the official structures.[34]

This is a revolutionary age. Gurvitch's conception of social structure and of social reality in its entirety could be helpfully applicable to the events transpiring in Cuba, South America, the Far East, Africa, and the Near East. More will be said about the values of this theoretical outline in the final chapter. A moving passage from *La vocation actuelle de la sociologie* illustrates what has just been said. It is an apt description of this revolutionary world:

> One finds in the total social phenomena as they are expressed in the macrosociological frameworks, other factors which lead to radical change: it is the constant testing by fire of the "mobile and fluctuating forces" of the "diffused milieux"; these are "complete and complex reactions" of individual and collective minds, as well as by "corps of members," they are the fugitive instants of social

---

[34] Cf. Merton, *Social Structure* . . . , pp. 3-117.

life, where groups, societies, humanity realize a consciousness of themselves and of social life, outside of the expected, the predictable, the anticipated. These are the terms of Marcel Mauss, the creator of the phrase, total social phenomena. Briefly, it is the perfectly unexpected element, the element which is completely unforeseen, discontinuous, whole and concrete, and inseparable from a totality *en marche*. This totality is where the collective effort is stripped of every superficial layer, where the *acte*, inventive liberty, decision-making liberty, and creative liberty cause an eruption in the social life beyond all that is foreseen. This igniting material is the permanent element of disruption present in the life of social totalities *en marche*. They can not be captured by any conceptualization or expression. They subsist in the total social phenomenon, be it global or partial, macrosociological or microsociological. Outside of the structured or structurable elements, and even the a-structural, this inflammable material exists which can cause an eruption even at the most unexpected moments. In this respect, every structure —despite the a-structural elements which enter into its structuration, destructuration and restructuration and despite certain efforts and certain observable movements which are immanent to them —is a tributary of the total social phenomenon as such, which it transcends while always at its base is this volcanic phenomenon which can never be fully expressed by the structure above.[35]

One may sense immediately the character of Gurvitch's approach in reading this passage. It is a *tour de force*. It shows the influence of the revolutions, the thought of Bergson, the phenomenologists, Fichte and Karl Marx. Proudhon and St. Simon are present also. Certainly Emile Durkheim and Marcel Mauss figure prominently in this definition of social structure.[36]

Gurvitch finds it acceptable to use the terms *political structures, economic structures* and *religious structures* because one is talking about real groupings in concrete sit-

---

[35] *La vocation* . . . , I, 438-439.
[36] Cf. Chapter II for a discussion of these various influences.

uations and not simply about activities and functions as such. To illustrate, crafts, professions, farms, workshops, factories, industrial enterprises, banks, trust and cartels, are all groupings involved in economic activity. It is legitimate, then, to speak of economic structures. However, if one is using the term in the *abstracted* sense of cultural structures or technical structures or juridical structures, one has left the realm of *reality* and entered into a kind of idealism.

Structure for Gurvitch is not an abstract concept like *type* but rather is real, a concrete manner of establishing some kind of tentative equilibrium. This is not the same thing as a stabilization. The following definition ensues from all that has been said:

> Every social structure is a precarious equilibrium, constantly being renewed; this equilibrium is composed of a multiplicity of hierarchies at the heart of a total social phenomenon of a macrosociological type; the structure is only a weak substitute of this phenomenon. This equilibrium is specifically made up of hierarchies of the depth levels, of the manifestations of sociability, the means of social control, social times, mental colorations, modes of division of labor, of accumulations of goods, and if the situation calls for it, of functional groupings, classes, and their various organizations. This equilibrium of multiple hierarchies fortified and cemented by the patterns, signs, symbols, regular and habitual social roles, values, and ideas in brief, by the cultural works which are proper to these structures, and if they are global, by an entire civilization which invades them and in which they participate as both the creator and benefactor of these cultural works.[37]

A constant dialectic goes on within the structure between *acte* and work. This dialectic makes it possible for the social structure to serve as a point of reference for other creative acts as well as the means by which global societies may be catalogued according to types. This is important for sociology since it links sociological analysis with history and political economy.

Social structures, because of their concreteness, do not

[37] *Traité* . . . , I, 214.

lend themselves to statistical analysis alone. Such methods of quantification are useful while studying the more superficial layers of social reality: e.g., the ecological factors, technical and economic patterns, and regular patterns of behaviour. But these multiple hierarchies, arranged as they are in a precarious equilibrium and representing only one aspect of the total social phenomena, must be studied by more effective means. The methods of history, ethnology, economics and political science are required if such a study is to be carried out successfully. This total method will be discussed after the types of global structures have been described.

2. GLOBAL STRUCTURES

This survey of Gurvitch's sociological theory comes to a close in the consideration of the types of global societies. These frameworks for total social phenomena are the most immense in breadth, the most imposing in structure, the richest in content. They are the possessors of the sovereign power (social) over every functional grouping, every social totality, every sector within their domain. This means they hold the supreme juridical sovereignty over groupings of locality, including the state, no matter the extent of the latter's coercive power. The global social structure can hold the economic power as well but this is not always the case. This distinction will become clearer as the types are analyzed in the following sections.

Ecologically these global societies are extremely extensive in their influence. Examples would be modern-day nations, the ancient empires of the Middle East or the former kingdoms of the Orient. Only the Greek city-states and the Roman city-states at the beginning of their history were small in size.

Each global society participates in the creation of and benefits from a particular culture. The global structure and its civilization are not the same nor can they be separated and studied independently. This position held by Gurvitch separates him from American sociology. As previously stated, Gurvitch is in agreement with the basic position of the French school of sociology. This school has never separated society and culture. In terms of the relationship between social structure and civilization,[38] Gurvitch says it is

---

[38] The terms *civilization* and *culture* are used interchangeably in Gurvitch's language.

false to confuse the two, since there are more social structures than civilizations. Furthermore, the civilizations form the material by which these structures are held together in their tenuous unities. However, each civilization is produced by the structures themselves. The essential point is these cultural products, designated together as the civilization, survive the structures. So it is, Gurvitch finds Toynbee's famous study of the twenty-one civilizations of history an unfruitful exercise, since they are viewed in the abstract without taking into consideration their social structures as Gurvitch views them. Conversely to study the types of global structures without taking into account the cultural bonds or products in which they participate neglects a whole area of the total social phenomena which is essential to a clear understanding of social reality. The best way to see these two elements, the social structure and its corresponding civilization, is once again by the dialectical approach. Their relationships are similar to those between the individual and society. A reciprocity of perspectives is essential once again if one is to grasp the totality of these intersections.[39]

In order to establish a typology of global societies, concrete structures are essential for this kind of abstract generalizing. Every global society is structured. No longer is the framework simply structurable as was the case with groupings. The global society is the most concrete macrosociological expression of the total social phenomena. Taking into consideration the role of culture in this structuration process, it becomes clear that "the global structures are normally more solid and more resistant than the partial structures." [40] With the exception of revolutions which violently attack the global structure, these structures have a much slower movement of structuration, destructuration and restructuration.

To study these global societies while noting the necessary relationship with civilizations as such, a definite alliance with history and ethnology is required. Both history and sociology study the total social phenomena. Both find the concrete global societies the richest domain for their study. Both discover these structures approaching the character of being unique and irrepeatable. History especially affirms this fact. Both need each other. History is interested in

[39] *Déterminismes sociaux* . . . , p. 194.
[40] *Ibid.*, p. 195.

showing the continuity which exists between various structures, in other words, seeing their singularized movement or what Gurvitch sometimes calls their *conjunctures;* sociology emphasizes the discontinuity of these same structures. It is interested in establishing types, in taking out time slices in order to observe the total social phenomena carefully and objectively. This relativism is a necessary corrective to the singularizing method of history which often leads to a dogmatic determinism of the Marxist variety.[41] More will be said later in the section on method concerning this necessary alliance between history and sociology.

Gurvitch sets up eight criteria for establishing types of global structures:

1) How are the functional groupings hierarchized?

2) How do the forms of sociability combine in the society and in the particular groupings?

3) How are the depth levels accentuated? Which level gets priority?

4) What is the stratification of the division of labor and the accumulation of goods?

5) How are the means of social control hierarchized?

6) What cultural works cement the structure together?

7) What is the scale of social times?

8) How are the various social determinisms ranked?[42]

From these criteria Gurvitch sees four types of primitive (archaic, in his word) and ten types of historical or *civilized* structures. Four of these latter are in competition at the present time. Why make this separation? There are basically three reasons for considering the archaic apart from the historical types. First, the archaic society lacks the characteristic of a nation (*pays*); it also lacks an *historical sense.* Second, there is a predominant or at least partially predominant presence of tribes, clans and bands. This is completely changed when one reaches the study of historical types. Third, there exists a subconscious character to human liberty in the archaic types, while creative freedom is consciously affirmed in historical types. These latter two distinctions are exceedlingly relative.[43] The consciousness of human liberty has led Gurvitch to prefer the term *Promethean* as a descriptive word for historical societies.

[41] *Ibid.,* pp. 196-197.
[42] *Traité* . . . , I, 217-218.
[43] *Déterminismes sociaux* . . . , pp. 198-199.

> We believe . . . it is more precise to designate them by the term Promethean society. We name them thus because one discovers within them the Promethean element of collective and individual consciousness concerning the capacity of human liberty for an active and effective intervention in social life.[44]

This human liberty can cause either constructive or destructive change. It can even be a causative factor in the splitting up of these global societies. A dialectic is observable, then, among tradition, reform and revolution. Such a dialectical tension assures a degree of continuity, since it points the way a society should go through either the transmission of tradition or a rediscovery of it.

Archaic structures are studied more by the enthnologist than the sociologist. Four archaic types are analyzed in Gurvitch's *Déterminismes sociaux et liberté humaine.*[45] However, we will concentrate on the Promethean types. The following global societies will be surveyed in the remainder of this chapter:

1. Charismatic theocracies.
2. Patriarchal societies.
3. Feudal societies.
4. Societies where the city state is in the process of becoming an empire.
5. Societies containing the early signs of a market economy; also known as enlightened despotisms.
6. Democratic-liberal societies corresponding to competitive capitalism.

(The final four societies are those presently in actual conflict.)

7. Economic societies corresponding to fully developed and organized capitalism.
8. Fascist societies based on a techno-bureaucracy.
9. Planned societies guided by the principles of state collectivism.
10. Planned societies guided by the principles of pluralistic collectivism.[46]

These societies will be taken up in order. This theory of global societies is the result of Gurvitch's most mature and disciplined thought. There are exciting prospects for the

---

[44] *The Spectrum* . . . , p. 105.
[45] Cf. *Déterminismes sociaux* . . . , pp. 200-222.
[46] *Traité* . . . , I, 218.

future of sociological analysis in this typology. This will become evident as the description unfolds.

1. *Charismatic theocracies.* An extremely relative homogeneity and a tenuous unity are a result of the identification of the State and the Church in the organized person of the Living King-Priest-God. This complex *institution* has supremacy over all the other groupings. "These dynasties of power express through their representatives have a character which is both supernatural and charismatically personal." [47] Examples of this type of global society include the ancient civilizations of Babylonia, Assyria, the Hittites, Egypt, Persia, China, Japan, Tibet, India and the Khalifat of Islam from the eighth through the twelfth centuries. According to the criteria mentioned above these characteristics can be delineated:

(a) The state church is the dominant grouping. (b) The masses are of greater importance than the communities or communions. Solely among the priests and the initiates of certain cults does the researcher find the presence of communions. (c) As to the depth levels, organizations are in first place; then come the morphological level, beliefs, religious and mystical symbols, and a supporting myth system for these factors. (d) The division of labor is sharply underlined; certain techniques are highly developed, e.g., the embalmers of ancient Egypt. (e) Religion, magic and myths occupy the top positions among the means of social control. (f) As to cultural works, the mystical is predominant and impedes the development of the more advanced levels of cultural expression. (g) On the scale of times one finds "a mystical-mythological type of cyclical time accompanied by that of deceptive time in which the great organizations move" [48] occupying the top position. However below the global society's time the total social phenomena move in a different scale of social times which is in direct competition with that of the global structure. This scale shows a death struggle between the time in advance and that behind; this latter type is supported by the time of irregular pulsations. [49]

These theocratic societies give the appearance of being extremely stable and static in nature. However, there is the latent possibility of disruptive change and the constant

---

[47] *The Spectrum* . . . , p. 149.

[48] *Traité* . . . , I, 219.

[49] Cf. Appendix II, for a brief description of kinds of social time.

presence of change factors. Gurvitch provides for this by re-emphasizing the volatile and dynamic potentialities of the global phenomena which invade the structures and their organizations at every point. The social times listed above provide for exploring this even further. In this way he makes change implicit in his whole theory. The spontaneous levels are perpetually at work beneath the crust of civilization. The constant struggle for these societies is to deal effectively with these explosive areas. This is the great problem facing a civilization which struggles to survive, to continue, and to develop. Again, the interactive relationship, this time between the infrastructure and the superstructure, the organized and the spontaneous levels which were observed in Gurvitch's social law theory, describes this dialectic. The theme is consistent and persistent.

The unity of the charismatic society is especially tenuous because of the radical separation between the structure and its organized levels and the *total* social phenomena. The organizational level develops around the ascendancy of rationalism derived mainly from economic requirements, barter trade, the development of the individual rights and obligations incorporated in contracts, pledges and credit. The organization of irrigation systems, the building of pyramids and the requirements of royal life in general led to extremely sophisticated organizational procedures, processes and controls. However, within these structures great heterogeneous masses of conquered peoples and slaves existed. "The charismatic theocracy does not have as calm a life as one would logically expect. They fly apart at different junctures and undergo revolutions. This is proof of the intense invasion by their subjacent total phenomena." [50] A patent illustration would be the collapse of the Old Kingdom in Egypt. Little is known as to why this happened, but a period of feudalism did set in, which underscores the disintegration of the old structures.[51]

2. *Patriarchal societies.* In this type there is very little observable difference between the structures and their total global phenomena. Obviously the structure is based on the exclusive preeminence of the patriarchal family group. The territorial area can be large. Blood relationship is the means of unity and the way to define membership rights.

---

[50] *Traité* . . . , I, 219.
[51] Cf. Jacques Pirenne, *The Tides of History*, Volume I (New York: E. P. Dutton and Company, Inc., 1962), pp. 33-46.

"The preference is for the male filial relationship whether polygamous or not." [52] This patriarchal grouping absorbs all the other groupings. "All the economic, political and religious activities are united in the very structure of the domestic-conjugal family, the patriarch being at once father, property owner, entrepreneur, priest, and political leader." [53] In this society, religion loses a considerable part of its mystical quality and is subservient to the patriarchal family. It serves as a kind of ethical insurance policy. Examples would be the type of structure emerging from the *Old Testament* and those found in the *Odyssey* and the *Iliad*. Once again the following outline emerges when the criteria are applied: (a) The domestic family is the dominant grouping. (b) The *We* predominates over the other forms of sociability and community over mass; communion is scarcely perceptible, and the passive *We* outweighs the active form. (c) In terms of depth levels, certain traditional patterns and mores have priority. These are rooted in custom rather than procedure and ritual. Gurvitch comments that many sociologists and philosophers have over-generalized from this type of structure. They have thought that every society is traditionalist, routinized, immobile and stagnant, or *closed* in the Bergsonian sense, because of these characteristics of patriarchal society. The second level emphasized in this type of society is the morphological. Next come the symbols, more rational than mystical, and social roles. (d) In terms of the division of labor, technical skill is of very little importance. The social division of labor is limited to the established relationships based on age, sex and inherited position, whether slave or freeman. Very little social mobility exists. The accumulation of wealth is de-emphasized and then is measured in terms of cattle and slaves.[54] (e) Among the types of morality, traditional morality and that of idealistic and symbolic images occupy first place. Such types of morality are the most important forms of social control. Certain forms of knowledge, e.g., common sense, perceptive knowledge of the external world, nascent knowledge of politics, follow as means of social control. A rudimentary educational system, an early form of common law, plus a moralistic religion

[52] *The Spectrum* . . . , p. 157.
[53] *Ibid.*
[54] *La vocation* . . . , I, 457.

serve as the other forms of social control in this society[55]
(f) Cultural works include only certain epic poems recited
as songs and dances. Written language, religious services,
rites, and orders just about complete the cultural heritage.
(g) The scale of social times shows the time of long duration and in slow motion and the time behind itself combined
with a seasonal cyclical time based also on the religious
calendar as the most important types. Their only competition comes from the time of irregular pulsations resulting
from the intrigues which arise within the patriarchal family in the struggle for power. This especially develops
among the first-born and the younger brothers who are
denied inheritance due to the laws of primogeniture. Another source of aggravation comes from the natural calam-
ities of famine, flood, epidemics, soil depletion, invasions
and wars.[56]

3. *Feudal societies.* The environment changes radically
in this type of society. This society tries to hide the very
sharp cleavage existing between its structure and its underlying total social phenomena. In contrast with the charismatic theocracy which, in appearance at least, exhibited a
solid unity, the feudal structure contains a pluralism of
hierarchies of groupings and means of social controls. These
are often in competition. For the first time one sees a set
of complex equilibria. Another dramatic difference between this type and that of the charismatic theocracy is the
role of the global phenomena. The turbulent, volcanic,
highly explosive nature of the global phenomena in the theocracy is reversed. These characteristics are the properties
of the feudal structure while its global phenomena live in
the social times of long duration and slow motion, regressing to the point where the past dominates the present and
the future.[57]

European feudalism (the tenth to the fourteenth centuries) has been studied at length by historians and provides a superb example of the pluralism which characterizes this type of structure. This extreme pluralism is not
found in the feudal structures of Egypt, Japan, China and
Russia. Nevertheless, the tendencies are present. Five
different competing hierarchies are observable in European
feudalism: (a) The federation of military groupings based

[55] *Déterminismes sociaux* . . . , p. 235.
[56] *Traité* . . . , I, 220-221.
[57] *Traité* . . . , I, 221.

on vassalage or the system of fiefs. (b) Patrimonial groupings formed out of the hereditary patterns that developed
to meet the economic problems of land ownership. (c) The
groupings headed by the monarchical state. In the feudal
structure this was least effective, since power was fragmented. (d) The ecclesiastical hierarchy of the Roman
Church, the most important structure within this feudal
society.

> The Church is considered above all as the visible
> incarnation of the *corpus mysticum* integrating in
> its unity the plurality of groupings and their hier-
> archies. She seeks to utilize this position to assert
> herself as a superfunctionl body *par excellence,*
> representing the total, global phenomenon. More-
> over, after numerous statements and struggles, the
> Church finds herself strongly limited by the mil-
> itary preeminence of the feudal chain and by the
> economic and eventually the cultural superiority
> of self-emancipated cities.[58]

(e) The federation of the free cities and their hierarchies
of groupings. In the European feudal structure, the free
cities acquired an independence with sufficient power to be
serious competition for the Church, State and the whole
system of vassalage.[59]

According to the criteria established by Gurvitch to
classify these types, the profile of feudal society would look
like the following:

(a) The various hierarchies of groupings listed above are
in competition with each other. The particular social and
historical conjuncture determines which hierarchy is in
first position.

(b) The *We* has priority over the *relations with the
Other.* The communities as degrees of the *We* are highly influential. Sometimes this *We* is actively expressed in the
cities, cooperating enterprises, brotherhoods, associations,
and religious orders; other times it is passive as illustrated
in the manors, among the vassalage groupings, in the villages and conjugal families. These *We's* are often limited
by the passive masses of the embryonic territorial states
and the radical communions within the body of the Church.

(c) The depth levels accentuated are social roles, certain
collective attitudes, mystical and rational symbols plus the

---

[58] *The Spectrum* . . . , p. 164.
[59] *La vocation* . . . , I, 464-465.

underlying values espoused by the collective mind. The organizational and morphological levels become competitive.

(d) The division of technical labor is rudimentary but the division of labor is pronounced.

(e) In terms of social control, art, religion and law surpass education and ethics in importance.

(f) As to cultural works, the products of feudal society are outstanding. They result from the synthesizing of various "cultural" influences which went to make up the stream of feudal life, e.g., Hellenistic, Roman, and Germanic. The whole magnus of cultural splendor derives from this synthesis and the dialectical relationships which were lived out between the various hierarchies of groupings.

(g) The time scales of this global structure find a deceptive time veiling certain surprises. This time comes from the great organizations of the Church, free cities and the feudal structures themselves. It combines with the time of alternation between advance and regression. This is a natural result of the conflicts between the various hierarchies plus the rise of the territorial state, the Crusades, and the beginnings of the market economy in the free cities.[60]

The time scale of the feudal global phenomena is different. Here the situation is reversed. The unexpected, the tentative and the explosive are not present. Instead the times of long duration, turned back on itself, and cyclical time (seasonal and religious) predominate. This is a heavy weight on the times of the global structure. The conflicts between the global structure and the subjacent total social phenomena provide the ignitible material precipitating social change.

4. *Societies in which the city-state is in the process of becoming an empire.* This type of society exhibits very little separation between the social structure and its subjacent global phenomena. This global society is illustrated by the Greek *polis* of the seventh through the fifth centuries B. C., and the Latin *civitas* in the early days of the Roman republic. Certain cities of the Italian renaissance are also examples of this type.

The territorial group predominates in this type over other particular groupings. This supremacy of the city-state precipitates an emphasis upon secularism and rationalism. There is a victory of the natural over the supernatural. In-

---

[60] Cf. Robert Heilbroner, *The Making of Economic History* (Englewood Cliffs, New Jersey: Prentice-Hall, 1962), pp. 45-71.

dividualism is also evident in the founding of Roman law, the *dominium* and the *imperium*. In Greece this same individualism is a prime factor in the system of law, philosophy, art, customs, morals and trade. The Italian renaissance is a restatement of this classical Roman and Greek spirit.

Technical knowledge remained far behind the advanced position of philosophy and science. This led to little division in technical labor. Social labor had a marked differentiation. So it was that horses were only used for ceremonial purposes in ancient Greece and slaves were hired to do manual labor considered beneath the dignity of the Greek city-state citizen. Accumulation of goods was principally in the hands of the commercial interests of the cities. Merchants thrived on the maritime industry of the Greeks.[61] Military conquest brought great wealth to Rome. Gurvitch denies the existence of social classes in Greece and Rome. His thesis has been expressed in the section on the definition of social class. Basically, this phenomenon only arose with industrial society.

The general characteristics of this type of global society are arranged according to Gurvitch's criteria.

(a) The *polis* dominated all groupings. Its power was pervasive. "Only the conjugal families and hereditary groupings were impervious to the city-state." [62] Even the atomized individuals were effectively controlled.

(b) The *We* was strongly limited by the *relations with the Other*. "Such interindividual and intergroupal functions predominated over all partial fusions. From this was derived the broad accentuation of individualism found at all levels and in all forms." [63] The rational and active communities at the heart of the city dominated the *We* expressions. Such types united easily with the *relations with the Other*. These rational communities also led to the development of organizations, secular social control through a judicial system, and the phenomenon of political democracy.

(c) The depth levels were so arranged that patterns, rules and signs possessed a rational character and occupied the most important positions. Such depth levels based on reason and human will provided the humanistic confidence which pervaded these societies. The potentiality of man

[61] *The Spectrum* . . . , pp. 122-123.
[62] *Ibid.*, p. 124.
[63] *Ibid.*

and his society was optimistically viewed. Organizations occupied the second rung. Then came rational ideas and values. Scientific knowledge, art and law were preferred. "There was a preference for a collective attitude which had confidence in new experiences, original judgment and intuition." [1] The morphological level remained very important; social roles accenting the creative side rather than routinized behaviour were preferred. Hence, the orator, sage, philosopher and reformer were all important in these societies.

(d) The division of technical labor was retarded, social labor extremely advanced. The accumulation of goods has already been noted.

(e) Knowledge, law and art were on top of the means of social control.

(f) The Greco-Roman civilization was a reality. Their cultural works were extraordinary.

(g) The social time scale showed their structures affirming both the time ahead of itself and the explosive time of creation. There was a real consciousness of this time. But these times did not achieve success. A struggle ensued with the time behind and turned in on itself, the time of long duration and partially with the deceptive time of organizations. The global phenomenon once again lagged behind its structure in support of the creative and goal-seeking social times.[65]

5. *Societies leading to the birth of capitalism and enlightened despotism.* This society historically supported an alliance between the territorial state and the bourgeoisies of the rapidly growing cities. Such an alliance dominated all other groups. The Church, the military, and most economic groupings, viz., workers in the manufacturing plants, were subservient to this union of the bourgeoisie and the monarchy. For the first time in history one can point to the rise of the social classes. From this development class conflict ensues.

> The territorial monarchy supports the common bourgeois people, the industrial capitalists, merchants and bankers (the king borrows money from the latter, wealth having increased in particular after the discovery of the New World). The mon-

---

[64] *Ibid.*, p. 125.
[65] *Traité* . . . , I, 225.

archy struggles againt the nobility, the military, and both the workers and peasants.[66]

The pattern becomes clear. The industrialized areas begin to flourish. Change is rapid. The state plays the role of a kind of apprentice-sorcerer. Improvement is technological know-how and means for the accumulation of wealth make the whole society more dynamic and moving. However, the global phenomenon slows down this drive towards "progress." The non-industrialized and stagnant rural areas limit the thrust of rising new industrial groups.

The basic philosophical orientation is a radically rationalistic Prometheanism. Man is cajoled to believe he can attain success through the rational application of his will and ability. Success is his if he works diligently and is frugal in his living. There is a similarity here with Weber's idea of the "protestant ethic." "Time is the most precious thing; it is the producer of wealth and power." [67] There is no place in this kind of society of the indomitable will for the lazy, the sluggard, and the irrational in their employment of time.

What are the traits of this society according to the criteria for analysis?

(a) The territorial monarchy dominates every level or grouping. An *official* hierarchy of groupings includes the nobility, the clergy, the Third Estate and the peasants.

However this "official" structure is threatened by the nascent social classes rising to power in the cities. "New economic enterprises of great scope, manufacturing, factories, maritime commerce . . . at first favored by the monarch become hostile to him." [68] This is brought out in their reluctance to approve either war or the maintenance of a privileged nobility.

(b) The passive masses are the most influential among the *We's*. Partial fusions are limited by the active *relations with the Other*. Such passive masses are found in the state, urban life and partially in rural life. The capitalistic enterprises are also the foyers for these *We's*. The *relations with the Other* are especially active in the whole of economic life. To reiterate, this limits the active *We's*.

(c) At the top of the depth levels technological and juridical patterns are firmly entrenched. They are basically

---

[66] *The Spectrum* . . . , p. 130.
[67] *Ibid.*, p. 131.
[68] *Ibid.*

creative and attack the time-worn customs in both the juridical means of regulation and in the ways of conducting economic life.

The morphological level follows. Manual labor and the problem of recruitment make this important. Third place is occupied by organizations and social roles. Lastly, symbols, rational and creative ideas and values prod the members of society to take the initiative in controlling their natural enviroment.

(d) Technical labor's division is much more developed in this society than social labor. Emphasis on the accumulation of wealth increases.

(e) As to social control, knowledge and law are competitors for the first rung. Within these, scientific and technical knowledge are in competition with philosophical knowledge; law is expressed through legislation and royal ordinances. Second place belongs to education as the universities begin to free themselves from the influence and control of the Church. The last rungs are left to morality, art and religion.

(f) This cultural framework is permeated with a triumphant naturalism, a growing individualism and the tantalizing idea of *Progress.*

(g) The social time scale finds the time alternation between advance and regression and the time of irregular pulsations at the top. The cities versus the rural areas would be an example.[69]

6. *The democratic-liberal societies corresponding to developed competitive capitalism.* This type of society dominated the United States and Europe at the close of the nineteenth century and the beginning of the present one. The state became democratic, dominated by the principles of the Declaration of Independence and the Declaration of the Rights of Man and of the Citizen (1789.) This democratic, secular territorial state was the predominant grouping but its power waned from that of enlightened despotism. Powerful grouping which opposed it grew up out of the industrial enterprises. Technological patterns and business-oriented frames of reference became decisive influences. This was the period of the complete development of the machine. Technology was the foundation of prosperity. Nations entered into competition on an economic level. Competition increased within these societies. Acute social prob-

[69] *Ibid.,* pp. 132-133.

lems arose out of this extreme competitiveness. This society is the epitome of capitalism. Its basic characteristics are easy to outline.

(a) The territorial state, democratic and secular in character, remains at the head of all functional groupings. Its position of supremacy is tenuous. Industrial enterprises, trusts and cartels, labor groupings, and financial organizations (in the broad sense here) undermine the stability of the territorial state's hold on this top rung. The social classes move into contention for the first time threatening the foundation of the hierarchy. The techno-bureaucrats begin forming a rival class which is still seeking the ascendant position.[70]

(b) Generally, the active masses are favored by this society. The bourgeois class does support certain communities through its economic structures, e.g., employer organizations. The proletarians, on the other hand, lend their support to some communions observable in labor unions and political parties which represent labor. The *We* in general is limited by the *relations with the Other* which are expressed in the intergroupal and interindividual nature of competitive enterprise.[71]

(c) Technical and economic patterns are more strongly accentuated than any other depth levels. Here Mumford, Ogburn and Veblen are right in their basic assessments of capitalistic society but only this particular type. Other forces in the collective persons of social classes, labor unions and political parties play such vital roles, have such creative and explosive collective attitudes that they must be put in second place. The organized level is in the next position. The morphological and ecological factors are still important but occupy a less important role.

(d) This type of society has a full division of both social and technical work. This is the significant contribution of the technological age.

(e) Social control comes through scientific knowledge, followed closely by political knowledge, or ideology, in the strict sense of the word. Secular education, law (legislation), moralities of aspiration, and symbolic ideal images all belonging to the bourgeois class, follow after knowledge.

(f) The cultural works are permeated by a scientism or cult of scientific knowledge which leads to a heady faith in

[70] *Traité* . . . , I, 228.
[71] *Ibid.*

the belief that every problem can be solved. This becomes the mark of society, its cement and integrating force.[72]

(g) The time ahead of itself finally comes to the fore in this type of global society. However, the time of alternation between advance and retardation poses a constant threat. Certain privileged groupings at the heart of the bourgeoisie resist any pretentions towards change; overproduction and decrease in profits also are causative factors. The time of irregular pulsations is a companion of economic crises. The ups and downs of the economy in the United States during the last fifty years provide a good example of this type of time. The class struggle, difficulties and conflicts resulting from colonial expansion, create the milieu for this latter time of irregular patterning. The huge economic organizations hide underlying forces which could cause deep changes as well as veil those tendencies which would limit "progress."

7. *Managerial society corresponding to organized capitalism.*

The United States, Germany before and after Nazism, and in a certain sense Great Britain before World War II would fit this type of society.

> The economy is no longer abandoned to free competition; it is planned in the private interest of trusts, cartels and companies with the aid of the State which puts its vast bureaucratic machinery at the disposal of the employers.[73]

(a) The state is under the control, at least partially, of private corporations which regulate and plan for all other groupings. They use every means to corrupt these other functional groups.

(b) The passive masses are unchallenged. They are successful in forcing back the communities.

(c) Among the depth levels the economic organizations predominate. Technological patterns and economic patterns, followed by political and public relations slogans diffused by technical means, come next in importance.

(d) Technical division of labor is somewhat curtailed by the augmentation of automation. "This has repercussions for the social division of labor since labor must be redistributed." [74]

---

[72] *The Spectrum* . . . , p. 139.
[73] *Ibid.*, p. 142.
[74] *Ibid.*, p. 143.

(e) The social control is headed by technical knowledge. Education and teaching reflect this type of knowledge in a uniform type of education. Morality, law and religion follow on the heels of these two forms of social control.

(f) " 'Technical civilization' dominating not only the social controls but 'human relations' themselves, causes the triumph of the 'instrument over the act.' " [75]

(g) The time ahead of itself is in a top position since this is a type of planned society. However, deceptive time at work in the organizations, the time of irregular pulsations active in the masses, and the time behind itself, always a part of management and the bureaucracy, do battle with the first place time. In the final analysis the time which belongs to the "machine" supplants them all. The members of society, collective and individual, serve as "sorcerer's apprentices" to these engines of control.

8. *Fascist societies.* These are recent phenomena. They are still present. Emerging nations in the areas of rapid social change are particularly susceptible to these regimes. Moreover, when deep economic crises hit, the passive masses rise to prominence, making the modern capitalist society prone to "radical" solutions which promise to alleviate the conditions of *angst* and anger.

Facist societies' structures consist of "the complete fusion of organized capitalism with the totalitarian State, led by the techno-bureaucratic groups linked with the organizational machinery of trusts, cartels, banks, administration and a highly specialized military.[76]

Gurvitch sees the leader, *der Fuehrer,* as a semi-charismatic demagogue who is only a straw man for these great organizations which control and dictate. These groups enslave all levels and classes of the population. The voluntary organizations are dissolved. The techno-bureaucratic organizations and groupings rely on a planned economy. They arrange all for their own profit. "The chauvinist and racial mythology, the slogan of the 're-establishment of order' and the faith in national independence, abundance, 'public salvation' . . . are only screens behind which hides the techno-bureaucratic authoritarianism." [77]

This structure differs little from the organized capitalism described in the previous section. The criteria for analysis

[75] *Traité* . . . , I, 230.
[76] *The Spectrum* . . . , p. 145.
[77] *Ibid.*

reveal about the same results. However, there are these differences: this fascist structure combines a kin dof mystical or mythological emotionalism with cynicism and super-organization. "Its communions are based on hate and an artificially inspired ecstasy; it declares war on every particular grouping which is outside the governmental machine; it shoves law and morality to the last rung of social control." [78] An artificial mythology is substituted which becomes its art form; military and atheletic parades express this art. Even education becomes a kind of drill.[79] Moreover, the basic unity is illusory. The fascist leadership unleashes forces which are ultimately beyond its control. Each of the great organizations, the techno-bureaucrats in particular, move in different social times. The dictators think they are in control of the time and that their mastery is complete; however, they are living an illusion which grows more grotesque as the crises worsen in the face of desperate decisions the poor leadership.[80]

9. *The planned society according to the principles of the centralized collectivist state.* Russia and China are examples. Their satellites of course would fit into this type. Yugoslavia is a case apart and will be discussed in connection with the next type. Gone are the bourgeois class and capitalist enterprises. This type's ideology rejects the absolute nature of private profit and industrial feudalism. Hence, the proletarian class, either alone or in combination with other groups, is the "official" dictator. "This dictatorship is not exercised by the proletariat themselves, but the communist party which becomes the supreme organ of the state, an organ charged with controlling the complete planning of the economy." It is also the creator and promulgator of the official 'party line." The proletariat does not control directly either the techno-bureaucracy, the state or the party. Certain professional organizational men, social engineers, are in control. Liberty and freedom are only promised for the second phase of communism when the class warfare will be ended and the state will have disappeared as an essential organ of control.

[78] *Ibid.*, p. 206.

[79] *Ibid.*

[80] Cf. C. N. Parkinson, *The Evolution of Political Thought* (New York: The Viking Press, 1960), pp. 238-304 for an excellent description of this whole process.

The following characteristics describe this structure:

(a) The single party controls the state and this latter dominates all other functional groupings.

(b) The masses are emphasized. They are sometimes active and other times passive. There are occasional active communions, especially within the party and in the *kolkhoses*.

(c) Centralized planning controls the arrangement and content of the depth levels. This planning is directed not only at economic life but the total life. Hence symbols and ideas become important. Organizations are essential for planning.

(d) Increased division of social and technical labor becomes an integral part of collective planning.

(e) Political knowledge is the first means of social control and scientific knowledge comes next. Humanistically oriented education follows and a morality based on ideal symbolic images with emphasis on creativity occupies the next rung. Art and law are last in importance.[81]

(f) As to culture, there is a real effort to synthesize humanism and technology, though without apparent success.

(g) The time scale is complicated. Explosive time of creation based on the ideals and values of humanism and the time ahead of itself which is guided by creative and novel plans for "programs," find themselves in competition with other times. Once again the deceptive time of the huge organizations, and the time of alternation between advance and retardation brought on by the relative success of the various plans which are implemented, as well as by the struggles among the several classes and groups occupy leading positions. There is a dissatisfaction among the proletariat in terms of their actually controlling the global structures; passive resistance exists on the part of the peasant classes. The impact of this is especially evident on the agricultural programs of both the Soviet Union and China.

Gurvitch contends that in order for the time of creation and the time ahead of itself to succeed, it would be necessary that the organizations be in the hands of the proletariat themselves and/or the peasants. Nor can they be dominated by the techno-bureaucrats or a powerful single party if this is to come to pass. "It is difficult to judge if these condi-

---

[81] Cf. Parkinson's work once again for an interesting discussion on the role of religion in the Soviet Union. His thesis is that Communism is a bona fide religion and hence, would be a means of social control.

tions have a chance of being realized in the near future and if the subjacent total social phenomenon to this structure reveals a sufficient dynamism moving in this direction." [82]

10. *Planned societies according to the principles of decentralized, pluralistic collectivism.* As yet this society has never been realized. There are examples in the world at present which give cause for including this in the list of types. Certain tendencies can be seen in the popular democracy of Yugoslavia,[83] in the Scandinavian countries,[84] and in Great Britain, which point to this decentralized planned society. This global society would try to effect a balance between industrial democracy and political democracy.[85]

The process of planning would move from the bottom to the top, the reverse of the Russian communist experiment. "It would commence with the general councils of control and the management of the local enterprises, passing on to the councils of industry and the regional economic councils, in order to arrive at a central economic council." [86]

Ownership would be federalized. This means that property be both individual and collective. The means of production would belong to these decentralized councils. Every person would participate individually and collectively in this ownership process. The state would be decentralized and its power would be balanced by the power of this separated economic organization. An impartial body would be established to rule on conflicts between the state and the economic council.[87]

The structures would have the following traits according to Gurvitch's criteria:

(a) The economic groupings would be arranged in one hierarchy; the locality groupings form another. The former would limit the latter (the state) and vice versa.

b) The communities and communions would be predominantly supported.

(c) The depth levels emphasized would include economic

---

[82] *Traité* . . . , I, 232.

[83] Cf. *The Atlantic Monthly*, CCX (December, 1962), 74-142.

[84] Cf. Marquis Childs, *Sweden: The Middle Way* (New Haven: Yale University Press, 1936).

[85] Harold J. Rutenberg and Clinton S. Golden in their works on industrial democracy indicate more concretely what Gurvitch is pointing to in this type of global society.

[86] *Traité* . . . , I, 232-233. Cf. Gurvitch's *La déclaration des droits sociaux* (New York: Editions de la Maison Française, 1944).

[87] *The Spectrum* . . . , p. 212.

planning based on the consent of the governed; open, versatile, creative values and ideas, innovating and unexpected roles, diverse types of federalist organizations would be in ascendancy. Competition would come from certain patterns and rules at the juridical level.

(d) The division of technical work would be more and more limited by automation; however, the social division of labor would be accentuated.

(e) The hierarchy of social control would find knowledge stripped of its political overtones and a choice would be given between knowledge of the *Other* and of the *We*. Law in its different forms would also occupy this first rung. Morality (creative morality, morality of virtues and imperative morality in particular) would come next, followed by education and art.

(f) A new humanistic civilization would be produced. All of the techniques, the means of controlling nature, the tools of creating a wholesome environment would be placed in the hands of mankind.

(g) For the first time the time of creation and the time ahead of itself would vie seriously for first place. However the time of alternation and the time behind itself could present some powerful competition. Conflicts are possible and probable between the multiple groupings which would be active in this type of society. Also the majority would conceivably make a mistake as to what would be best for them in a given situation. Any society which would develop a juridical system to promote justice would tend to favor a time behind itself. This is the very nature of "juridical restraint." [88]

The struggle to keep the separation between the structure and its global phenomenon will always pose problems. Gurvitch ends by declaring he is in no way interested in proposing this as an ideal type of global society.[89]

This brings to a close the description of the macrosociological view of social reality. This concludes the descriptive analysis of both the horizontal and vertical aspects of social reality. This tapestry of social life is of one piece. It is a totality. When these various parts are considered together the web of social relationships, the interpenetrations and fusions of individuals and groups, they create a many-

---

[88] *Traité* . . . , I, 233.
[89] *Ibid.*

colored design that reveals certain patterns, certain regularities, certain observable characteristics. This whole is social reality. These many parts are held together by a dialectical process. In graphic form these dialectical relationships can be viewed in this way:

THE VERTICAL   1) The Ecological Level

	2) Organizations	
	3) Social Patterns	
	4) Patterned Collective Behaviour	
	5) Social Roles	

THE HORIZONTAL

Social bonds	Macrosociology	Global
Microsociology		Structures
	6) Collective Attitudes	
	7) Social Symbols	
	8) Creative Collective Behaviour	
	9) Collective Ideas and Values	

10) The Collective Mind

This diagram shows the intersecting of the vertical and horizontal aspects of social reality as Gurvitch has described them. At any point along the continuum the vertical total social phenomena are discovered. They are related through the dialectical processes which we will describe in the next chapter. We would underline once more the symbolic nature of this description of social reality as Gurvitch conceives it. To use the terms *depth levels,* or *moving from the superficial to the more profound,* is in no way to make a value statement. This is simply one way of dealing with the extremely difficult material which makes up social reality. Nor is this diagram to suggest a static quality to society. These intersecting relationships are dynamic and moving. "All of these depth levels interpenetrate; more than this they are in perpetual conflict, tension, and threatened by estrangement or antinomy. The degree of their discontinuity and continuity, their mutual implication, or their polarization is a question of fact, and fact only." [90] Experience alone will provide the know-how to deal with the effervescent, continuously varying and changing combinations of these strata which roughly follow the contingent outlines of their different frameworks; always it is necessary to remember the Protean nature of the total social phenomena with their capacity to resist every attempt at containing them. Such combinations, therefore, vary according to the types of frameworks and the historical circumstances.

The dialectical method, Gurvitch contends, is the means by which the sociologist may at once describe the individual parts of social reality while holding to a view of the whole.

[90] *Déterminismes sociaux* . . . , p. 103.

CHAPTER VII

THE DIALECTIC:
EXPLANATION AND APPLICATION

The constant task of this study is to describe the nature of social reality. This exploration thus far has revealed a reality which is in Gurvitch's terms constantly moving, tension-filled, fluctuating, renewing, threatened by revolutions, in short characterized by a dynamic quality which St. Simon has called *société en acte*. This view of social reality then is dialectical. Such a dialectical character requires a special approach. It is this approach which must now be described.

First, the dialectic concerns social reality. This means that such a reality is conceived or studied in its totality, in its various dimensions, expressions and manifestations. As a real movement the dialectic is the way (*dia*) followed or taken by human groups. "According to the beautiful formula of Jean Wahl, 'The dialectic is a pathway. Moreover, in the very word dialectic, there is this idea of *dia*, through. The dialectic is a way rather, than a point of arrival.' " [1]

Each of these totalities (groups and global societies) is made up of collective and individual consciences, or in a larger sense, the total psychological phenomena and the multiple significations which these consciences grasp and by which they are influenced or affected. "In other words the dialectic as a real movement concerns a very specific reality, human reality, which is par excellence, social reality." [2]

If the first aspect of the dialectic is to assert its parallelism with social reality, the second logical step would be to see it as a method. Gurvitch contends that this is the means by which to grasp the basic reality of social groups as totalities. Here the essential unity of the subject and object

---

[1] *Dialectique et sociologie*, p. 2.
[2] *Ibid.*, p. 179.

is explicitly affirmed. There are several characteristics which help to clarify this term as a method. First, it denies every position which is rigidly held or unquestioningly espoused. The dialectic destroys every type of intellectual sclerosis. Such "mummification" (a favorite word of Gurvitch throughout this whole discussion) impairs sociology's ability to grasp these totalities as *dynamic* wholes, as well as to understand their various parts.

Furthermore, this dialectic as a method is predominantly negative in spirit. It must circumvent every propensity towards establishing laws, strictly formal abstractions, or superficial divisions which would undercut the basic *realness* of groups. The rational and the logical are insufficient. He would never deny the proper role of reason and logic. He finds them inadequate alone; they have their place in the formulation of theory and the expression of certain ideas about social reality, but they fail to do justice to the full-orbed nature of social reality. This is very close to the widely accepted distinction between deductive and inductive reasoning. Gurvitch is saying that the deductive, though essential in the building of hypotheses, is incomplete. The total social phenomenon is so highly complex the only recourse is to the dialectic, alone sufficiently competent and imaginative to grasp the idea of social reality *en marche*.

The dialectical, moreover, constantly struggles against every attempt to simplify social reality, to crystalize or anesthetize it or limit knowledge about it. "The dialectic focuses on the complexities, sinuosities, flexibilities and constantly renewing tensions, along with the unexpected turns of events of social reality; all of these must be taken into account to comprehend such social entities." [3] As a method it reveals the constantly changing character of human experience. The content of that experience (midpoints between the immediate and the constructed, in Gurvitch's terminology) and the frameworks which encompass this experience—such frameworks make it possible to construct a typology of social experience—are constantly varying and dynamically related. Obviously, Gurvitch's definition of the content of experience is very close to that of Henri Bergson. A two-fold application of the dialectic emerges from this description thus far: first, it shows the types of movement which reality takes; and second, it is the means by which such movements are studied. Thus, the natural sciences find

---

[3] *Ibid.*, pp. 180-181.

some processes of the dialectic applicable since all experience is colored by the human factor. All experience is human experience, according to Gurvitch.[4]

"The striking affinity which exists between the dialectic, as much a method as a real movement, and experience . . . comes from their both being attached to the human factor." [5] In another place Gurvitch explains this more fully as he describes what he means by experience. Experience has several levels, the immediate, the mundane and the constructed, e.g., the scientific. Experience is so rich in content it escapes the easy reduction to certain "given and observed facts" in a scientific induction as the positivists would assert. Nor is experience merely "the reflection guiding the sensations by the intermediary of associations, the position of Locke and Hume." [6] Neither is it based on isolated sensations which are mechanically united as Condillac illustrates in his philosophy. The partisans of empirical research in sociology, especially among many Americans, suffer from this kind of reductionism. They think they are free from presuppositions with their emphasis on objectivity and quantification, but this in itself reveals a preconception.

Gurvitch's persistent criticism of this all too simple reductionism on the part of a large segment of American sociology has been effectively re-enforced in C. Wright Mills's writings. Mills calls this movement "abstracted empiricism." Though the practitioners of abstracted empiricism believe they are free from any philosophical presuppositions, in reality they espouse a particular position at the very outset. "What they have done in brief is to embrace one philosophy of science which they now suppose to be The Scientific Method . . . its most decisive result has been a sort of methodological inhibition." [7]

Mills explains that this loyalty to "The Method" sorely limits the kinds of problems which are studied by social scientists. Those problems are mostly irrelevant; they lack the classical concern of social scientists; they fail to examine the struggle for survival.

Gurvitch vigorously underlines the notion that the social scientists have a different domain for their study than the

---

[4] *Ibid.*, p. 181.
[5] *Ibid.*
[6] *Ibid.*, p. 7.
[7] *The Sociological Imagination*, p. 57.

physical scientists. The study of social facts calls for a different approach than that used by the physical and natural sciences. Moreover, the latter's method has undergone serious changes since the turn of the century. There is no longer a single method, only a basic attitude which can be called scientific. Polycarp Kush, Percy Bridgmen and William Beck attest to this. "There is no 'scientific' method and that which is called by that name can be outlined for only quite simple problems." [8] As one writer has put it, "Scientific problems are solved by collecting data and by 'thinking about them all the time.' " [9]

The basic approach for problem solving in the social sciences is more an attitude or a posture than it is a set method. It is an atmosphere in which exploration for truth may be made. It is much broader than so often conceived. The important thing is to be consistent with the elevated aims of classical social study or critical analysis in the finest sense of the word. What are the characteristics of this scientific ethos? This is the question which concerns Gurvitch as he attempts to correct what he sees as a stultifying narrowness in social science research.

As previously stated in Chapter IV, a dialectical tension exists between method and object of study. In the social sciences the object of study is social reality in all its depth and breadth. This reality is far from being simple, static and stable as a field of investigation, but is a fluid, dynamic, ever-changing, explosive domain requiring a method of observation and comprehension equal to such a task. The method adequate to fulfill this aim, Gurvitch contends, has to be dialectical. Furthermore, the goal of social science is to discover the truth about social reality. Such an aim of objective truth requires a loyalty to certain notions which make this exploration possible. The classical atmosphere of science involves opportunities for independent dissent, tolerance for the other person's point of view, a respect for reason, integrity, fearless observation, careful validation of hypotheses, the invitation to imaginative speculation and open discussion. These classic characteristics are implied in Gurvitch's dialectic. He attempts to demolish every acquired concept which is crystalized and hardened. This is

---

[8] Quoted in *Ibid.*, p. 58.

[9] Abraham Wolf, "The Scientific Method," *The Encyclopedia Britannica*, Volume XX (Chicago: The Encyclopedia Britannica, Inc., 1955), 125.

the point he makes in asserting that the dialectical approach is primarily negative. Absolutes are impossible. Only probabilities and relationships are possible to the scientist. This has become patently clear in atomic physics.

However, the dialectic suffers from certain stereotyped ideas about its nature. When one hears the word he assumes it is a philosophical position. This is unfortunate in the light of twentieth century physics and the critical analysis of the dialectic itself. It is when one settles on a particular operational process of the dialectic and sees this as the *passe partout* to the solution of every problem in social reality, that subjectivism and dogmatism enter. Several operational processes are possible. They all belong to the dialectical method. Sometimes all are used; other times only one or two suffice. Furthermore, the number of processes is not limited; new ones can and will be discovered as this quest for truth continues. At present there are five distinct types of dialectical processes. These will be discussed below. Before this is pursued, one final comment must be made about the general posture or attitude of the social scientist in the classical sense.

The social scientist, because his field of labor is human reality, cannot enclose himself in a laboratory, where conditions allow more objectivity, fairly rigid control, and repetition of circumstances. There is no escape from the human condition. Those whom he examines are thinking, willing, conscious persons—he is also part of this same humanity. He is *engagé*. There is no alternative. This is the essence of the dialectic. The processes of dialectical investigation lend themselves to the tasks of the social scientist. They enable the researcher to move beyond the sterile dichotomy made famous by Einstein, "For science can only ascertain what is, but not what should be, and outside of its domain value judgments of all kinds remain necessary." [10] This is a popular way of resolving the problems between ethics, theology and science, but Gurvitch would state that this is too neat a division. Man's existence militates against such a precise separation. By seeing the relationship of values and method as dialectical, one has a more realistic estimation of the human condition. Classical social science included this element of involvement. The early social scientists were engaged thinkers and scholars. They were ac-

[10] Quoted in Paul F. Schmidt, "Ethical Norms in Scientific Method," *The Journal of Philosophy*, LVI (July 16, 1959), 644.

tive in political life. They were far from being a-political and spiritually destitute. Humanity mattered. In this period they were intellectually concerned even though less sophisticated in their technological skills. Gurvitch, in his approach, seeks to reaffirm this inescapable human coefficient. His own life as well as his method of analysis and study illustrate this concretely.

1. THE OPERATIONAL PROCESSES OF THE DIALECTIC

A recurring theme in Gurvitch's analysis of social reality is the presence of the unexpected or the unanticipated. In his critical review of current sociology, Gurvitch complained that too few sociologists have paid enough attention to this aspect of social life.[11] Experience is infinitely varied and the changes which take place within a social whole are continuous. The dialectical method takes into consideration these infinite variations; it is at once empirical and realistic because of this attribute.

To be empirical does not mean to espouse the philosophical position of the positivists or the "abstract empiricists" active in the United States. They would assert that the only thing necessary is to gather the given and observable facts into a nice neat pile and make some generalizations from the findings. Social reality is considerably removed from this view. This is at once too limiting and too simple. It forsakes any real effort at analysis and explanation. Gurvitch contends his view is broader, that his "scientific approach" is not limited to this abstracted empiricism, and that the operational processes go much further in attempting to understand. This is the first step towards explanation.

All experience is dialectical. Gurvitch means that experience must be "managed" in part to be observed and explored. This means that experience is abstractly reconstructed by the various sciences. These constructions are the essential expressions of the immediately experienced. This also implies there are intermediary positions between the immediate and the superficial or the constructed. Though these constructions are multiplied and multiplied, they can never contain the full richness of experience. Experience is a kind of Proteus. "It escapes us when we think we have

---

[11] Robert Merton's idea of "serendipity" comes close to this requirement. Cf. *Social Theory* . . . , pp. 103-108.

caught it; we are dupes when we believe we have penetrated its secret; we are victims of it when we believe we are free of it, if only for a moment." [12]

Again, this is why experience cannot be reduced to one theory. As soon as one advances a particular theory of experience he has slipped into dogmatism. Whether one calls it sensualism, associationism, positivism, pragmatism, phenomenology or existentialism, the result is the same. "One deforms experience, arrests this experience, destroys its unpredictability, the infinite variety, and the unexpected aspects of its very frameworks." [13] Experience, to labor the point for just a moment, is uncontainable. Experience, then, plunges the researcher into the dialectic. It is the sole method which can deal with such a variety. The variety itself is dialectical.

This whole argument is clear when one realizes that the dialectic and experience are both attached to humanity. Everything that is touched by the human condition is also within the spheres of the dialectical and experience.

> Experience is always human; it is never sub-human or super-human. It is the effort of men, the *We*, of the groups, classes, and entire societies to be oriented in the world, in the social world first, but also, by this intermediary, to be oriented in the natural world. It is the social praxis, at once individual and collective, which Karl Marx insisted upon with a particularly persuasive force. Scientific experience itself—not only in the social sciences, but in the natural sciences—remains essentially a "human experience." It bears the imprint of the human, the social, and the historic reverberating in the natural world.[14]

This statement is an excellent summary of Gurvitch's essential position. Five operational procedures of the dialectic clarify the complexity of these relationships and tensions.

I. COMPLEMENTARITY.

Gurvitch points to Niels Bohr as one of the founders of the idea of complementarity. According to Bohr there are

---

[12] *Dialectique et sociologie*, p. 8.
[13] *Ibid.*
[14] *Ibid.*

two sets of phenomena which can be interpreted in terms of contradictory theories (wave and particle). These were obtained under experimental conditions impossible to carry out simultaneously. He says explicitly, "They cannot be comprehended within a single picture, but must be regarded as complementary in the sense that only the totality of the phenomena exhausts the possible information about the objects." [15]

From this Gurvitch argues for his emphasis on relativism and realism; or put another way, he argues contextualism. This is not a new concept. Whitehead and Mead preceded him. There is little doubt he was influenced by Mead whom he admires greatly. This idea of complementarity is a common-sense scientific tool. The toleration of one person by another requires some sort of complementary understanding. How could differing views exist side by side unless this were so in everyday life? It is logical to believe that if one were to examine certain phenomena from several perspectives or positions, the data accumulated and the generalizations coming from such observation would be more accurate and valid. Contradiction is part of social life and this contradiction, when it is included in analysis, makes the study much more relevant and authentic. This is certainly one of the basic ideas implicit in this notion.

> We cannot know an object in complete isolation either from ourselves or from other objects. It is the perceptual context, that is, the object in the context, or taken for granted. Objective relativism . . . emphasizes that this is indeed a context, with transcendent ontological status in and of itself, but only a part of a totality of objective appearances defined by their relations to one another, that is to say defined in various contexts. [16]

Social life is of such a nature the conceptual framework must be coherent and wholistic in its approach, since the proper domain of sociology is the real social group. It is a totality because of the dialectical tensions at play within its interior life holding the various parts together, bringing order out of human variety. The dialectic of complemen-

---

[15] "Discussion with Einstein," in *Albert Einstein, Philosopher-Scientist*, ed. by P. A. Schlipp (Evanston: The Library of Living Philosophers, 1949), p. 210.

[16] Patricia J. Doty, "Complementarity and its Analogies," *The Journal of Philosophy*, LV (December 4, 1958), 1103.

tarity explains this movement in part but it is only a first step. The other kinds of dialectical process explain further. There are different types of complementarity. First, the type which reveals at first contradictory alternatives which turn out to be complementary notions or hypotheses; on closer scrutiny for instance, the dichotomy between comprehension and explanation is a false one. These two interact constantly, in fact complement each other. They are necessary to one another.[17]

A second type of complementary dialectic works in a reverse sense. This is best explained by several examples, e.g., the relationships between effort and resistance, the given and the constructed, the mediary and the immediate, the continuous and the discontinuous, the superficial and the profound, the qualitative and the quantitative. A common way of describing this type is the use of the continuum which plots an infinite number of positions between the two polar positions. There is an element of compensation in this type. The discontinuous must be compensated by the continuous or order fails to materialize. Without order the group ceases to exist as a real unity. For instance, there is a compensatory relationship between the *We* and the *relations with the other*.[18]

The third type of complementary action, controlled always by the situation, causes the polar points to pull together (go in the same direction) or pull apart, though always as a compensatory action. In some ways this is the sense in which Toynbee puts forth his famous doctrine of "challenge and response." For instance, the morphological and ecological factors are such that certain responses, certain compensations must be made to meet the population explosion which is occurring in a country of ever-decreasing arable land. The way in which the various depth levels, e.g., roles, symbols, collective attitudes and values respond, whether in a compensatory action towards each other or of separation, depends upon the various social and historical conjunctions. This third type is also illustrated by the way in which an individual balances the various roles he is asked to play. "One can play an important role as a scholar or professor and succeed at playing only a minor one in his political party, labor union, or his own home." [19]

---

[17] *Dialectique et sociologie*, p. 193.
[18] *Ibid.*, pp. 194-195.
[19] *Ibid.*, p. 196.

II. MUTUAL IMPLICATION.

This second kind of dialectic concerns those elements which on first sight appear to be heterogenous or opposite. However, upon a closer look, they illustrate a mutuality, an interdependency in which they are partially immanent in one another.

One of the best illustrations of this is the relationship of the social and the psychological. It is impossible to understand how these sets of phenomena intersect and relate without recourse to this type of dialectic. See Chapter III for a detailed discussion of this.

Another apt example is the mutual implication of culture and society. It is really foolhardy to try and separate them. Culture finds its framework in the social structure; the binding materials of society are the works of civilization. Though a structure from time to time may be destroyed by its cultural content, a new structure is soon formed to contain these new arrangements and hierarchies.

III. AMBIGUITY.

Gurvitch takes Freud's important finding and applies it to social reality. Complementarity fails to explore the profound levels in the relationships between the individual and collective minds. Mutual implication as well does not go far enough. The destiny of man which has caused him to live in societies, or in various *We's*, i.e., groups and social classes, involves a further dimension, the presence of *ambiguity*. This ambiguity can eventually lead to ambivalence. This represents another process of the dialectic. At the heart of social groupings are friends and enemies, feelings of love and hate, comfort and insecurity. These are the conditions which belong to ambiguity. Take for example the polar attributes of the organized and the spontaneous within social reality. Excessive rigidity of the organized leads to a critical and disruptive explosion at the spontaneous level. Or, the situation can develop where the explosive elements are so prevalent as to threaten the unity of society. Frequently both conditions are present and a tug of war begins which leads from ambiguity to ambivalence and finally to polarization or the complete juxtaposition of the elements. Gurvitch asks how else it is possible to study the relationships of three elements such as the mass, communion, and community without recourse to this dialectic of ambiguity. The three are present at the same time and require the researcher see them all as they relate to each other. Obviously there are striking contradictions, but this is the truth about society. It behooves the social scientist then to adopt some means whereby he can take into account this ambiguity. Such a means would help the social scientist escape the pitfall of placing a value judgment on one type of fusion in the *We*. Only then can empirical research be carried out in a truly "scientific" fashion.

Examples of this type of dialectic would be relationships formed by contractual agreements or credit arrangements, or any kind of legal bond. There are points of integration where the two parties agree; there are points of disagreement as to interpretation of set clauses and the means of executing the document. Ambiguity can lead to ambivalence when either individuals or groups or even global societies, at once are attracted and repelled by each other. In other words, there are times when the separate entities or individuals are burning with curiosity, other moments when they are indifferent, times when a spirit of friendliness prevails, other junctures when backbiting and hypercriticism rules. Persons can be enemies now and friends later; there can exist within the same person and persons sympathy and coldness, love and hate.

All of these relationships of ambiguity plus those of mutual implication and complementarity can become antinomic. When this happens polarization obtains. This is the next type of dialectical process.

IV. THE DIALECTIC OF POLARIZATION.

Polarization is the usual type of dialectic when one thinks of this term. Gurvitch makes it plain these antinomies, dichotomies or opposites are not sacred. They only tell part of the dialectical story. The mystical, sacrosanct connotations about this process must be eliminated. A simple synthesis in the Hegelian-Marxist dialectical sense is untenable. Social reality gives little evidence that such antinomies are always present in clear, sharp form. It all depends upon the circumstances, situations, or *Sitz in Leben*. The tensions between the several factors or aspects are relative; they are observable in different degrees of intensity. Sometimes they reach the proportion of polarization; other times they exist as ambiguities or mutual implication or evidences of complementarity. The paradoxical often resists the dialectical process of polarity.

Always there is the element of surprise. Sometimes one would think, upon first examination, polarity holds, but closer analysis reveals a less intense process. On the other hand, the relationship between the individual and society seems to be solved quite easily by the process of "reciprocity of perspectives," but there are occasions when the individual senses an acute separation or alienation from society. The dialectic of polarity helps to understand this.

Another example where this process is particularly valuable is the presence of revolution within a given social structure. This dialectic is operational for analyzing the present situation in Africa, South America and Southeast Asia. These are areas of conflict, disintegration and "rapid social change."

Technology in the Western world threatens to create a more acute alienation than Marx ever envisioned. This alienation involves cultural works, social structure and technological know-how. "Is it not necessary to insist on the fact that in order to study seriously the situation in which our societies are struggling, the use of polarization is essential?" [20] Our age reveals a critical, ever-widening abyss between technology and the other cultural works.

Finally, this dialectical process is very useful in examining the problems of acculturation, particularly pervasive in every part of the modern world.

V. THE DIALECTIC OF RECIPROCITY OF PERSPECTIVES.

This process of reciprocity concerns those aspects of a social whole which relate to each other in such a way that both total identification and separation are denied. They are mutually immanent. There is a parallelism and a symmetry between them which is more or less rigorously maintained.

Gurvitch maintains this is no *solution-clef*. It lacks universal application. Yet like the notion of the collective mind and the importance of social law before it, there is a certain primordial quality to this process for Gurvitch which resists denial.

This process explains the centripetal force of a group, for example. Still it would be in error to deny the constant possibility of surprises, or the unexpected which can enter a

---

[20] *Dialectique et sociologie*, p. 211. Cf. also Association internationale des sociologues de langue française, *Structures sociales et democratie économique* (Brussels: Institut de Sociologie, 1961), pp. 269-280.

given situation and wreak havoc with the symmetry and parallelism implied in the reciprocity of perspectives. The hyper-empiricism in its radical dialectic takes these possibilities into account. The reciprocity of perspectives takes its place alongside the other types of processes. In the final analysis, the concrete experience of the living social reality will determine the type(s) of dialectic operating in that particular, peculiar and specific historical-empirical situation.[21]

This ends the presentation of these various operational procedures. This method is an approach to analysis. Inherent in this role are limitations. Such a method describes *what is*. It stops at the threshold of explanation. It assembles the data, describes what is happening. Explanation is subject to a different set of rules. It is concerned with *why* and *whither*. This is the subject of the following section. Before moving into the rules of explanation, it is best to summarize what the dialectical method accomplishes.

a) The method apprises the social scientist of the nature of social reality in all its explosive and revolutionary movements, its ebb and flow, its dialectical character.

b) It describes the movements of structuration, destructuration and restructuration. . . . This includes a view of the total social phenomena moving towards existence as a totality and being split apart by the opposite force of anarchy or disintegration.

c) This method shows that the various types of groupings and societies are more than mere images. They are concrete points of reference for analyzing the real social entities in all their fluidity.

d) Finally, the dialectical approach only leads to explanation. Its sole job is to describe. Assigning other roles to this phase of the sociological enterprise is invalid. It still remains descriptive. "The most beautiful girl in France is no more than what she is." [22]

Many sociologists try to go beyond description even though they operate within the framework of a method whose limit is in gathering data and preparing the soil for explanation. There is only so much an approach can tell the researcher.

---

[21] *Ibid.*, p. 218.
[22] *Ibid.*, p. 219.

2. EXPLANATION IN SOCIOLOGY [23]

Any discussion of *explanation* in science must take into consideration the whole idea of determinism. Two conclusions follow: a) "It is impossible to detach the notion of determinism from the concrete and real frameworks which it directs. Such a determinism is limited by the time in which it lives. The outcome is a pluralism of limited, relative and varying partial determinisms which are distinctly different in each concrete universe, each specific world studied by a particular science." [24] b) The technical processes or descriptive tools by which to explain these determinisms vary according to the same criteria. New tools will have to be covered as knowledge expands. Causal laws, functional laws, evolutionary laws, laws of statistical probability, singular causality, tendencies towards regularity, functional correlations or direct integration in the totalities are all possible. One or several may apply in one situation. Others will fit other circumstances. Contingency limits coherence. This is the central problem of explanation.

This double contingency does not deny there are concrete wholes which have certain patterns, certain regularities plus a certain coherence. However, a paradox obtains: at one and the same time there exists a coherent contingency coupled with a contingent coherence. Such a paradox is consistent with those other ambiguities, e.g., *discontinuous continuity and continuous discontinuity, qualitative quantity and quantitative quality.*

Gurvitch's definition of determinism hammers home this relative and limited pluralism.

> Determinism is the integration of particular facts into one of the real, multiple frameworks or concrete universes (actual, known or constructed) which always remains contingent; it (determinism) situates these facts, that is explains them in relationship to its understanding of the framework. This integration presupposes, in effect, an understanding of the relative cohesion of the contingent framework in question, plus its unfolding life

---

[23] This section is largely taken from the *Traité* . . . , I, 236-250. This represents the first systematic discussion of the rules for explanation in sociology. Previous reviewers of his work did not have access to this latest addition to his thought.

[24] Cf. *Déterminismes sociaux* . . . , pp. 9-40.

within one or several of the temporalities. These latter are seldom singularized and never uniform.[25]

Straightway one notices the close alliance between comprehension and explanation. Gurvitch sees these dialectically related. Each is part of the other. It is fruitless to separate them. "It is as impossible to explain without understanding the framework, as it is to comprehend the relative coherence of this latter without reaching some conclusion as to the manner of integration that is explanation." [26] Max Weber comes under attack by Gurvitch for his loyalty to Dilthey, who separated explanation from comprehension by subsuming both into the latter. Dilthey's explanation was mechanistic. He failed to realize that in order to explain anything one has to have an understanding of the framework itself which in turn presupposes the framework is *real*. Weber reintroduced explanation into sociology by subsuming it under the comprehensive interpretations of the internal meanings of behaviour. He thereby transformed comprehension or Dilthey's intuitive understanding of *real totalities* into a subjective introspection of the internal meanings of individual behaviours and their liaison with spiritual meanings, thus fragmenting and demolishing these frameworks of social reality which must serve as the basis for explanation.[27]

A tight predictability is out of the question in most cases. Only rare circumstances will allow this type of conclusion. The social sciences are particularly removed from such hope. The determinisms are much more relative, numerous and consequently limiting. Increasingly it becomes obvious, as Gaston Bachelard was wont to say, that sociology's task is "to find the hidden." [28] This is a difficult assignment. What is real rarely becomes evident from mere surface estimation. Hence, Gurvitch asserts his depth sociology and his empirical-realist dialectical method are justified.

The ways in which explanation is erroneously attempted are explained in Chapter III.[29] Explanation in sociology is so often betrayed by false assumptions or total dismissal. Explanation is desperately needed today. The threatening contemporary problems of fascism, technocracy (even so-

[25] *Ibid.*, p. 40.
[26] *Ibid.*
[27] *Traité* . . . , I, 239.
[28] *La vocation* . . . , I, 5.
[29] Cf. above, pp. 110-112.

ciology in certain areas has become the servant of power), social revolutions in countries where a proletariat is nearly non-existent, e.g., Russia, China and most of Asia, all await sociological analysis and explanation. Such an explanation is dependent upon an adequate theory. Only a valid theory is able to produce working hypotheses. Such hypotheses provide guidelines for research whereby comprehension of social frameworks and explanation through certain conceptual tools can be realized. False hypotheses are better than none at all. At least they will indicate the superficial nature of a considerable amount of generalizing and serve to point one's efforts in the direction of unveiling the hidden. In sum, to distrust theory is to render explanation impossible.

3. THE RULES OF EXPLANATION IN SOCIOLOGY

A. Harking back to one of the basic notions in Gurvitch's *L'idée du droit social,* each social element stands in relationship to the next larger context. Hence, the microsocial aspects are integrated in groupings, the groupings in social classes, the groupings and social classes in global societies. The movement of explanation is from the abstract to the concrete. The totality tends to predominate over the separate elements, the whole over the partial. The total social phenomena are global. This view of the totality is possible and the ability to control these phenomena depends upon certain points of reference which represent partial manifestations of these concrete *total* phenomena, e.g., the *We,* groups and classes. These frameworks suggest the complex character of the total social phenomena. The various depth levels and the a-structural, structurable and structured elements are in ceaseless tension with each other.

B. To study these total global phenomena requires the researcher go through the intermediary of their structures. Since the global society is always structured, this step is a logical one. Two exigencies hold for this rule: 1) The structure must always be seen as an intermediary; its character is supple and dialectical. It cannot serve as the basis for sociological explanation. The total social phenomena alone can do this. 2) Neither the social structure nor the total phenomena should be confused with their types. The various types are only operational conceptions constructed for purposes of grasping these concrete and real entities.

C. The changes and reversals within each global structure are explained by the conflicts between the structure a᾿ιd its subjacent total social phenomena. Each structure serves as a category of explanation depending upon its type, "the character, force, feebleness, relative changeability or immobility of the organizations supported by it." [30]

D. One must include a detailed consideration of every partial structure though the global is pre-eminent. These partial structures and partial expressions of the total social phenomena have built-in conflicts and tensions. Examples are the conflicts among the classes, the struggles among groupings at the interior of the social classes and the opposition among the various *We's*.

E. A sociological study must take every depth level into consideration. The myopic study of one level fails to see the whole. This view of the whole separates sociology from the particular social sciences. Furthermore, it underlines the necessity of sociology's working closely with the particular disciplines which are branches within sociology. Explanation can only come from such cooperation. Once again the variability of the social determinisms is accentuated by this approach, since the arrangement of the depth levels in a hierarchy changes with each type of global structure.

F. One must distinguish between social determinisms and sociological determinism. The former are the abstract determinisms belonging to the individual depth levels and to the a-structural microsociological frameworks which encompass the forms of sociability. The sociological determinism belongs to the properly sociological realities in which these social elements are integrated. It does not always follow that the concrete global societies reveal the most vigorous and consistent type of determinism. Certain uni-dimensional determinisms (a one depth level type) provide manageable areas for quantitative analysis. The ecological level especially is open to this type of study. However, most laws of probability are inapplicable for global structures. Of necessity the sociological determinisms are dialectically oriented since the conflicts and tensions among the global, uni-dimensional and micro-determinisms do not abate as the drive towards sociological explanation continues. Again the structural framework is all important. For purposes of understanding and explanation social and sociological determinisms are better kept conceptually separate.

---

[30] *Traité* . . . , I, 242.

G. Causal laws are extremely rare in sociology. Such laws resist every scientific effort. There is too much discontinuity, too much contingency and lack of repetition in social reality to generalize in *this manner*. Even a singular causality linked to just one particular social structure is suspect. The singular causality tends to become increasingly individualized. If one goes from the ecological to the deepest level this becomes manifestly true. The same holds when moving from the uni-dimensional to the multi-dimensional, from the partial to the total. There is too great an abyss between cause and effect for such a conceptual tool. It is simply inadequate. Sociological explanation must rely on other means. History provides the best clue.

H. Three processes hold for sociology, since causality reveals precious little: (1) functional correlation, (2) tendency towards regularity, and (3) the direct integration in the whole.

(1) *Functional correlation.* This process of explanation concerns two or more elements which demand being integrated in the same totality. Hence, the mystical form of knowledge is often linked with the most intense type of *We,* the communion; the rational form of knowledge is more than likely integrated in the community; the symbol and the symbolized have a like correlation. These examples resist putting one aspect before the other; nor are they reciprocally causal. Neither are they constant, since other variables could affect the total situation.[31] These functional correlations will become apparent upon examining the concrete entities, whether partial or global. Mannheim observes that, "Every social fact is a function of the time and place in which it occurs." [32] In other words, the two or more elemen fit. They can be correlated. This is the sense in which Gurvitch uses the term.

(2) *Tendency towards regularity.* While the functional correlation is a substitute for causal and functional laws, tendencies towards regularity are substitutes for evolutionary laws. "These tendencies are the patterns in which totalities move, certain approximate directions, though they are always ambiguous and tentative. In each type of global structure, and even at times in certain sectors of the structure, several contradictory regularities exist simultane-

---

[31] *Déterminismes sociaux* . . . , pp. 64-65.
[32] Cited in *Social Theory* . . . , p. 21.

ously." [3] These patterns apply only at the macrosociological level. A contemporary example would be the contradictory technocracy or towards a pluralistic democratic economy, or patterning of capitalist society. It can go in the direction of technocracy or towards a pluralistic democratic economy, or in the direction of communism. Capitalist society can persevere or take an unexpected turn. Patterns are still present. They are tendencies and nothing more. Within certain limits the diverse aspects of social life, whether economic, political, juridicial, moral, religious, cognative or esthetic, can be stated in this manner. Each type of global or partial structure contains certain tendencies towards regularity. One can only ascertain their success post-factum. Then the results are always contingent and tentative.

(3) *The direct integration in a social whole.* There are certain elements which are directly explained by the social framework. One takes them for granted. Gurvitch points out it is not by chance that sexual habits differ or relationships between different generations vary, or expressions of affection are dissimilar among different societies or even among social classes within the same society. It is sufficient to say this is a process of sociological explanation. "Neither the causality of the framework in question, nor the particular functional correlations need be considered." [34] These facts are integrated directly and naturally. They belong. This is Gurvitch's conception of *verstehen.* Here is the internal significance of the real group. However, he stops abruptly at this juncture. He is careful to avoid any total separation of *comprehension* and *explanation.*

I. Sociology must see the necessary collaboration between historical and sociological explanation. Experimentation needs to be distinguished from observation. The former has had little success in sociology. At least when analyzing group, class and global phenomena such a method is inoperative. This behooves sociology to see the invaluable assistance which history can offer. Historical causality places more emphasis on continuity. It is more singularized and more tightly integrated. There is less "recurrence of states" in historical description. History deals with those factors which never repeat themselves. Hence, historians have a better chance of explaining *why* than sociology. The discipline of history has wrongly waited for sociology to

---

[33] *Déterminismes sociaux* . . . , p. 65.
[34] *Traité* . . . , 244-245.

provide the ultimate explanation. Sociology must depend on history for necessary help. "For it is from the total concrete situation and its strictly singular, rigorously non-recurring causality . . . that one can arrive at certain explanations which are more in keeping with the human condition." [35] The relationship between history and sociology has been discussed previously. It is enough to say that a paradox exists which can only be overcome by a cooperation between the two disciplines. History through its method which places emphasis on continuity and singularity studies a reality which includes tendencies towards discontinuity and pluralism. Sociology emphasizes the discontinuous and follows a typological approach as social reality tends more towards continuity and unity. In essence the two approaches complement each other. Each must rely on the work of the other. Conflict is unrealistic. Both study the total social phenomena. Answers to the questions of *why* and *whither* depend on their close collaboration. Gordon Allport's work on prejudice contains an approach to that problem which is very similar to that which Gurvitch is proposing here.[36]

4. AN EXAMPLE OF EMPIRICAL RESEARCH

The foregoing discussion of Gurvitch's dialectical method and his follow-up rules for explanation in sociology serve as a backdrop for the following analysis of certain empirical trends which have developed from Gurvitch's theory.

Previously Gurvitch advocated certain methods of sociometry, but only with his characteristic reservations and additions.[37] Since we are dealing primarily with the macro-sociological frameworks we will look at a project concerned with a group's knowledge of the *other*. Parenthetically Gurvitch places great emphasis on the use of role-playing, psycho- and socio-drama. He has suggested using the theater as a valid means to study the microsociological elements or social bonds. "There is a striking affinity between real social life and the theater." [38]

---

[35] *Ibid.*, p. 245.

[36] *The Nature of Prejudice* (Garden City: Doubleday Anchor Books, 1958), pp. 201-212.

[37] *Sociometry*, XV, 1949, "Sociometry in France and the United States." Gurvitch edited this volume and wrote the initial article.

[38] Cf. *La vocation* . . . , I, 272. P.-H. Maucorps and used Gurvitch's categories in his "Sociometric Study in the French Army," Sociometry, XVI, 1950, pp. 48 ff. Also see Jean Duvignaud, *La Sociologie du Théatre* (Paris: Presses Universitaire de France, 1966).

In his introductory remarks to the National Research Center project, Gurvitch asserts the approach to the knowledge of others has changed in this century.[39] The rejection of Neo-Kantianism and the rise of phenomenology suggest the outlines of the change. Max Scheler is especially important for Gurvitch. In *The Nature of Sympathy*, Scheler states the problem: "The difficulties . . . are mostly self-engendered, owing to the assumption that each of us is 'primarily' aware only of his self and its experiences, images, etc., are related to other individuals."[40] Scheler rejects such a starting place for the knowledge of others. Inference, analogy and empathy are equally invalid. We cannot know other minds this way.

> The problem as stated in these arguments is a pseudo-problem. It is generated by a false, prejudicial reading of reality. For it proceeds on the assumption that we first know only our own selves and must grope our way to the knowledge of others with the help of some artificial theory.[41]

The important thing is such a knowledge of the other is prior to knowledge of one's self. We are in direct contact with other minds from childhood on. They are part of our *immediate experience*. We don't infer other selves from our own self. We are fully immersed in a community of minds from the outset. The conscience or mind is not closed in on itself. It is *open* to *others*. The mind directly and immediately experiences others. Scheler's realism becomes apparent. There is a specificity to the knowledge of others. Gurvitch is basically in agreement with this psychology, but he parts company with Scheler on two issues. First, he feels Scheler identified the intuitive with knowledge; second, Scheler conceived the "openness" of the mind in terms too narrow, relying solely on sympathy and love. Experiences of the other are much broader and more complex. For example, the other appears in social reality as father, brother, stranger, companion or rival. The intuitive is a direct apprehension of the other. "Knowledge on the other hand en-

[39] Jean Cazeneuve, Paul-H. Maucorps and Albert Memmi, "Enquête sociologique sur la connaissance d'autrui," *CIS, XXIX* (Juillet- Decembre, 1960), pp. 137-156.

[40] Translated by Peter Heath (London: Routledge and Kegan Paul, 1954), p. 238.

[41] Max Scheler, *Man's Place in Nature*, translated by Hans Meyerhoff (Boston: Beacon Press, 1961), p. xviii.

tails reflection and the elaboration of systematic images of the other based on judgments which pretend to be true." [42] Gurvitch thus sees this in a dialectical manner. Direct apprehension and knowledge are two different ways of *knowing* the other. They are both relevant and present. There is a constant movement back and forth between the two experiences. The processes of complementarity, mutual implication and polarization are at play. Such dialectics also apply when analyzing the variations among transcendance and immanence, homogeneity and heterogeneity, among the self, other, and the *We*. The degree of their integration in particular groups, social classes and global societies also requires the dialectic.[43] These global societies are limiting factors to the rise of spontaneous images of the other within the more restrained groups active in their midst.

The knowledge of others lends itself particularly to empirical research because there is an especially close correlation between this knowledge and the specific reality in which it resides. Hence, particular groups possessing a structure are better suited for these initial studies. First, from a technical standpoint all the participants of a group can be interrogated. This eliminates the guess-work so patent in superficial sample polling procedures. Second, each group is a member of the same global society and is strongly influenced by it. Third, these groups include microcosms of sociability which in turn are part of real groups; they are likewise part of larger entities.

The basic results of this study are simple: considerable variations are observable in the ways in which the other is experienced. The central hypothesis is validated, that a positive correlation exists between the forms of knowledge and their social frameworks.

I. THE MECHANICS OF THE STUDY.

The central aim is to test two ways of apprehending or perceiving the other: by intuition and by knowledge. An interview was devised and tested in the Lycée Louis-le-Grand. Refinements of the interview ensued from findings there.

Next eight groups were chosen. They can be broken down into four categories. These are: a) intellectual—two groups, a philosophy class in the Lycée Turgot and a company of actors from the *Théatre d'aujourd'hui;* b) *indus-*

---

[42] *CIS,* XXIX, 138.
[43] *Ibid.*

trial—four groups, one on the assembly line at the Renault plant in Paris, one semi-assembly line group at the same plant, one group working in a foundry (Aciéries Legenisel-Blanchard) and a group of research engineers, chemists and their assistants at the Centre de Recherche Péchiney; c) administrative—one group of administrators involved in the direction of a technical school; and d) rural—a small village, Seine-et-Marne.

These eight groups were subject to depth interviews by the research team. Each member of each group was interviewed. Definite directions were given to the interviewers, thereby reducing the subjective factors to a minimum. However, a certain spontaneity was encouraged, enabling the interviewer to assess the individual personality factors. The questionnaire was not conceived as a rigid instrument but a framework for guiding the interviews. The questions for these interviews are included at the end of this section.

Four themes were spelled out in the study:

I. The first one sought to measure the direct intuition of the person. Among the questions explored with the interviewees were, What was striking about the other persons? and What were they like at first glance?

II. The second theme aimed at discovering the role of ideal images or stereotypes of the other. This explored the importance given to social prestige, situation in the group, conversations with fellow members and common work. The key question was this one: Upon reflecting further, what permits you to arrive at a more precise image of the other?

III. The third theme oriented the interview in such a direction as to determine how the knowledge one has of the other person changes. Furthermore, how important are the mutual estimations of each other?

IV. The fourth theme dealt with communication and knowledge. How important were verbal communication, gestures and the circumstances in which communication is attempted? How easily and rapidly was the knowledge of others consummated?

II. CONCLUSIONS DRAWN FROM THIS INQUIRY.

a) The factors which affect the way the other is perceived vary according to the type of grouping involved. This became especially apparent with the first theme. The intellectuals and the industrial groupings were particularly different. The rural group was a case totally apart. (See the graphs at the end of this chapter.) The type of grouping, though less apparent in the other themes, still was a decisive factor. The resemblance and dissimilarity factors were different according to the specific groups.

b) A general consensus grew out of this study concerning the importance of both verbal and non-verbal communication. The slow introduction of change in the image of the other was preferred over brutally rapid social change. There is little doubt the global societies exert the strongest influence.

c) The study showed conclusively how impossible it is to validate theories which are too general. The variations are apparent even among groups of the same global society.

d) Finally, each group reveals a marked character. *The intellectuals:* placed a greater emphasis on physical appearance and social attitudes. Less importance was attached to overt behaviour. They defined their image of the other by noting how he differed from them. They placed only a relative importance on the circumstances of life in the group; they had less difficulty with abrupt changes, but were never quite *certain* about knowing the other well.

The industrial participants: placed greatest value on the behaviour of the other and very little on his physical appearance; they showed ambivalence concerning the role of similarity and dissimilarity in the estimation of others. The same holds for the slow or rapid change in the image of the other. They placed greater confidence in their own judgments of others than the estimations these others had of them.

Administrative participants: were sensitive to the behaviour of the other. Physical appearance was of little importance; however, social attitudes carried considerable weight. Specific aspects of their group life were important; they rarely modified their notions of the other once these had been clearly defined. They, too, placed more confidence in their own estimations of others than vice-versa. Conversations and communication based on gestures were important in building the image and knowledge of others.

Rural groups: direct apprehension was barely discernible; their knowledge was based mostly on similarity or an analogy with themselves and correspond closely with the stereotype dictated by the global society. Only the women did not fear being known of what they really are. They placed less emphasis on verbal conversations; consistent behavior with the global society's expectation was of basic importance.

In conclusion, parallels can be drawn between industrial and administrative groupings. Intellectuals and rural participants were diametrically opposed. However, the main hypothesis holds. Each specific group manifests its own way of apprehending and knowing the other.[44]

The approach which this research team took in studying the knowledge of others would be a useful method for sociologists and social psychologists studying such problems as race relations and the impact of technical change on cultural patterns. One of the basic dilemmas of our time is the lack of adequate knowledge—both intuitive and reflective—of the other person. Perhaps such research would enable contemporary man to ferret out some of the individual and collective bases for hatreds, conflicts and irrational behavior.

III. THE QUESTIONNAIRE.

Theme I: What strikes you about your work partner?
  a) His physical appearance
  b) His facial expressions
  c) What he says
  d) What he does
  e) His attitudes towards you
  f) His attitude towards other fellow workers
  g) His spirit of cooperation within the group
  h) His spirit of cooperation within your particular work team
  i) His attitude towards his superiors
  j) His attitude towards his subordinates

---

[44] *Ibid.*, pp. 152-153. Cf. *CIS* XXXII (January-June, 1962), 135-176, for an excellent bibliography of the sociology of knowledge. This was compiled by the research team at the Centre National. Other recent research projects using Gurvitch's categories include: P.-H. Maucorps and René Bussoul, "Jeux de miroirs et sociologie de la connaissance d'autrui," *CIS*, XXXII (January-June, 1962), 43-60; Monique Vincenne, "La ville et les paysans," in *Ibid.*, pp. 125-134; Georges Kavadias, "L'étude de la circulation des hommes et des biens, point de départ d'une enquête de sociologie rurale," *CIS*, XXX (January-June, 1961), 167-174. Also note the bibliography contained in Gurvitch's last work, *Les cadres sociaux de la connaissance* (Paris: Presses Universitaires de France, 1966).

Theme II: On reflecting further, what permits you to reach a more precise image of the other? Was it ———

  a) His resemblance or difference in terms of yourself?
  b) Because he had to be or did not have to be your work partner?
  c) The degree of his influence in your group?
  d) The conversations that you had with him?
  e) The work in common which you did with him?

Theme III: When you believe you possess a precise image of the other, how is this knowledge modified?

  a) Does it change slowly or rapidly?
  b) Under the influence of what circumstances?
  c) Do you believe you are often wrong in your impression of others?
  d) Do you consider your comrades are often wrong about their estimations of you?
  e) Which is most frequent: that the other is wrong about you, or that you are wrong about them?

Theme IV: Communication and Knowledge

  a) Do you enter rather easily or with difficulty into congenial relationships with your fellow workers?
  b) Rapidly or slowly?
  c) Does the exchange of words always help you know your fellow workers better?
  d) If no, give example(s) of the case where verbal communication did not aid in this knowledge, or even undermined it.
  e) If yes, give example(s) of conversations or discussions with your fellow workers which helped you to know them better.
  f) Classify in a hierarchy the subjects of the conversations and discussions which were most revealing for this knowledge.
  g) Does non-verbal communication with your fellow workers permit you to know them better?
  h) If yes, what forms?
  i) Under what circumstances?[45]

---

[45] *Ibid.,* pp. 153-154.

FIGURE ONE

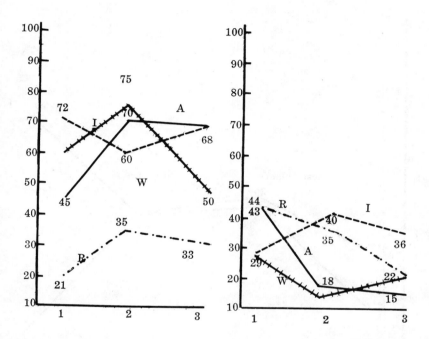

The Interaction of the Options (Yes and No) and Certain Elements in Apprehending the Other

Legend: The figure at the left represents the percentage of positive responses (concerning the relative importance of the factors dealing with the knowledge of the other) and is marked by the numbers on the vertical line; the figure on the right represents the percentage of negative responses.

The numbers under the horizontal line represent the three factors considered: (1 = physical, 2 = behaviour, 3 = social attitudes).

The intellectuals (I) are represented by dashes (— — —).

The workers (W) by a plus sign + + +).

The rural (R) by dots and dashes (— . —).

For example the rural curve has a maximum positive response towards behaviour of 35%. The same holds for the workers; but their percentages for positive responses in favor of behaviour are considerably greater (75% in terms of the behaviour of the other).[46]

---

[46] *Ibid.,* p. 142.

FIGURE TWO

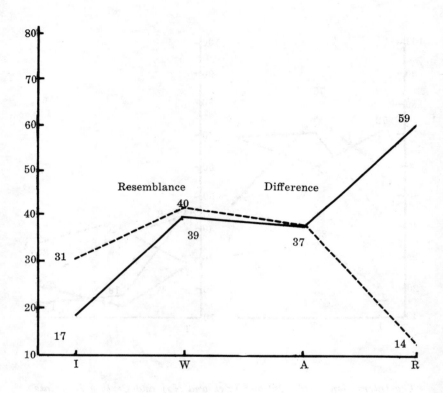

The Interaction of the Options "Resemblance-Difference" and the Collectivities

Legend: The horizontal line carries the four types of collectivities. The vertical line represents the percentages of responses.

Very clearly this shows the greatest difference between the two curves is in relation to the responses of the rural group (R). Considerable importance is given to resemblance and little to the differences between them and the other or neighbor. At the left of the table the two curves are noticeably separated. Such is the case of the intellectuals (I). In the center, the opposite holds for the factory groups (W) and the administration (A). The curve of responses in favor of resemblance and the curve of responses insisting on differences are at just about the same level.[47]

_____
[47] *Ibid.,* p. 144.

FIGURE THREE

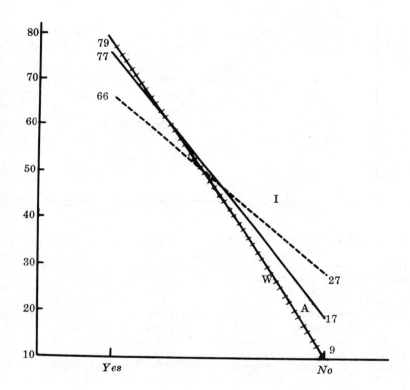

The Interaction of Options and Types of Collectivities

Legend: Below the horizontal line, the options "yes" and "no" are given; the vertical line gives the percentages of responses. Dashes = intellectuals; straight line = administration; pluses = workers.

The "yes" and "no" here correspond to Theme II. The difference between the positive responses and the negative ones is less prominent on the intellectual curve than the others.

The rural group was not considered in this question.[48]

---

[48] *Ibid.*, p. 145.

FIGURE FOUR

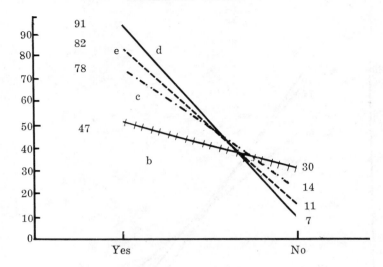

The Interaction of Options and Certain Factors in the Knowledge of Others

Legend: Conversations (d) straight line; work in common (e) dashes; role in group (c) dashes and dots; ideal companion (b) pluses. Below the horizontal line, the responses "yes" and "no"; the vertical shows the four factors in knowing the other envisioned in Theme II (the factor "resemblance-difference" has been envisioned in part).

The percentages of responses are important for each collectivity.

Clearly the curve of response dealing with the importance of conversations (d) denotes the maximum approbations (91%) and the minimum of negative responses (7%) while the ideal companion reveals on the contrary the minimum of "yes" (47%) and the maximum of "no's" (30%).[1]

---

[1] *Ibid.,* p. 146.

TABLE FOR THEME III

Rapidly	Slowly
I = 30%	I = 33%
W = 30%	W = 49%
A = 40%	A = 57%
R = 24%	R = 42%

FIGURE FIVE

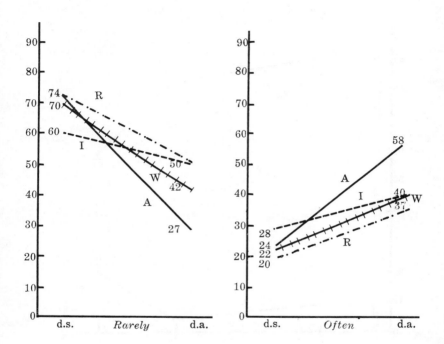

The Interaction of Options (Rarely-Often), Propositions (Fear of being wrong concerning his own judgments of the other; fear of error concerning the judgments of the other of himself), *and the Types of Collectivities Represented Here as in Figures One and Three.*

Legend: Below the horizontal line the propositions: d.s. (fear of error in terms of himself, formulated in this question, "Do you believe you are rarely wrong or often in error in your knowledge of the other?") and d.a. (fear of being wrong in the judgment of the other formulated in the question: "Do you consider that the others are rarely or often mistaken in their judgment of you?"); the vertical line gives the percentages of responses.

To illustrate the curve of administrators (A = straight line) reveals a great confidence in their own judgments of the other and a considerable fear of error concerning the estimations of others of themselves.[49]

---

[49] *Ibid.,* p. 148.

FIGURE SIX

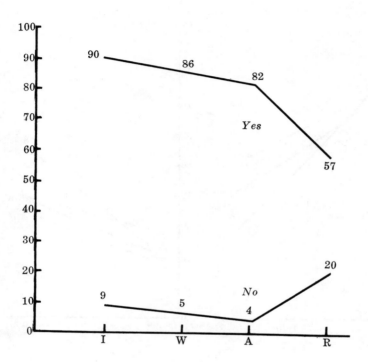

Conversations and Knowledge of the Other. The Interaction of the Option (Yes-No) and the types of Collectivities.

Legend: Below the horizontal line, the type of collectivity is represented; the vertical line give the percentages of responses.

The "Yes" curve is shown as a straight line, that of "no" as dashes. The question posed was that of the importance of conversations in the knowledge of the other. A minimum separation exists between the two curves when considering the rural group, while the distinction is uniformly quite sharp for the other three types of collectivities.[50]

---

[50] *Ibid.*, p. 150.

FIGURE SEVEN

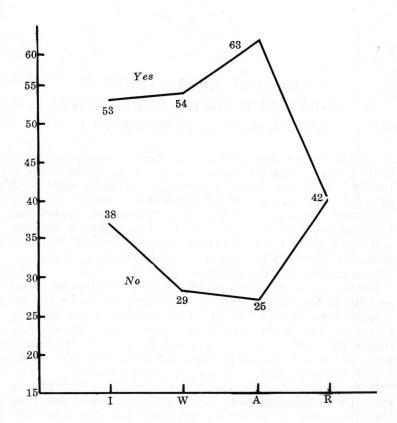

Communication without Words

Legend: Below the horizontal the different types of groups; the vertical represents the percentages of responses (*positive* = yes; *negative* = no) to the question: "Does all types of communication without words among fellow workers permit them to know each other better?"

The maximum separation between Yes and No clearly is evident at the administrative level, while as to the rural group the two curves are joined.[51]

---

[51] *Ibid.*, p. 151.

CHAPTER VIII

A CRITICAL EVALUATION OF GURVITCH'S SOCIOLOGY OF THE TOTAL SOCIAL PHENOMENA

Gurvitch's sociology of the total social phenomena represents a new approach to social reality. As he views it, social reality is dynamic, vital, and complex. It is fraught with paradoxes and aspects of the irrational, a reality which is constantly moving, changing, progressing and regressing, basically unpredictable, yet exhibiting an essential patterning which enables the researcher to make certain tentative generalizations. It is a reality at once frustrating and enticing, mysterious and challenging.

Gurvitch has gone beyond the mere description of social reality. In the very process of such a description he has developed his method of study. That method is tied directly to the kind of social reality he views. This method challenges the current trends in sociology. The social reality with which it interacts is much different from the static, functional notions of many contemporary theories in American sociology. For one thing, it is a reality. This idea is more than an appellation. Gurvitch is in agreement with Emile Durkheim that social groups are real. They are more than the sum of their parts. They are more than mere aggregates of interacting members.

Along with his realist approach, Gurvitch asserts the basic unity of social reality. He dissects it long enough to provide some categories of empirical research but he quickly re-asserts the fundamental unity of the social phenomena. An aspect of his method then, is to study the various elements of social reality at once individually and as a whole. He is a *Gestalt* sociologist.

The pluralism within social reality is vertical and horizontal. Such a pluralism is many-sided, intensely relative, and requires a hyper-empiricism linked with a radical dialectic to study the totality encompassing such a plurality. The concept of the total social phenomena serves as the working hypothesis for this approach. To understand how he arrived at this notion we have plotted his early work in philosophy leading to the more specialized study in jurisprudence. In this final chapter we will discuss analytically and critically certain areas of his thought. We can consider here only a limited number of his most important ideas.

1. SOCIAL LAW

Gurvitch's early work in legal studies led to his theory of social law. This is one of his most important contributions. The scope of his study, the challenging possibilities of his ideas, the daring aspects of his social law theory indicate the stature of his scholarship and value of his work. Significantly this idea of social law was conceived during the 1920's and carefully elaborated during the early thirties.[1] The closest approximation in America to his thesis, is that of Robert M. MacIver. The latter's *Web of Government*[2] is a classic in the field of political sociology. So much of what Gurvitch said in the thirties is echoed in this volume. The significance of Gurvitch's efforts has not been appreciated heretofore. We have sought to suggest the importance of what this political sociologist has to say concerning the origin of law, its authority and the various types of law.

His clear logical discussion of social law, justice, natural law, the relationship of justice to the moral order is a welcome addition to contemporary legal debates. Gurvitch sees social law as ontologically prior to all other forms of law. This is an important notion in his sociological theory concerning the realness of groups. The collective mind is ontologically prior to the other levels of social reality. The total social phenomena, total because of the collective mind, are ontologically prior to all other phenomena. Gurvitch is affirming an old conception so ably expressed by Roscoe Pound, that all law is social. The earliest civilizations which appeared in the river valleys of the Nile and the Tigris-Euphrates clearly show the origins of law went hand

---

[1] In a personal letter Gurvitch makes it clear that he has gone beyond many of the ideas of Social Law. He states: "I have confused communion and the *We*. I ignored the liaison of law with its social structures. I was unjust to both St. Simon and Marx. The ensemble is too dogmatic."

[2] New York: The Macmillan Company, 1947. See especially Chapters 1V, V, and VI.

in hand with the growing complexity of civilization and the need to define and regulate. Law is a part of social regulation. But there is an informal aspect to law. Codification comes at certain junctures in history. But these codifications are simply that. They summarize and systematize the "firmament of law" which is already operative. They are not new systems of law conceived *de novo* first articulated by some Pharaoh or Babylonian monarch. In this sense Gurvitch is indeed correct. Social law is ontologically prior to every other kind of law.

Gurvitch goes much more deeply into the "phenomena of law." He separates law from justice, long enough to see that law is the instrument of justice. The goal of law is to implement justice. What is justice? Gurvitch defines justice as the attempt to establish order, peace and security in the social whole. This means that some type of arrangement must be worked out to assure the mutual realization of claims and duties is arrived at by a consensus which speaks of an underlying set of values for the society. These values Gurvitch calls *normative facts*. These normative facts are the content of authority. This is why people obey. These are the roots of law-abidingness. Moreover, law if it exists, must be effective. All law is positive law. This means it is indigenous to the society to which it owes its existence.

Another approach is to see the depth levels in this analysis. The fundamental source of law is the normative fact which in essence is a result of consensus on the part of the social group. The social group created these values, and the values in turn create the social entity. They have an integrative function. The normative fact is a product of the group mind. It is a first step in the direction of generalization, removed from the white heat of the moral experience itself. Such a moral experience is individual and a-logical. This is the level of the immediate, the intuitive, the shatteringly real. Logic cools and generalizes. The normative fact represents the first step in the direction of greater generalization and abstraction. The moral, if it is to be effective, says Gurvitch, must be relativized. The next step up from the normative fact is that of justice which in turn finds its greatest rationalization in law. These depth levels in juridicial experience are easily transposed into social life in all its aspects. This is the very development which Gurvitch's thought follows.

2. NATURAL LAW

Natural law in the classical sense is inoperative to Gurvitch's way of thinking. It is inoperative since it fails to be effective, he argues. It does not apply in a positive sense. It lacks specificity and concreteness. If universality is desired, if the existence of a law to which all mankind can turn is the goal, then such a law must be discovered within the social milieu of mankind as a whole. Gurvitch provides a solution to this question and at the same time he answers those critics who accuse him of making social law a new natural law since he has declared it to be ontologically prior. This has already been discussed and illustrated. As to the universal claims, the same would hold as obtains within a given society. This is best described by viewing social law as a series of concentric social rings. This recalls Eero Saarinen's memorable statement: "Always design a thing by considering it in its next larger context—a chair in a room in a house, a house in an environment, an environment in a city plan." [3] In Gurvitch's terms, a given social law promulgated by a particular social grouping has validity only if it is considered within the context of the next larger grouping. Hence, the particular social grouping is included within the social class, which in turn is incorporated with the given global society which has its existence because of the international society whose validity undergirds the normative fact of the society. The reason for this is obvious. There are competing claims and duties which must be worked out; consensus has to be reached. Such a consensus results in the normative facts which are then translated into justice which is in turn implemented by a system of law.

Now, what is happening in contemporary society is the rapid progress towards an international community which is creating a consensus of moral values resulting in certain normative facts that have positive validity, are real, because they are effective. This is an exciting development. The rise of regional communities, illustrated in the European Economic Community, is one example. But more than this, the coming of age of the scientific ethos has so permeated the life of modern societies that this is rapidly becoming the basis for the normative facts on an international level. The values inherent in the scientific approach are

---

[3] *Time*, July 2, 1956, p. 51.

very nearly ubiquitous. Such values include honesty in reporting, open-mindedness, tolerance, good-will, open-endedness on a theoretical level, objectivity, invitation to discussion and criticism, open covenants, no secrets, no deals, and total freedom of discrimination with respect to race, creed, or national origin. For those committed to personalistic ethics, this ethos underscores such values. Hence, Gurvitch seems vindicated. From a sociological point of view, his apparent radical positivism in no way undercuts the possibility of a universal set of values which would give rise to a natural law in this narrow sense. Such a law would be at once the creation and the creator of the international community. This is both anthropologically and sociologically sound. This notion has important values for the fields of political sociology and juridical sociology.

However, there are two places where Gurvitch asserts a natural law theory. This he does unwittingly. There is a certain sense in which one cannot escape natural law, a natural law in the generic usage of the term.

First, Gurvitch maintains that justice is a way of settling the attributive-imperative *dichotomy* of human society. Each individual has certain rights within society but also certain obligations. Whenever such an assertion is made, natural law is present. There is a certain inevitability to the whole notion of natural law. It is a part of the human condition. If man makes decisions based on values then he is within the scope of natural law. He has a set of priorities operating for him and they are in part reflective of his society, in part reflective of mankind in general. The differences occur in making the general applicable to the particular but this does not deny the general. Man requires this. When he denies such a natural law he leaves himself open to chaos and disintegration. The nineteenth century wedge of logical positivism resulted in the nihilism of Nazism and fascism in the twentieth century. World War II's end brought a whole new movement in response to this condition. Its roots also are discoverable in the nineteenth century. The name given to this new movement is existentialism. Certainly it harks back to the ancients and up through the history of intellectual thought looking for those key thinkers and works which give the position historical validity. Such support is available. But the important thing to realize in existentialism is that despite its adherents' desire to deny every liaison with natural law theory, what they have done in *essence* is to create a new natural law expression relevant for the present age! Such a law is discoverable once again in the nature of things, in the nature of man, in the very condition of his existence. Such an existence is dialectial, dialogic, interdependent and dichotomized. The new natural law is based on relations, tensions, on the movement between subject and object, or as Martin Buber puts it, between I and Thou. Accordingly, an individual becomes a person insofar as "he steps into a living relation with other individuals." Society emerges as a reality "insofar as it is built out of living units of relation. . . . Only men who are truly capable of saying Thou to one another can truly say We with one another." [4] "The community is built up out of living mutual relation, but the building is the living effective Center." [5]

Out of this personalistic dialectic emerge certain affirmations about man. They are in the form of rights. Now to assert the attributive-imperative is to arrive at a natural law level of thinking. One cannot declare there are certain rights and then in the next breath deny natural law. Whenever rights are affirmed, natural law exists.

> A judgment about the good for man cannot be both rendered and not rendered at the same time. If it is rendered, and supposed to be within the competence of reason, reference is somehow made to the nature of man, whatever account may be given of how this is known. Entailed in any serious utterance about the rights of man (unless of course one wishes to base the rights and the dignity of man on revelation) is some conception of human nature, and so of the natural law. Nothing hinders such judgment being uttered *in medias res* in a personal moral dilemma or in judicial decision.[6]

Gurvitch fits into the new natural theory in a vital way. What he has said about social law undergirds his estimates of man's nature and his firm conviction in seeing to it that justice is established in the gate. His stand on the irresponsible action of the OAS in France during the Algerian crisis

---

[4] Martin Buber, *Between Man and Man* (Boston: The Beacon Press, 1955), pp. 203, 176.

[5] Martin Buber, *I and Thou* (New York: Charles Scribner's, 1961), p. 45.

[6] Paul Ramsey, *Nine Modern Moralists* (Englewood Cliffs, New Jersey: Prentice Hall, 1962), p. 214.

is indicative of his conviction. Whenever one is involved in asserting this is wrong and proclaims that injustice is loose in the streets, he is saying something about general principles, a natural law.

The second way in which Gurvitch actually sustains a natural law follows from his social law theory. Though he constantly reiterates that social law is no more important than contractural or individual law one has the distinct impression, after having read the various volumes which he wrote on the subject that underneath he favors social law and sees it as the basis for all law. Isn't this a real assertion of natural law, since social law as the underlying source, becomes the general principles upon which all decisions of fact are made depending upon the situation? Gurvitch's admission of rights and his obvious preference for social law are mutually complementary. This fits the individual-collective reciprocity of perspectives. This agrees with Buber's thesis in *Between Man and Man*: individualism and collectivism, if either is overemphasized, can vitiate community. Individualism understands only a part of man and collectivism understands man only as a part.[7] Buber goes on to see organic community comprising communities which are smaller and smaller but all encompassed in the wider circle of the global community. This is very similar to Gurvitch's idea of the circles of influence and control moving from the microsocial to the macrosocial.

Certainly one of the crises which modern man faces is the crisis of law. Gurvitch contributes some important ideas to this discussion of law. In his article on natural law in the *Encyclopedia of Social Sciences* he suggested that the renewed interest in natural law in recent years is a direct result of this predicament. Gurvitch himself has been aware of this interest. His discussions have explicitly reflected this awareness. They encourage our own participation.

3. THE TOTAL SOCIAL PHENOMENA

Both Martin and Toulemont in their studies criticize Gurvitch for his depth sociology. "Has Gurvitch presented clear criteria of division among his different levels? Though they can never be separated and always imply one another, he always insists on the tensions and conflicts between

---

[7] Buber, *Between Man and Man*, p. 200.

them," [8] which suggest their distinctiveness. Toulemont puts the question in a slightly different way. "The fact that Gurvitch never establishes real abstractions, but always stops somewhere in between the abstract and the concrete, has led to definitions which are hazy, elastic and elusive." [9] Toulemont goes on to ask if a scientific work can be carried out under such conditions. Clear cut abstractions are essential for valid scientific exploration. Granted, the conceptual tool is of necessity abstract. But an essential question remains: how abstract must it be to be useful? How closely must it correspond to nature? If one moves too far in the direction of abstraction he has removed himself from the whole domain of the real world. Such heady flights can be made in two ways: by a transcendental, general theorizing which rides comfortably above the vicissitudes of everyday life; or by the narrow abstractions of little concerns or projects which separate one from the total view, resulting in a fragmented labor. Both are equally irrelevant. Gurvitch has attempted to walk between these two pitfalls. This is the whole burden of his theory. This is the meaning of the term total social phenomena. The phenomena are varied but there remains a basic unity. He has sought to come to grips with the problem of unity versus diversity. In democracy this is expressed in the unending attempt to reach some consensus or unity without uniformity. Uniformity is an invalid way to look at social reality. Still there is a tentative, persistent unity which asserts itself, is stronger than those forces which would destroy or pull apart. Social law is one aspect of the positive factors producing unity. The centripetal forces are stronger than the centrifugal ones. What causes this? A single glance at social life begins the explanation. First, one notes the obvious. He confronts the organizations. He studies their activities. He reads the world almanac, gathers data from the encyclopedias, carries on research projects which plot the demographical facts of life, but only the surface manifestations have been touched. There is obviously much more. Gurvitch notes that classical sociologists asked certain probing questions which sought to get beneath the facade. He cites the works of Proudhon, Marx, Spencer, Cooley, Durkheim and Mauss which give clues to a vertical view of social reality. Below the crusted layers of society the vol-

---

[8] Martin, *Depth Sociology* . . . , p. 78.
[9] Toulemont, *Sociologie et pluralisme* . . . , p. 246.

canic, the spontaneous, the moving and dynamic are at work. Furthermore, the irrational had to be dealt with. Contemporary sociologists are perplexed by these irrational phenomena which threaten their scientific labors. The patterns are confused. They fail to show a clear cut configuration of movement which lends itself to predictability or social engineering. Mathematical formulas fail to describe adequately. The human coefficient, the engaged character of social science or the nature of its object of study eludes and escapes the researchers much as did Proteus of old. The natural temptation is to select those problems, create those universes which lend themselves to the rigid notions of a scientific method indicated by nineteenth century physics. The social sciences have allowed themselves to be caught in this type of trap. Gurvitch submits an answer. He asserts the central problem is the lack of a theory which takes into consideration, 1) the actual nature of social reality and, 2) the development of a method of study which can explore this reality and understand its inner workings. The presupposition of such a theory is that the approach must be structurally oriented. Or, put another way, the giveness of the social entity must determine the way in which it is studied. This is in keeping with the great traditions of Marx, Proudhon, Cooley, Durkheim, Weber and Mauss. *Sitz im Leben* is ultimately determinative. Though the total social phenomena are being considered in this section, the structural or horizontal manifestations of these phenomena are so closely linked to this whole discussion that it is necessary to underline the relationship.

The question remains, does Gurvitch present a picture of social reality which is useful to sociology? Is this a valid approach? Is it scientifically verifiable? Martin contends it is "doubtful depth sociology will be accepted as the theoretical basis of sociography." [10] He asks what are the criteria which justify stratifying social reality into a number of depth levels? Is there some principle of order? Does it resemble geology? Is there some kind of logical relationship between the various levels? Martin rejects accessibility as the criterion. He finds little help in an approach which states that "the deeper levels of the collective mind require more effort to be grasped and studied scientifically." [11] For example he explains, under certain circumstances, the or-

---

[10] Martin, *op. cit.*, p. 76.
[11] *Ibid.*, p. 79.

ganized level of social reality is harder to describe than some of the deeper levels.

This fails to meet the argument as Gurvitch has advanced it. He has in no way denied this possibility. He has always maintained this is a revolving and moving hierarchy. Here Martin has misunderstood one of the basic notions in this vertical view. The historical circumstances, the conjunctures of time and place determine which level will be on top, and what levels will follow. During a particularly revolutionary era, the more spontaneous strata will be emphasized. The feudal global structure for example exhibits an entirely different arrangement of depth levels than that of contemporary industrial capitalism. Accessibility then holds. Martin has neglected to see the importance of the historical dimension.

Now, as to the question of this depth sociology being scientifically valid, one must make a closer scrutiny. The aim of sociology is to describe and to explain social reality. Gurvitch is concerned with those of the fraternity who have become so eager to be about the task they have jumped on their horses and ridden off in several directions without first devising a plan concrete enough to be relevant to what is and yet abstract enough to be scientifically useful. Gurvitch in his appropriation of the felicitous phrase of Marcel Mauss, the *total social phenomena,* has taken off from a classic position. He is indebted to Durkheim for his realism, Proudhon for his analysis of conflict, Bergson for his dynamism, phenomenology for the understanding of the subject-object relationship in observation and description, and Fichte for the emphasis upon action as the ontological ground.

He is proposing nothing new. He is simply bringing together certain crucial ideas which have been fermenting in this century to such a remarkable extent that if these categories are studied and applied seriously sociology might have a chance of coming of age during a time when it is so desperately needed.

Gurvitch is in good company. The Lynds in the Middletown books, the pioneer work of Znanieki and Thomas in their study of the Polish peasant, the subsequent community studies developed on these foundations and recent efforts particularly in cultural anthropology illustrate clearly that this approach is taking hold[12] Gurvitch is a systematizer in the finest sense of the word. He would reject the use of this term, but what he is doing is exactly this. He is providing a much needed frame of reference for the study of social reality in its totality *and* in its infinite variety. A catalogue of some of the best work in recent years suffices to support this contention.

Oscar Lewis' *The Children of Sanchez*[13] is such an example. The book is about a poor family in Mexico City. This is a kinship grouping in Gurvitch's terminology. What Lewis accomplishes is to see this kinship grouping as it encompasses the total social phenomena within its global society (structure), social class, and in its relationships with other groups. His study catalogues the social bonds at the center of this kinship grouping, the social times in which the members live, the hierarchy of social determinisms, the measure of freedom and the interplay of the organized and spontaneous. This study has a ring of authenticity to it. It is neither a fragment nor an empirical abstraction. The author refused to succumb to some method which might have revealed certain quantitative truths but missed the real life of the family. The study comes from a descriptive effort in depth sociology. Gurvitch would praise this effort. Oscar Lewis has come to grips with the total social phenomena. It was an arduous task. It took several years to complete. He used a tape-recorder to gather his data. Such a device served his purposes well in this study. It may not work in the next. Here are his words:

> I offer a deeper look into the lives of one of these families by the use of a new technique whereby each member of the family tells his own life story in his own words. This approach gives us a cumulative, multifaceted, panoramic view of each individual of the family as a whole, and of many aspects of lower-class Mexican life....[14] As I became aware that this single family seemed to illustrate many of the social and psychological problems of

---

[12] Cf. Severyn Bruyn, *The Human Perspective in Sociology* (Englewood Cliffs, New Jersey: Prentice Hall, 1967). This very important work appeared too late to incorporate many of the author's valuable insights.

[13] New York: Random House, 1961.

[14] *Ibid.*, p. xi.

lower-class Mexican life, I decided to try to study in depth.[15]

Here then is one modern study which follows very closely the theme that has run throughout Gurvitch's work. The headings are missing. Nowhere does one find each level of social reality set apart. This is not necessary. The point is a total approach was taken. Lewis would probably resist the assertion that groups are real, that culture and society are inextricably bound together. This is beside the point. The evidence from this study corroborates Gurvitch's main contention. The total social phenomena are ontologically prior. There is a ring of reality to what Lewis reports.

An entirely different approach is followed by James Agee in his much neglected study *Let Us Now Praise Famous Men*. Once again this is an authentic piece of writing and reporting. Sociologists would throw up their hands in despair at the subjective tone of this one. Still, when one has completed the reading of this work done in the 1930's in collaboration with the renowned photographer Walker Evans, he is convinced he has a clear idea of what life was like among the white tenant farmers of the American South. This impression is inescapable. James Agee with a poet's vision and sensitivity has carefully, meticulously described what he felt and saw. He and Walker Evans lived among these people for several months. They came to know their very existence. Again the subject-object dichotomy is destroyed. The end result is full-bodied and the life of this people, crystal clear. Fragmentation in research has been avoided. Yet, specifics have been included. Research need not be sterile and pedantic. The categories of the total social phenomena are missing in an explicit manner but when the total assessment is made they are all there. The kinship grouping, the grouping of locality, and the voluntary groupings of various modes of access and rhythm are studied in relation to each other, to their larger structures, to their historical circumstance and in their social bonds. The way in which they balance these various phenomena and microsociological elements are then spelled out. The structures, groups, and social ties are real.

Or again, turning to the sociologist, Irwin T. Sanders, in his study, *Rainbow in the Rock*,[16] gives a lesson in the

[15] *Ibid.*, p. xix.
[16] Cambridge: Harvard University Press, 1962.

271

analysis of the total social phenomena. Greek village life is observed in all its depth levels from the most superficial on down to the least perceptible and more spontaneous. These are not Sanders' categories but they are discernible if one carefully looks at his method and the descriptive analysis he offers.

Max Lerner in his highly successful *America as a Civilization*,[17] asks certain questions of every civilization. In essence these questions deal with the total social phenomena. A cataloguing of these guiding principles illustrates this very well.

> The questions I ask about Americans are those one would have to ask about the people of any great civilization. What are their traditions, biological stock, environment? How do they make a living, govern themselves, handle the inevitable problems of power and freedom? How are they divided into ethnic and class groupings? What are they like in their deep and enduring strains? What is their life history like, in its characteristic phases from birth to death? How do they court, marry, press their creativeness in art and literature? What are the connective and organizing principles that hold their civilization together? What gods do they worship, what beliefs hold them in thrall or give them strength, what attitudes do they own up to, what convictions animate them, what culture patterns do they move in, what dreams are they moved by, what myths run through their being, what incentives propel them, what fears restrain them, what forms of power invest their striving, what tensions and divisions tear them apart, what sense of society cements them? [18]

Clearly these are questions which have a striking similarity to the depth levels. They even move from the superficial to the more profound. In sum the approach which Gurvitch takes is not revolutionary. It compares with the work of cultural anthropologists in the United States though his theory is generally more systematic and explicit. His hypotheses for research contain exciting possibilities. It is important to see his close affinity with cultural anthropology. Though he chides the American school

---

17 New York: Simon and Schuster, 1957.
18 Max Lerner, *America* . . . , I, x-xi.

for its culturalism and spiritualism, he admits this affinity. Sociology in Europe resembles much more closely the United States work in cultural anthropology than it does American sociology. Most French sociologists would agree. Raymond Aron, speaking before a colloquium on social science in France made this point explicitly. In the discussion which followed Aron's presentation, Gurvitch was quick to point out his basic agreement with Aron.[19] This is a capital distinction and if it were widely understood, it could lead to some fruitful exchange of ideas and research. Sociologists in the two countries simply fail to communicate on the same wave-length.

Aron in this article makes some other comments about American sociology which Gurvitch has emphasized throughout his own works. First, American sociology has little interest or inclination to study social structures from an historical orientation. It has preferred to analyze the American society as a contemporary industrial nation. The historical roots of this society are considered of little importance. This historical question will be the burden of a later discussion.

Second, Aron points to American sociology's propensity to nominalize. There is very little emphasis on the *realness* of groups. "American sociology is profoundly analytical and seeks to dissolve the totalities . . . into as many elements as possible." [20] These elements are then clarified from many different points of view. Social groups lack realness in American sociological parlance.

Finally, Aron asserts the American school tends to insist upon the empirical and the experimental. It shows an intransigent inclination to fragment, to quantify, and to measure. The criterion for its being a science rests upon this empirical base. There is a shallowness to this approach. It lacks a view in depth. It is too analytical. In a way, this method suffers from the familiar *paralysis of analysis*.

> The centipede was happy quite
>   Until a toad in fun
> Said, "Pray, which leg goes after which?"
> That worked her mind to such a pitch,
>   She lay distracted in a ditch,
>   Considering how to run.

---

[19] Raymond Aron, "La sociéte américaine," *CIS* (XXVI, 1959), 55-68.

[20] *Ibid.*, p. 66.

This fragmentary, rigidly empirical approach frustrates communication and valid scholarship. "Sociologists cannot evoke the vibrant reality of a particular whole. . . . For one thing they atomize and isolate. What we need is the organic reality, the way it really is." [21] Gurvitch has sought to answer this criticism. He sees social reality in depth levels: this contributes to deepening the sociological analysis; he asserts the necessity of viewing social reality as the total social phenomena: this means studying these various phenomena for themselves but always from the perspective that "in reality" they are an organic whole.

Are the levels in depth distinct? Is this a hopeless taxonomic structure which reflects an empty formalism? Constantly, Gurvitch's critics have leveled the charge that he is a formalist whose categories are impractical and irrelevant for empirical research. Nowhere is this criticism advanced with greater intensity than when confronting the concept of the total social phenomena. A recent review of the *Traité de sociologie* is a good example. The reviewer, Everett K. Wilson, states: "Each section contains a historical note with critical comments followed by a systematic discussion revealing Gurvitch's propensity for taxonomies and typologies." [22] Further on he observes, "One is impressed with the deft taxonomic legerdemain, and struck with the cavalier sweep across data-free centuries." [23]

These comments have appeared frequently among Gurvitch's critics. They are impressive criticisms. We can agree with Gurvitch's initial aim to look at both the superstructure and infrastructure of social reality. His first concern was to look at the organized, the more rigid, the more obvious manifestations of social life in relationship to the spontaneous, dynamic, and volatile aspects which are at play beneath the surface. His studies in social law had led to these two general levels, the organized and the spontaneous. Trying to provide a theoretical structure for studying social reality which contains these two levels meant middle range abstractions for the purposes of carrying out research in these areas. Are Gurvitch's theoretical

---

[21] A. H. Halsey, a review of *Campus USA: Portraits of American Colleges in Action* by David Boroff (New York: Harper and Brothers, 1961) in *American Sociological Review*, XXVII (June, 1962), 419.

[22] In *The American Journal of Sociology*, LXVIII (Sept., 1962), 252.

[23] *Ibid.*

categories i.e., depth levels, sufficient and clear enough to answer this need?

Though Gurvitch's whole approach is the right one as far as we are concerned, certainly we must take issue with him at certain junctures. We are aware of his general desire for in-depth studies of social phenomena. However, does an in-depth study necessitate arranging such phenomena in depth levels, much as in geology? What reasons are there for putting symbols and roles at different depth levels? These two types of phenomena deal primarily with the *horizontal* relationships of persons and groups. Why do the total social phenomena need to be hierarcherized? The key notion is relationship between the various phenomena. Furthermore, depth studies essentially mean seeing these various relationships among the several components such as roles and statuses and social classes. The ten depth levels make the whole theoretical structure extremely complicated, if not unmanagable. The division of the total social phenomena into the two general strata, superstructure and infrastructure, is consistent and provocative. However, to attempt to place these phenomena on a vertical scale becomes tremendously involved. Gurvitch is not clear what constitutes significant distinctions among the different levels. Though he places these phenomena on a hierarchy, they have no structure without the horizontal plane, i.e., microsociological frameworks. Gurvitch is guilty of the same error he chides the American sociologists for committing when they separate culture and society. The vertical represents the cultural content, the sinews and flesh of social reality; the horizontal represents society, or the social structure, the framework by which such phenomena find definition and concrete expression. They are so intertwined there is little theoretical distinctiveness. What we need are the dialectical processes of reciprocity of perspectives and mutual implication to bring these two aspects together. Seen another way the superstructure represents structures, social frameworks; the spontaneous level represents the cultural content. Gurvitch includes something else: the spontaneous-structured tensions speaks of the exogenic, irrational, creative actions which seemingly defy definition and give social reality its Protean nature. The total social phenomena are overlapping and interactive. To separate them into ten distinctive strata for purposes of empirical research is taxonomic and formalistic. Depth sociology is possible without this exercise. Dialetical sociology remains the essential perspective.

To conclude, let's say the vertical view holds in terms of trying to go beneath the obvious, to explain the spontaneous, to understand a group's realness which is predicated on the collective mind. The interlacing of the vertical and horizontal in a general theoretical framework provides a fresh look at the problem, suggests the work necessary to describe these phenomena, and explains how they do relate.

Only a few of Gurvitch's categories have been tested empirically. By and large they have remained outside the research centers. His theory as it now stands, is too heavy and complex. It is cumbersome. It requires a careful reworking to put the theory into managable research problems.[24] Gurvitch's fertile sociological imagination has given us the broad strokes. Reality testing this theory requires careful, diligent work. The point is, it is worth doing.

4. THE REALNESS OF GROUPS

Gurvitch maintains that sociology as a science is impossible without going beyond nominalism and seeing the realness of groups. The emphasis upon structure is one such way of overcoming this nominalistic dilemma.

Gurvitch's macrosociological theory has only appeared in recent years. He devised several typologies for empirical study. These give research direction. Gurvitch adopted the typological approach because it allows him to use the comparative method. He contends typology in sociology is possible since it falls between a thoroughgoing generalizing method of the natural sciences and the singularizing method of ethnology. A typology projects the existence of particular groupings, or types of groupings which fit a set of criteria. To be sure, they must be studied in and for themselves but they also have a general similarity with other groups of the same type and function. These types are discontinuous. This would seem to shut sociological research

---

[24] From another perspective there is a positive way to look at Gurvitch's taxonomy. This represents a middle or intermediary theory which Robert Merton is so fond of advocating as the end point of sociological theorizing. Gurvitch's taxonomic typology could be a place to begin in putting his view of social reality to empirical testing. This, in fact, is what he says his typologies and hierarchies represent. They are tentative research designs.

See below, p. 52 for references to some empirical studies using his categories.

off from history; on the contrary, the very types themselves are derived from the study of history. The data often
come from history. Part of the study in depth must maintain a close cooperation with the historical view of a structure. The real collaboration comes from both history and
sociology studying the total social phenomena. History sees
these phenomena in their continuity. Sociology must look at
the data as a slice of time, living within its own hierarchy
of social times. The two disciplines complement and mutually reinforce each other.

Now consider their realness. There is growing support
for the notion that groups are real, that groups are more
than the sum of the individual participants. A collective
personality exists which is distinguishable from the individual personalities. However, most American sociologists have
been reluctant to affirm this concept outright. They have
been repelled by the theory of Durkheim with its spiritualism and its separation of the whole or the collective from
the individual. They have had just cause to be wary of this
reductionism. Gurvitch has provided one of the finest cri-
tiques of this position which appears in sociological literature. Moreover, he has sought to overcome this difficulty.
His solution to the problem of the collective reality resides
in his definition of the collective mind. He views the individual and social minds from the standpoint of modern
theories in psychology. The mind is no longer closed but
open. Hence, the reciprocity of perspective or the dialectic
of mutual implication is possible. The individual and the
collective are inseparable entities; each is immanent in the
other. This is different from interactionism. Open consciousness or conscience makes this possible. It is fruitless
to study them separately though they may be abstracted
from each other for scientific purposes. However, recall the
diagram in Chapter III which shows how the total social
phenomena are related to the total psychical phenomena.[25]
The latter are included within the former. At least this is
the ideal conception. These are related only partially in
much research being carried out today. The trend is towards this more "open" approach.

Among American sociologists Charles Warriner has
openly espoused a realist position.[26] This is essentially the

---

[25] See pages 121-122.
[26] "Groups Are Real: A Reaffirmation," *The American Sociological
Review*, XXI (October, 1956), 549-554.

Durkheimian solution. Going back to the earlier discussion in Chapter IV it was clearly spelled out that Durkheim's conception relied upon this symbol-making attribute. Gurvitch submits a devastating argument. The symbols themselves suggest a deeper unity. They make imperative the existence of the collective mind. This is Gurvitch's solution. It will have to be examined critically.

The arguments which are raised against the realness of groups follow from "common sense." Such solutions are suspect since science relies upon an attitude of systematic doubt. Stuart Chase tells the story of a scientist and his friend who were driving in the hills of Wyoming. Nearby they saw a flock of sheep.

"They've just been sheared," said the friend. "They seem to be, on this side," replied the scientist.

Science leaves no room for absolutes. Not only this, the witness of common sense is frequently unrealiable. Common sense suggests the world is flat but scientific knowledge tells otherwise. Common sense declares the individual is real but groups are not. Further exploration reveals something else. Four basic propositions are commonly advanced to refute the existence of groups.

1. We can see persons, but we cannot see groups except by observing persons.
2. Groups are composed of persons.
3. Social phenomena have their reality only in persons, this is the only possible location of such phenomena.
4. The purpose for studying groups is to facilitate explanations and predictions of individual behaviour.[27]

Proposition number one fails to convince since it is based on the faulty logic that only what can be seen is real. There are many scientific facts which are accepted though they escape senses. More than this the limitations of our perception make it impossible to take the whole phenomenon in at once. In mathematical terms man's "sight comprehension" can only take a limited number of articles. This does not deny that more than, say, twelve or thirteen can be comprehended given the right tools and concepts to extend such comprehension. More than this, there is sufficient evidence, a sufficient view to lead one to conjecture that this or that is true. "The fact we cannot directly perceive their unity does not detract from their essential empirical reality; it merely

---

[27] *Ibid.*, p. 552.

reflects the human limitation." [28] The very same thing can be said about groups, or about the human personality. One cannot possibly see the whole complexus of the human person but it is no less real because the perceptive "equipment" has definite limitations. From partial observations the researcher postulates a conception of what is observed. More data are collected. The conception is validated. This conception then becomes a perception for all intents and purposes. This conception-becoming-perception process is followed unconsciously during the daily rounds of life. A stereotype is such a perception. Science constantly attempts to base its conception-perception upon a wider base of facts.

The second argument contains the basic nominalistic problem. Persons are more concrete and less abstract than groups. Yet personality has already been seen to be a complex phenomenon (a total psychical phenomenon). The whole person is conceived though one fails to perceive every aspect. This proposition really dichotomizes the individual and the group. Underneath it is a denial of the "reciprocity of perspectives." Gurvitch always goes further. Such a reciprocity is more than an interaction of the individual and the group. He maintains there is an immanent presence of each in the other. This immanence then logically leads to the existence of a collective mind alongside the individual mind. Warriner does not go this far. He states, "There is much evidence to show that interaction results in new phenomena which are emergent in the situation and not explicable by reference to the persons as they exist prior to the interaction." [29] He is saying that the combination of factors results in a compound which has a totally different character. With this Gurvitch would agree. It is Durkheim's basic formula. However, there is a danger here which will become evident in the discussion of the next proposition.

Staying for the moment with this nominalistic problem, Gurvitch and Warriner attack a central weakness. They see the problem as a direct outcome of confusing substance and form. The physical materials—steel, plastic, rubber, and aluminum—from which an automobile is made would fail to denote auto unless they resembled the notion of auto. More precisely there are structural parts to an auto which immediately set it apart from all other objects. A fender,

---

[28] *Ibid.*, p. 553.
[29] *Ibid.*

hood, grill are a part of the idea of "carness." Now then, to say that groups are composed of persons, tells us nothing about groups as such. These are materials common to several phenomena, but does not "indicate the structural components that are involved in groups as a particular kind of unity and reality." [30]

The third argument falls into place, "the only existence of social phenomena is in the individual." Here Warriner and others approach a serious difficulty. First, however, it is imperative to see the question. This proposition maintains that group products, cultural works, are only real so long as they are present in the individuals which make up the group. Here Warriner says the confusion comes from failing to discriminate between knowing and internalization . . . a person may know cultural forms, beliefs, and patterns and know when they are appropriate . . . without these becoming an integral part of his own personality." [31] This almost parallels Gurvitch's distinction between intuition and knowledge. However, this is exactly what is lacking in Warriner's otherwise very helpful analysis. In order for him to show that these social phenomena have a reality of their own he has had to make the same mistake which Durkheim did. The reality of the group transcends the individual persons. He tries to overcome this by distinguishing between actor in the situation and person, but this seems to be a semantic solution and fails to meet the persistent problem. In fact, to say the actor in the situation carries the phenomena of the social grouping is to enter once again the nominalistic fallacy. Gurvitch's solution seems the best possible answer to this unrelenting question. The open conscience or mind, both collective and individual, which enables a partial fusion of the individual and collective minds, meaning a mutual immanence governed by the degree of openness which the minds possess, overcomes at once the dual error: the individual alone is immanent in the collective (the nominalistic fallacy) and the collective alone is immanent in the individual (the transcendent fallacy). Modern existentialist thought and research have made it possible to assert this concept as a basis for the realness of groups. The collective mind has a reality but it pervades the individual minds to the extent of their openness. When the openness is direct, the pres-

---

[30] *Ibid.*
[31] *Ibid.*

ence is intuited. When openness is partial the minds are only partially grasped. This requires the levels of knowledge operating through symbols, sign and signals, and other social phenomena to translate the mutual implication into reality. All of these variables are dependent upon the structure and situation.

The fourth proposition is already answered. The purpose in the study of groups is to learn more about group phenomena, not to explain individual behavior as such. This latter is the proper domain of psychology. Of course, they intersect and Gurvitch sees them as concentric circles with the social phenomena having a wider influence. Gurvitch has placed the vocation of sociology on the block. If groups are not real, then there is no possibility for sociology being a separate discipline outside of psychology. If groups are real, then it behooves the sociologist to develop a theoretical scheme which will enable him to carry out empirical research in a systematic manner aiming at the explanation of group phenomena. Such an explanation is desperately needed. The essential value of this realist position is twofold. First, it gives a proper domain to sociology and it gets at the truly social phenomena which have escaped social scientists for so long. Second, this dialectic of mutual implication affirms the realness of the human personality alongside the realness of the group. The human person is not just an actor, abstracted in an effort to explain the distinctiveness of the social group. The person is real and by virtue of the open conscience or mind he "intends" the collective mind and it in turn grasps the individual minds which are heterogeneous to it. The collective mind is a result of the partial fusion of the individual consciences. It is a mutual participation in the same mental object. This indicates the basic error in Warriner's argument. How is communication possible between individual consciences since the very symbols which they use must possess the same meaning and this meaning cannot be agreed upon unless there existed prior to this an interpenetration or partial fusion of the consciences? This undergirds all symbolic communication. This property of openness is the attribute of intuition. Such an intuitionist interpretation of the conscience or mind which sees it as latently open makes it unnecessary to postulate the transcendence of the collective mind or to support such transcendence with a metaphysical argument. This approach says intuition is one aspect of the psychical life.

Such an intuitionist approach saves the collective mind, the most profound level of the total social phenomena, since this notion makes possible the existence of all the other levels. It undergirds the whole idea of real social groups. If the collective mind is denied, then the problems discovered in Warriner's thesis are encountered.

Obviously the realness of some groups is more evident than others. Social classes in the United States lack a realism which social classes in France exhibit. Some means of showing the degrees of such realness needs to be specified. Gurvitch tries to do this emphasizing the role of symbols and more precisely in introducing the distinctions of mental states and mental acts. These have to do with the degrees of intentionality which in turn have to do with the intensity of fusion and subsequent interpenetration. Mental states as explained in Chapter IV are the result of partially open minds. Here symbols would be more important. This seems to be the level at which Warriner is operating. Mental acts have to do with the more open minds which directly grasp the object. Intentionality is strong. The degree of fusion is intense. Martin sees these mental states and mental acts as parallel notions of Merton's latent and manifest. Whether this be so or not, these distinctions are important to the whole work of Gurvitch. Does his method help to ascertain the degree of fusion, interpenetration and realness of social groups? This will have to be explored.

5. THE EMPIRICAL-REALIST METHOD

In terms of method Gurvitch is following a pathway traversed by such disciplines as psychology and psychotherapy. These latter have been receptive to the modern movements of existentialism and phenomenology. Gurvitch is taking the lead in sociology. He has sought to use certain ideas which phenomenology and existentialism present. He has made an effort in drawing from these sources to be scientific and to steer away from any philosophical bias. Americans have found it difficult to overcome a built-in suspicion of such movements as these which have arisen in Europe since the last war. However, these are methods of study which promise to revolutionize work in the social sciences. Because Gurvitch's whole method incorporates many aspects of these movements it is important that his work be studied carefully. He is on the threshold of an important new way of studying social behavior.

Gurvitch's whole method is more empirical than one would first suspect. The radical nature of this empiricism comes from his desire to know social groups for what they are. This means steering away from any preconceptions about what the group ought to look like or superimposing a theory upon it. This method seeks to ferret out the total social phenomena of groups. A pet system of thought cannot be protected. Technique for its own sake must be rejected. It has its limitations. There is no desire to explain the life history of a group according to the teachings of one school of thought, according to the idiosyncrasies of a philosophical position or the esteemed schema of a certain set of categories. Instead Gurvitch through his method wants to understand the life history of a social grouping from the standpoint of its own being. The beginning point is ontological. Gurvitch rebels against every notion which would see this social group from a tailored set of preconceptions or attempts to fit it into one's own propensities. This is why he has often struggled to change his thought when he has discovered himself espousing some philosophical position.

Gurvitch then seeks to work out his theory from the standpoint of the concrete, real social group. Hence, he cuts below the problem which has plagued western man, that of the subject-object dichotomy. He denies the idealist-materialist conflict. Social reality is inconceivable from either pole. It is incomplete if viewed as simply subject or object. Here Martin makes a fundamental error. He claims Gurvitch's whole method is subjective, placing the burden upon the observer. He asks if this is a very helpful way to develop a science. The discussion here on method (Chapter IV) makes it clear such a distinction between subject and object is *passé*. Social reality is not a bundle of static, rigid, material substances but an emerging, dynamic, always-becoming total phenomenon. The collective mind as the ontological fact, and the total social phenomena as the ontological reality are subject to the spontaneous, the free will of the individual and collective minds. Such spontaneity is the only thing which will explain social change. It is the dialectical, dynamic, ever-renewing aspect of social reality. The approach to such a phenomenon must be dynamic, since the "object" of study is dynamic. If one looks only at the essences—the substances of social reality—he will be able to describe *some* characteristics, make *some* abstract generalizations which will be *true* but miss reality. A conclusion may be statistically accurate but still fail to grasp the *essential*, authentic nature of the phenomenon. Gurvitch sees that what is true, in an abstract sense, is dialectically related to what is real. This is the whole burden of his typological method for sociology. It stands midway between the essentialist and realist positions. This explains why Gurvitch is impatient with those sociologists who would select phenomena which lend themselves to control and analysis and the formulation of abstract laws. Whether the data has relevancy to reality itself is unimportant to them. Hence, abstraction can be piled upon abstraction without touching reality itself.

Gurvitch is interested basically in discovering the living social reality of modern civilization and to do this he proposes a study in depth. There is a group experience which can be described and explained. This is the proper domain of sociology. The group is more than an abstract material object or a thinking, subjective mind; it is an experiencing being. Because Gurvitch bridges the gap between the subject and object in social science research, he releases the researcher from the bondage of viewing only the external objects. There is a vast inner reality, the depth levels which need to be opened and described. This means the hidden becomes most important. What is on the surface is only a partial story. The objective phenomena are not denied; they are put in parentheses while one examines more carefully the lower depth levels.

Relationship is a key idea. This is the brunt of Gurvitch's insistence upon seeing these total social phenomena within their social framework and their historical situation. But more than that, this relationship means seeing the sociologist's role as a participant in the very object which he is examining. The old notion that the less one is involved in a situation the more he can fathom about it is untenable. To be sure, one must be certain he understands where he is and what he is and the presuppositions upon which he works, but this does not require detachment and abstraction. If such a view is taken then the net result is "a handful of seafoam" to use the analogy of Rollo May.[32] Para-

---

[32] *Existence* (Glencoe, Illinois: Basic Books, 1958), p. 27.

phrasing T. S. Eliot, it would be like trying to dissipate a fog by throwing handgrenades into it.[33] The Protean nature of social reality is, to say the least, overwhelming. The only way to get at these phenomena of the social is to see the relationships both contextually and as an observer. The social scientist must devise a scheme which will take him to the depths of social life where the irrational, unconscious, spontaneous, and creatively revolutionary are at play. These are below the crust of civilization, or what appears to be. This method will have to be centered on being in and of itself. Such a method will have to recapture some of what has been lost in the transition from an earlier philosophical theory reflected in the work of St. Simon, Proudhon, Marx, Ward, Cooley and even Durkheim, to the empirically centered approach which split the material and the ideal, restricted the scientific method to a set pattern of processes based on quantitative analysis and thereby deprived sociology of the other aspects of social reality which these techniques could not uncover.[34] There is a deep seated feeling in social science today which fears the presence of irrational factors; such factors upset comfortable notions concerning social causality and generalization.

Gurvitch has devised a method which takes into consideration these irrational elements. The hyper-empiricism and radical dialectic provides the *modus operandi*. It also frees the sociologist from a fragmentary abstractionism or abstract empiricism. This is the natural result of a method which is tied to rigid processes based on quantitative analysis. This dialectical approach unites "science and ontology." [35]

A social whole can only be understood within the context of its existence. This means a social group first must be accepted as real. Moreover, the sociologist, though he collects a considerable amount of data about a particular entity must recognize that he still is unable to grasp the reality of that collectivity. Understanding and knowledge are separate. To gather data about some group is important but this data will have little meaning until one has encountered the group itself. This is the whole message of studies made by such social scientists as Oscar Lewis, Ir-

---

[33] T. S. Eliot, editor, *Pascal's Pensées* (New York: Dutton Everyman Paperback, 1958), p. xiii.

[34] Cf. S. Bruyn, *op. cit.*

[35] May, *Existence*, p. 39.

win T. Sanders and Margaret Mead. "Knowing something involves a dialectical participation with the other." [36] The purely technical will be insufficient to see what really is. It is false to assume a thing is real only if it can be quantified. This is to reduce it to some manageable abstraction. Then comes the task of persuading oneself what he has abstracted is the real thing. "Society is like love and consciousness . . . to abstract them is to lose what we have set out to describe. . . ." [37] The end is to describe what ontologically is. This means seeing that residue of being after all the layers are removed (in essence the collective mind), within the context of *its* world. The social group and its world are unitary. This is the meaning of the two views of social reality, the vertical and the horizontal. They are always dialectically related. The vertical implies the horizontal and the horizontal the self. One cannot exist without the other, and they are only understandable in terms of each other. The same holds for the relationships of the individual and the collective. Probably the dichotomy of the individual and society resulted from the subject-object separation. They are interpenetrating and mutually supportive. This is the whole meaning of reciprocity of perspectives. It is one process of the dialectical method. The others are variations on this essential theme. These have been described in Chapter VII.

The dialectical method reflects the requirements of the field of study. This dialectic is two-fold: it applies to the relationship of the method as a tool with its object of study, social reality. It also describes the relationship of observer and observed. This same method is one way of seeing the different levels and their interrelationships. It enables one to describe the horizontal frameworks and note their interdependency. Finally, it is a way of seeing the individual parts and yet understanding their basic unity. The centrifugal forces are present but the stronger ties are those which bind. The relationship of the spontaneous and the organized, the hierarchies of depth levels, or social times, or types of knowledge, or kinds of morality or law, are describable because of this dialectical approach.

The processes of the dialectical method are important contributions to scientific literature. They need to be seriously considered. They are important because Gurvitch

---

[36] *Ibid.*, p. 40.
[37] *Ibid.*

has made a splendid effort to systematize and categorize the various approaches one must take in analyzing and observing a particular social phenomenon. For one thing it is always a total social phenomenon. Second, it is like an iceberg. Only the very top part is readily available. One must go beneath the surface to get at the real body of information. These processes should be of great help to the researcher in the field who is seeking to see these various relationships. The rich possibilities of this approach illustrate most decidedly that Gurvitch's theory and method could help correct the sterile tendencies of statistical sociology and bring sociological theory and research into line with the twentieth century.

The dialectical method, unfamiliar to most Americans and consistently passed up by them because of a natural tendency to assume this is another philosophical position, dispels any notions that Gurvitch is a formalist. Don Martindale in his book on sociological theory[38] classifies Gurvitch with the phenomenologists and as a formalist. The discussion on the relationship between "culture" and social structure has already served to show that such an appellation is unwarranted. Furthermore, the philosophical overtones of formalism with its emphasis on the static and those elements which can be quantified, are entirely alien to Gurvitch's whole position. His radical empiricism based on an unrelenting dialectic undercuts any description of his sociology which sees it as another formalism. Seeing it as such results from a mere surface acquaintanceship with Gurvitch's sociology; the essential thrust of his thought has been missed.

Martindale makes certain other serious errors in his interpretation of Gurvitch's ideas. The contention that Gurvitch is a formalist is not the least. He fails to translate *L'idée du droit social* correctly as the *Idea of Social Law*. Rather it becomes *The Concept of Social Justice*. His reading of Gurvitch is suspect. He goes on to list only eight depth levels to social reality; Gurvitch's works since 1955 contain ten. Martindale neglects Gurvitch's debt to Marcel Mauss and the whole concept of the total social phenomena which is the keystone to his theory.

Still, there is a persistent question which has to be faced when considering the whole corpus of Gurvitch's work.

[38] Don Martindale, *The Nature and Types of Sociological Theory* (Boston: Houghton Mifflin Co., 1960), pp. 276-281.

That question is, why has this sociologist been dismissed? Why do most American sociologists at least fail to take him seriously or even attempt to deal with him honestly? There are several reasons. The first, though a superficial reason, is nonetheless important. Gurvitch uses a language which is hard to grasp and until one has been able to get "inside" the structure and forms of his expressions, it is rough going. Undoubtedly many individuals have been frustrated soon after attempting to wade through one of Professor Gurvitch's closely reasoned, yet highly elevated volumes. A European would find the task much easier since he has generally been well-educated in the classics and in philosophy. Most sociologists in America are empirically oriented and consequently lack the necessary foundation in philosophy. Nevertheless, Europeans encounter difficulty in some rather specialized, if not esoteric, branches of philosophy. For example, Gurvitch was greatly influenced by Fichte whom many consider to be one of the most difficult philosophers to comprehend. Furthermore, Gurvitch waits for no one. He knows what he believes and he moves immediately into an explanation of this conviction he holds considering the nature of social reality. If he would have undertaken to do a more careful and elementary presentation of a number of the key concepts in his theory, his readers would be aided in grasping more easily the core of his thought.

Second, somewhat more profound than the first reason, but even so, a surface manifestation, Gurvitch has had a strong tendency to be hypercritical. There has been in his character and his presentation a natural aggressiveness, bordering on contentiousness, which alienated him from many of his contemporaries. Certainly the difficulty was not all one-sided. However, in reading some of the responses and open letters sent to certain individuals one gains the impression that part of his problem was self-inflicted. Moreover, his attacks upon certain theorists and positions were often caustic and acidic. As one of his students was wont to say about this procedure: 'un peu mechant.' Still, this was a recent development. One has the distinct impression Professor Gurvitch had been stung by this continued neglect and indifference to what he had to say. These hypercritical positions are his way of making a response to this devastating silence on the part of the American school.

Third, he rightly sensed in the account of his intellectual itinerary that sociologists consider him a philosopher who has somehow gotten in the wrong room and the philosophers have long since been convinced that he forsook their discipline for the greener landscapes of sociology. He had to go it alone most of the time. But more than anything else for Americans, the language which he employs connotes a philosophical bias or at least orientation, and there is no room in their sociology for that. Once a sociologist has made his peace with the presuppositions which he holds concerning sociology's task and his own role in that task, his philosophical speculation is ended. So reads the empiricist's manifesto. Gurvitch along with so many other Europeans— more implicitly for them than for Gurvitch—exhibits in his language a philosophical background which is replete with such words as dialectic, immanence, *total* phenomena, and complementarity. This is immediately suspect and usually he is a marked man thereafter. To wit, the American reviews of *Dialectique et sociologie,* a little volume dedicated to an exposition of Gurvitch's method, have all commented on its obvious philosophical character and have failed to see any relevancy for sociology or the other social sciences. The European estimations of this volume have praised Gurvitch's efforts. Several have commented that this is his finest book.

This radical separation between sociology and philosophy in America is beginning to be viewed with alarm by some persons. Edward A. Tiryakian in his *Sociologism and Existentialism,* especially seeks to realize a liaison between these two disciplines. He notes that the American school separated sociology from philosophy and gained for the former a separate existence with its own status as an empirical science. "But at what cost? It appears that, in the modern period, sociology has tended to focus on problems at the microscopic level. For most practicing sociologists social problems of global magnitude do not seem to exist." [39] Tiryakian goes on to say in a footnote that he only recently learned of Gurvitch's work and discovered they were generally in agreement.[40] More on the positive contributions of Gurvitch to this whole question will follow in the next section.

[39] Englewod Cliffs, New Jersey: Prentice Hall, 1962, p. 4.
[40] *Ibid.,* p. 7. See also Tiryakians article "Existential Phenomenology," *American Sociological Review,* XXX, No. 5, Oct., 1965, 674-688.

The fourth barrier to acceptance of Gurvitch's theory has been due to its emphasis on a concept of totality. Gurvitch is attempting to see groups as whole units, as collectivities, as real frameworks of social activity. This requires a *Gestalt* approach not only in an empirical sense but also in a theoretical sense. Consequently, Gurvitch cannot be content with partial theories, intermediary theories. He needs a view of the whole as a guideline or framework for empirical studies. Such whole theories are *passé*. At least they have been during this century. Now, however, one gets the distinct impression there is a growing sense of the need for more systematic and overarching theories for empirical research. Gurvitch's realist position concerning the nature of groups would require such a general theory; they go hand in hand.

Perhaps it is all a matter of perspective, but it would seem safer to start with a general theory, one that attempted to see the totality and "descend" from there into the more concrete and specific, minute, microscopic areas of research. The general theory could be corrected accordingly. The danger in relying on intermediary theory at best, is that one may get so involved and subsequently inspired by his empirical work in an intermediary area of research that he loses all touch with reality, social reality, that is.

Despite these barriers to the understanding and appreciation of Gurvitch's thought there are those who maintain that his theory is of little heuristic value or even worth serious consideration. This judgment seems based on little evidence of such "serious consideration." Having examined every review available by an American on Gurvitch's thought we reach the conclusion that the reviewers lack facts to back up their overwhelmingly negative reactions. European scholars have placed Gurvitch among the front ranks of theoretical sociologists. Until his death he was president of the International Association of French Speaking Sociologists.

Among the small number of reviewers who have honestly wrestled with what he says, there are those who find his work basically too abstract and manifestly deficient in empirical support. A paucity of empirical studies is noted. However, it must be underlined once again: his theoretical approach is gaining adherents; there are research projects underway. His sociological thought is growing, not waning, in importance in Europe.

6 A PHILOSOPHICAL POSITION

Throughout the descriptive analysis of Gurvitch's thought we had the distinct impression that despite every claim to the contrary the theorist was inclined to favor certain phenomena and/or positions. In his theory of law he has carefully disclaimed any preferences but there are indications that Gurvitch actually favors social law over individual law.

We observe the same thing when it comes to types of global societies. He obviously prefers the decentralized, federalist type of global structure. In a letter he makes it clear that the reason for his dissatisfaction with the Russian revolutions was their failure to maintain the locus of power in the hands of workers at the factory level.[41] His most recent writings also lend support to this contention.[42]

When it comes to morality, the creative, effervescent types are preferred. The same holds for social time. Those types which are beneath the surface ready to burst forth in an innovating manner are favored by Gurvitch. The same holds for types of knowledge. Even if one analyzes the depth levels he comes away with the impression that the more profound levels are preferable to a liberal mind.

There is a ready explanation for this. Gurvitch is reacting against the static theories prevalent especially in the United States. He has in mind both Parsons and Merton. Gurvitch would agree with Bennett Berger's statement: "Parsons seems 'unmusical' when it comes to matters of power; conflict is something a very important thinker like Marx wrote a great deal about and which Parsons consequently must take account of." [43] Gurvitch certainly steers away from this criticism. His great strength lies in the position which attempts to place emphasis upon both the spontaneous and the organized. There are two levels to social reality. This is the whole burden of his thought.

Gurvitch's denial that he espouses a philosophical position or prefers any one type of global society or morality or law is a contradiction with an important premise in his method. He maintains that the subject-object dichotomy must be overcome if sociology is to become a valid science. He then develops a dialectical method incorporating several processes which will uncover any inclinations towards cer-

[41] November 3, 1962.
[42] Cf. *Structures sociales et democratie économique*, pp. 269-280, and "L'effondrement d'un mythe . . . ," *CIS* XXXIII, 5-18.
[43] "The Study of Man," *Commentary*, XXXIV (Dec., 1962), 511.

tain dogmatic philosophical positions. Gurvitch's preference of these various types of phenomena is in no way dogmatic. The dialectical method is precisely designed to cut through any position which borders on becoming doctrinaire. The sociologist cannot escape his predicament, his involvement in humanity, in the very subject he is seeking to observe. The dialectical processes at once recognize this involvement and the necessity to be as "objective" as possible. Hence, Gurvitch provides in his own theory the solution to what now may be termed a "false problem." The time to be concerned about position-taking is when one is unaware he holds this or that attitude and begins to appropriate it for everyone else; or when he begins to read the data he has collected according to his favorite preconceptions. The dialectic guards against such prejudice, such subjectivity while at the same time recognizing it is foolish to believe the subjective can be wiped out, denied, pushed to the side.

To this problem Gurvitch has contributed a valuable tool for analysis and correction. It seems to be a contradiction to insist on setting aside one's own preconceptions. Gurvitch's own dialectic urges the sociologist admit them and allow the processes of dialectical critical analysis to clarify and correct.

7. INHERENT VALUES FOR CONTEMPORARY SOCIOLOGY

This final section deals with the most important contributions and values which come from Gurvitch's work for the contemporary task of sociology.

a) Gurvitch attempts to re-establish a link or bridge between the different social sciences and to relate sociology once again to history and philosophy. His general sociology is a synthesizing discipline. Groups are real and whole man is a unity. The science of man studies the individual and collective efforts at building a society. Norman Birnbaum points to Gurvitch's great contribution: "his distinctions represent an interesting attempt to deal with a fundamental problem—the unity of the social system—in a bold and critical way." [44]

The object of study for the social sciences and sociology is the freedom humanity possesses to create these societies and the obstacles encountered along the way. All the social

---

[44] Norman Birnbaum, *op. cit.*, AJS, LX, 199.

sciences, including history, study the *human condition*. This condition comes under the scrutiny of each in its own particular manner but always the emphasis is placed on the act over the product, the total or whole effort over the disparate activities. Moreover the compartmentalization of the social sciences is only relative since man is one and the various groups in which he acts cannot be permanently dissected. They are totalities. Society is *en acte*, it is becoming what it shall be. This is a central focus. Gurvitch's approach shows the possibilities of interdisciplinary study. He constantly underlines a necessary interdependence. He radically opposes any approach which would permanently dissect or which only partially views social reality, thereby distorting its real character. Moreover, in placing the emphasis upon existence, or being, or the human condition, Gurvitch brings the study of sociology in line with the essential nature of social reality. This is the character of society as observed today. The pace is fast. The emphasis must be placed on the dynamic and the creative, the spontaneous and the unexpected, the fluid and the dissonant, the ruptures and the discontinuous. This is reality. It is sensed by modern man. It appears in all he writes, expresses in art, lives in his industrial centers or experiences in the areas of rapid social change where the processes of structuration, destruction and re-structuration are especially evident. Somehow the study of depth levels, the search for the hidden, the uncovering of the irrational, typing the phenomena which the dialectical processes reveal seem to fit what society is. The structural-functionalist fails to capture this dynamic aspect, this spontaneous level, this infrastructure below the superstructure. Gurvitch has taken a symbolic notion of the total social phenomena. He has explained that it is a device or tool by which to understand these layers or levels to social reality. The ten levels are not sacrosanct. They can change, be altered by addition or subtraction. Such a concept is insufficient to capture the total aspect of social life. Even these ten levels, which are constantly changing and rearranging themselves in scales according to the situation and social framework, are more than their frameworks. They spill over, escape a complete encirclement. These frameworks are real enough but this does not mean they are structured. Only certain macrosociological frames are structured. This suggests an even further spontaneity and freedom. Determinism is relative alongside human liberty. They are interactive but the ontological priority is given to the element of freedom. There is a residue of freedom which persists come what will. There is necessarily a price to pay for placing the emphasis upon the spontaneous. The static or functional approach allows neater categories and abstractions. The spontaneous requires less precision but sees the social as a whole and notes the constancy of movement. Perhaps the choice must be made between a closer abstraction which tends towards looking at society in unreal categories both from the standpoint of spontaneity and totality and a view which notes change and contingency affecting the level of abstraction. Abstracted empiricism and static functionalism are the natural results of the former. On the other hand, Gurvitch's approach sees the social as it exists and sees it for its unity and wholeness, while emphasizing its discontinuity and fluidity. Vagueness and theoretical fuzziness are real dangers in the latter.

Sociology must not neglect the historical dimension. The data for establishing the typologies of groups and global societies come from the study of history. History studies the total social phenomena just as does sociology. Its emphasis is upon the continuous and hence its causal explanations are more sophisticated. Sociology must depend upon history to explain and clarify plus provide essential data. History is imperative to carry out any comparative study. Sociology provides history with categories, i.e., types of social groupings and social structures. It serves as a corrective against any tendency to dogmatize a position or reduce the causal factors to one or omit essential material. They are mutually supportive and if amelioration is to be effective, both must counsel. As for the other social sciences, they each study a single aspect of the total social phenomena and sociology reasserts their basic unity, ties the levels together, shows the way in which the data are functionally correlative. Sociology is the culminating point of the science of man. As suggested above, European sociology is very similar to cultural anthropology in the United States.

b) Gurvitch attacks the tendency towards abstracted empiricism. He sees that this fragmentation and atomization leads to even greater alienation and *anomie*. His solution attempts to fuse empirical research and theory into a dialectical whole. The great problem with American research is its inability to construct a systematic theory which leads in a logical and fruitful direction. Research is done with overemphasis on technique overlooking the ultimate goals and systematic views of social reality which then can be put to the test of empirical research. Gurvitch sees the ideal sociology as one which is totally empirical and totally theoretical. He would disagree with Robert Merton that the best one can hope for is an intermediary theory residing between a total view conceiving society as a whole and a conceptual position which is guided by the next statistical exercise. Gurvitch asserts instead that a view of the total social phenomena is possible; not only this, a systematic intermediary theory can be worked out which can be put to the test of empirical research. This is why his theory appears complex. He has attempted to do both and in view of recent projects carried out at the Centre Nationale des Recherches Scientifiques the validation of his approach is well under way. This is contrary to the uninformed assertion by Everett K. Wilson in the *American Journal of Sociology*:

> The *Traité* is in the middle . . . between theory and data, failing generally to meet Simiand's injunction "Pas de faits sans idées, pas d'idées sans faits". It will doubtless be contended that this is inevitable in a perhaps impossible undertaking: an objective overview of the field of sociology, as Gurvitch puts it. But this "middleness" may derive not only from the nature of French sociology, split as it is between provincial departments of philosophy and Parisian research centers.[45]

This is inaccurate. The new *Revue Française de Sociologie*[46] indicates that significant changes have taken place in France in terms of the relationships between theory and empirical research. Gurvitch's contribution was important in this respect. Recent issues of the Cahiers Internationaux de Sociologie show concrete research projects using Gurvitch's categories.[47] The 1963 editions of the *Traité* and

[45] *Op. cit.*, p. 252.
[46] Centre National de Recherche Scientifique, Paris.
[47] Cf. Jean Cazeneuve, Paul-H. Maucorps and Albert Memmi "Enquête sociologique sur la connaissance d'autrui, *CIS*, XXIX (Juillet-Decembre, 1960), pp. 137-156; P.-H. Maucorps and René Bussoul, "Jeux de miroirs et sociologie de la connaissance d'autrui," *CIS*, XXXII (January-June, 1962), 43-60; Monique Vincenne, "La ville et les paysans," in *Ibid.*, pp. 125-134; Georges Kavadias, "L'étude de la circulation des hommes et des biens, point de départ d'une enquête de sociologie rurale," *CIS*, XXX (January-June, 1961), 167-174.

La vocation . . . incorporate some of these data. Joseph B. Ford commenting on *Déterminismes sociaux* . . . made the observation that its major weakness was a lack of "solid contact with empirical data save where fitted or forced into molds of the author's increasingly intricate system of classification." [48] Increasing evidence points to empirical research designed specifically to test Gurvitch's theoretical concepts.

Gurvitch makes one final telling criticism at this juncture. He points out that the paucity of theoretical considerations has resulted in sociology becoming the pawn of technocracy. His thesis agrees with those of C. Wright Mills, Lorin Baritz and others. Sociology has become a servant of power. It is part of the manipulative process seeking to adjust workers to their environment, thereby maintaining the logics of size, functional efficiency and hierarchy now operative in the industrial order.[49] The lack of theory has led to a general indecisiveness as to goals and purposes. This has made sociology and the social sciences particularly open to use by bureaucracies of all types. "The phenomenological insistence on the concrete and immediate can contribute (if only indirectly) to a new humanization of sociology in a period when it has become another instrument of bureaucratization." [50]

c) Gurvitch's typology of global societies is especially challenging for sociology. This should provide a general basis for empirical research and augment comparative studies in whole cultures. We need such an emphasis. Edward Shils in *Theories of Society* makes the following comment:

> What is most obviously lacking in the present situation of sociology is a theory as to why and how one type of society yields place to another or why one type of society passes through one, rather than another, of alternative sets of sequences. This, however, has no chance of realization until the focus of the theory of action is widened to a macrosociological scope. The construction of a realistically differentiated typology

---

[48] *American Sociological Review*, XX (Oct., 1955), 599.

[49] Daniel Bell ,"Work in the Life of an American," *Manpower in the U.S.: Problem and Politics*, William Haber, ed. (New York: Harpers, 1954), pp. 3-23.

[50] Norman Birnbaum, a review of *Où va la sociologie française..* in *The American Journal of Sociology*, LX (Sept., 1954), 199.

of societies is thus once more thrust upon the agenda of sociological theory.[51]

The extraordinary thing about this quotation is that Shils is pleading for exactly the same thing Gurvitch has advocated. Gurvitch has gone further and worked out an imaginative, skillful, empirically supported typology of global societies. Shils and his colleagues seem unaware of this typology. In fact, the two volumes of *Theories of Society* do not once mention Gurvitch. In the long bibliography at the end of volume II Gurvitch's name is not included! Yet until his death in December, 1965, he was considered the most important theorist in Europe. This illustrates a strange myopia.

d) Edward Shils in his article in *Theories of Society* calls for another reform in theory: he laments that contemporary sociology avoids the temporal. "Its concepts have little time depth. . . . The temporal structure of an action or event has not yet been grasped." [52] Yet Gurvitch has devoted an entire book[53] to this subject; an important part of his theory attempts to meet this lacuna.

Gurvitch makes the observation that if social frameworks are real, if there are discernible total social phenomena which have realness, then it follows that such categories exist within certain times. Gurvitch comes to this conclusion after considering the problem of social determinism. Each category has its particular time and the various societies seek to harmonize the multiplicity of times within their life, each succeeding at this in a different manner.

The multiplicity of social times throws light on the whole problem of social change. It is imperative that one understands these various times and hierarchies of times if he is to succeed in effecting social change.

Professor Gurvitch has rendered an enormous service to those involved in the study and amelioration of the developing world or in understanding those regions undergoing rapid social change.[54] His social time theory would also be

---

[51] Talcott Parsons, Edward Shils, Kaspar D. Naegele, Jesse R. Pitts, eds., *Theories of Society*, (New York: The Free Press, 1961), II, 1444.

[52] *Ibid.*

[53] *The Spectrum of Social Time.*

[54] Note the work of Georges Balandier, particularly his *Sociologie actuelle de l'Afrique Noire* (Paris: Presses Universitaires de France, 1963). He has employed Gurvitch's categories.

helpful in studying full-developed societies facing the prospects of increasing technocracy, bureaucracy, automation, depersonalization, leisure time and alienation.

e) Professor Gurvitch's dialectic is broad enough to allow the unrelenting social problems to determine the approach to their study. He has steered clear of the strait jacket procedures implicit in a narrow conception of the scientific method. Moreover, he has emphasized the necessity of viewing each problem within the context of its social frameworks and historical situation. The abstraction is not ripped from reality but kept within it.

f) The basic emphasis on the spontaneous, exogenic, irrational aspects of social reality which Gurvitch makes is a welcome contribution to sociological exploration and explanation. This brings modern social science in line with twentieth century physics and overcomes a serious cultural lag. That lag is the gap between scientific knowledge of human behavior and technological know-how. Gurvitch has bridged this gap by underlining the human factor, by overcoming the subject-object dichotomy, by seeing the existential reality both of the human person as a total psychical phenomenon and social reality as a total social phenomenon.

g) Gurvitch's argument in favor of the realness of groups is one which should be given serious attention. His attempt is noble. Whether he succeeds in establishing the ground of the group's being as the collective mind should be the subject of theoretical debate. It is that important. Too few have bothered to wrestle with the notion. If the realism of groups is espoused, then it seems preferable to accept the notion of the open mind or consciousness. Indications point to this as a valid concept. A recent research project at the Centre National shows the reciprocity of perspectives is operative and interpenetration or fusion takes place.[55] The sense of the collective mind is more widely accepted then might be realized. Hans Kohn in his works on nationalism has consistently maintained this is a state of consciousness or mind. Such a statement presupposes the collective mind at the level of partial fusion in the *We*. MacIver and Page's use of "community sentiment" comes very close to the idea of the collective mind. In fact it seems impossible to conceive of this sentiment apart from some conception of the

---

[55] P.-H. Maucorps and Réné Bussoul, "Jeux de miroirs et sociologie de la connaissance d'autrui," *CIS*, XXXII, 43 ff.

collective mind. The following description of this sentiment indicates the challenge of this notion:

> A neighborhood is not a community because it does not possess a feeling of belonging together— it lacks community sentiment . . . locality, though a necessary condition is not enough to create a community. A community . . . is an area of common living. There must be the common living with its awareness of sharing a way of life as well as common earth.[56]

Durkheim is present here. Gurvitch's improvement on his predecessor's definition goes a long way in spelling out exactly what is the nature of community sentiment.

h) The total social phenomena as a notion is not as revolutionary as one would suspect on first glance. It is a helpful device by which to study the total aspects of a society or group. Mauss saw these total phenomena holding only for a global structure. Gurvitch goes further and sees these phenomena present in every kind of framework. Such an idea is accepted by most cultural anthropologists. Gurvitch's refinement of the notion and his depth levels make it a concept which could be of great use to anthropologists in their field work. Again, the social and cultural are integral. They interact and are necessary to each other in Gurvitch's scheme. His affinity with cultural anthropology is obvious.

i) Gurvitch illustrates the necessity of being intellectually and politically involved. He is not advocating that sociological knowledge have a political coloration. On the contrary, sociological knowledge pertaining to certain structures must be devoid of every philosophical bias. This is the task of the dialectical-empirical method. Such knowledge then is available for use by anyone. The sociologist should not feel, however, he is insulated from political affairs or isolated because of scientific endeavors. He has the same responsibility as any other person to take the knowledge and apply it according to his own conception of justice. Gurvitch advocates in the third colloquium of the Association internationale des sociologues de langue française on

---

[56] *Society: An Introductory Analysis* (New York: Holt, Rinehart and Winston, Inc., 1949), quoted in Elgin F. Hunt and Jules Karlin, *Society Today and Tomorrow* (New York: The Macmillan Co., 1961), p. 28.

the *Structures sociales et democratie economique*[57] certain radical solutions to save democracy from the impending threats of technocracy and technology. These are so serious that a sustained effort to decentralize national economies and place the decision-making in the hands of the working people is the only hope before the deluge. Sociologists' unwillingness to be politically engaged, to separate their tasks from every mention of values make this plea of Gurvitch especially significant. Such involvement is desperately needed from every level of scholarship.

j) Closely linked to the above observation is the task sociology holds in Gurvitch's scheme. To him it is imperative that sociology serve as a guide in integrating the social sciences. Moreover, it needs to take the lead in making some concrete explanations as to why and whither. The particular social science is limited to description and systematization of data. Only sociology can perform the integrative function. Sociology's analysis of the social structures enables it to see those forces which menace modern man. These are essential data. Man may choose what he will do once he has learned that truth. Sociology can provide him with certain facts and can suggest what possibly could happen. Certain tendencies are observable. Such tendencies are tentative and incomplete. Still they provide guidelines which could be of immeasurable assistance.

k) Gurvitch brings together the disciplines of philosophy and sociology. A persistent theme which appears in his theory is the desire to counter the fragmentary nature of the contemporary view of sociology's vocation. Certainly abstracted empiricism has led to a consideration of trivia. This has reached serious proportions in an age when mankind can ill afford to be concerned with the non-essential.

> The need to pose global problems, to seek the most general level of analysis, to develop a global perspective—all of which should be imparted by a philosophical background—is a necessity seldom considered. As a result, research projects accumulate, but are not cumulative. Sociological theory of a general and systematic nature is seen as something esoteric and recondite, not as a practical necessity to the development of sociology.[58]

---

[57] (Brussels: Institut de sociologie, 1961), pp. 269-280.
[58] Tiryakian, *Sociologism and Existentialism*, p. 4.

Philosophy has historically been concerned with an over-arching approach to the problem of human existence. Sociology with its object of study, social reality, requires such a synthesizing view. Both the notions of the total social phenomena, essentially a wholistic concept, and the idea that this social totality is *en acte,* are derived from philosophy.

Gurvitch makes it clear that the divorce between sociology and philosophy leads to serious repercussions for the task of sociology. First, he notes general theory is impossible without a philosophical orientation; second, research which is done without an adequate theoretical framework is often of poor quality and/or impractical. Gurvitch asserts 75 per cent of American sociology suffers from this condition. Third, efforts to eliminate philosophy from the discipline of sociology only leave the sociologist open to implicit or unconscious philosophical positions which often lead to three curses of American sociology: "technocracy," "testomania," and "testocracy." Finally a sociology divorced from philosophy so frequently issues into research projects which only rework previously accepted conclusions.

Gurvitch asserts that sociology and philosophy are naturally linked together for four basic reasons: their common domain of study is *la condition humaine;* their view of the phenomena is wholistic; symbols, ideas and values are important elements in their respective studies; lastly, the dialectical method sees the domain or object of study and the approach to this human milieu as inseparable. Both philosophy and sociology must admit this common element in their relationships. The dialectical processes encompassing a radical empiricism eliminate all propensities towards taking vitiating dogmatic positions.

Philosophy needs sociology for this very reason. In order that he may move beyond a narrow conception of the human condition, the philosopher is protected in his task by the dialectic. Sociology also provides him with a vast storehouse of data concerning social reality without which he cannot work.

Sociology, on the other hand, is indebted to philosophy for its means of synthesis, its conceptual framework for working out general theories which will spring sociology from the grip of both an empty abstracted empiricism and an ethereal theory out of touch with reality. Philosophy is indispensable in the study of those subjects included in the *sociology of the spirit* such as morality, law, religion, knowledge and art. Philosophy provides the schemata for classification.[59]

Gurvitch's discussion of this necessary relationship between sociology and philosophy warrants serious attention. It is central to his thought. In many ways it serves as the rationale for his approach. As a general theorist he stands in the tradition of the great French sociologists, Auguste Comte, St. Simon, Proudhon, Durkheim, and Marcel Mauss. Each saw the necessary liaison between these two areas of study.

---

[59] Gurvitch, "Philosophie et sociologie," *Encyclopedie française*, XIX (Philosophie et religion), 2615.

CHAPTER IX

CONCLUSIONS

Professor Georges Gurvitch has written a general sociology based on the concept of the total social phenomena. Social reality is split into two general levels, the superficial or organized exterior and the spontaneous stratum beneath. Appearances of phenomena suggest one thing. Always there is more than what is immediately perceived.

It is like looking at the Norte Dame of Chartres. From the outside we are aware of a general idea of the style and period of architecture, the placement of the church basilica, its bell towers, and its sculptured symbols. From such a perspective it is easy to describe the height of the windows, the number of doors, the materials which went into making the edifice. But this is not the cathedral. These are surface phenomena, the external details, the quantitative data. We enter the main door, and stepping inside gain a totally different impression. A life and spontaneity are present which we did not imagine before. Our view of the building has been transformed.

Such an analogy applies to Gurvitch's description of the total social phenomena. What appears to be may turn out to be very different once all the facts are in, once the search for the hidden, for the levels in depth has ended. The dialectical processes help us see some of these hidden depths. Dialetical sociology opens up a view of society as a whole in all its effervescent and vividly dynamic aspects. Underneath the crust of tradition and organization reside the well-springs of revolutions, of rapid change, the irrational roots of behaviour, the creative acts and attitudes. Together they provide the excitement and challenge to social science research, which in turn holds the clues to man's future.

Iris Murdoch, speaking of the art of prose, said in a lecture at Yale a few years ago, "To combine form with a respect for reality with all its odd contingent ways is the highest art of prose." [1] In paraphrase this statement, to combine a design of society with a respect for social reality with all its odd contingent ways is the highest art of sociological theory. Gurvitch has contributed to this art.

[1] Quoted by Granville Hicks in "Rector for a Dead God," *Saturday Review*, October 29, 1966, p. 26.

APPENDIX I. GEORGES GURVITCH'S INTELLECTUAL HERITAGE [1]

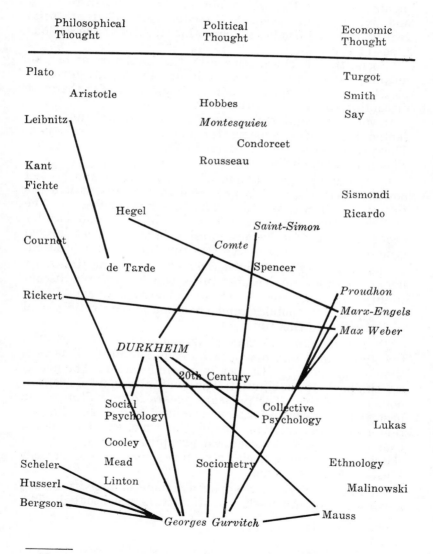

[1] Lecture notes, The University of Paris, November, 1956.

APPENDIX II. THE TYPES OF SOCIAL TIME

Social time "is the convergency and divergency of movements of the total social phenomena, giving birth to times and living within them." [1] Gurvitch contends that social reality lives and produces certain hierarchies of the various types of time.

"Social time is characterized by the maximum of human meaning which is grafted on to it, and by its extreme complexity. . . . Except for historic time, it is by far the most discontinuous of human times." [2]

In his *Déterminismes sociaux* . . . , Gurvitch first presented his general schema for the types of social time. These have been elaborated on in *The Spectrum of Social Time*, from which this discussion is taken.[3]

1) Enduring Time (Time of long duration and slowed down). Here the past is projected in the present and the future. Continuity is emphasized to a greater degree. The ecological level moves in this time. Kinship and locality groupings, e.g., family and rural village. The patriarchal type of global society places this time in the first position.

2) *Deceptive Time.* Under the veil of enduring time exist latent crises and unexpected turns which reinforce discontinuity. It is at once agitated and slowed down. Large cities, political "public," and charismatic-theocratic global societies live in this time.

3) *Erratic Time.* A time of irregular pulsation between the appearance and disappearance of rhythms. This is a time of uncertainty. Chance is a prime factor. The greatest emphasis is ambiguity. The qualitative and discontinuous are relative. The present appears to prevail over the past and the future. Patterns are hard to discern. Transition groups and relations fit into this time, e.g., technology, passive masses, non-structured groupings, emerging social classes, and waning social structures such as the present Western European ones.

4) *Cyclical Time.* An apparent image of activity masks a withdrawal into itself. Continuity is accentuated. The

---

[1] *The Spectrum* . . . , p. 27.
[2] *Ibid.*, p. 26.
[3] In *Déterminismes sociaux* . . . , pp. 38-40; *The Spectrum* . . . , pp. 28-33.

past, present and future are projected into each other. The chance element is weakened. The qualitative is highlighted. Mystic communions, churches, sects, and primitive societies fit into this type.

5) *Retarding Time, Time Turned in on Itself.* The adage, "time waits for no one," describes this type. Continuity and discontinuity fail to achieve a balance. Symbols fit this type. They are always outmoded at the very moment they become crystallized. Communities, professional associations, and academic faculties live in this time.

6) *Alternating Time.* The time alternating between retardation and advance. The past and the future compete for the dominant position. Discontinuity holds the upper hand. The qualitative and the element of chance are deemphasized. The victory of one over the other is always costly. Global societies incorporating an emerging capitalism are examples of types which live in this time.

7) *Time in Advance of Itself.* Discontinuity, chance and the qualitative triumph over their opposites. The future is present. The proletariat fit into this category of time as does competitive capitalism.

8) *Explosive Time.* In this time the present and the past are fused into the creation of the immediately transcendant future. Discontinuity, the contingent, and the qualitative find their maximum expression. This time gives rise to the acts of creation. Revolutions bring to the surface this type of social time. Creative communions live in this ambiance. In pluralistic collectivities this time is dominant. The global and partial structures are always in danger when confronting this time.

THE WORKS OF GEORGES GURVITCH

Books

La doctrine politique de Prokopovitch et les sources européennes (Grotius, Hobbes, Pufendorf). Dorpat, Russia: 1915. (In Russian).

Rousseau et la déclaration des droits. L'idée de droits inaliénables de l'individu dans la doctrine politique de Rousseau. Petrograd: 1918.

Otto V. Gierke als Rechtsphilosoph. Tubingen: Mohr, 1922.

Die Einheit der Fichteschen Philosophie. Berlin: Colligon, 1922.

Intrcduction to the General Theory of International Law. Prague: University Law School, 1923. (In Russian).

Fichtes System der konkreten Ethik. Tubingen: Mohr, 1924.

Proudhon und die Gegenwart. Archiv für Rechts und Wirtschaft philosophie, 1928.

Les tendences actuelles de la philosophie allemande. Paris: J. Vrin, 1930. (Second impression, 1949).

L'idée du droit social. Paris: Sirey, 1932.

Le temps présent et l'idée du droit social. Paris: J. Vrin, 1932.

Las tendencias de la filosofia allemana. Madrid and Buenos Aires: Losada, 1933.

Expérience juridique et philosophie pluraliste du droit. Paris, France: Pédone, 1935.

Essai d'une classification pluraliste des formes de la sociabilité. Paris, France: Alcan, 1937.

Morale théorique et science des moeurs. Paris, France: Alcan, 1937. 2d ed., 1948; 3d ed., 1961.

Essais de sociologie. Paris, France: Recueil Sirey, 1938.

Elements de sociologie juridique. Paris, France: Aubier, 1940.

Las formas de la sociobilidad. Buenos Aires: Losada, 1941.

Sociology of Law. New York: Philosophical Library, 1942.

La déclaration des droits sociaux. New York: Edition de la Maison Francaise, Inc., 1944.

Sociologia del derecho. Cordoba: Rosario, 1945.

La déclaration des droits sociaux. Paris: J. Vrin, 1946.

Sociologia juridica. Rio de Janerio: Kosmos, 1946.

The Bill of Social Rights. New York: International Universities Press, 1946.

(Ed. with Wilbert E. Moore) *Twentieth Century Sociology.* New York: Philosophical Library, 1946.

Initiation aux recherches sur la sociologie de la connaissance. Paris: Centre de Documentation Universitaire, 1948.

La dichiarazione dei diritti sociali. Milano: Editioni di Communita, 1949.

(Ed.) *Industrialisation et technocratie.* Paris: Armand Colin, 1949.

La vocation actuelle de la sociologie. Paris: Presses Universitaires de France, 1950.

Le concept de classes sociales de Marx à nos jours. Paris: Centre de Documentation Universitaire, 1954.

Déterminismes sociaux et liberté humaine. Paris: Presses Universitaires de France, 1955.

THE WORKS OF GEORGES GURVITCH

La vocation actuelle de la sociologie. 2d ed., 2 vols. Paris: Presses Universitaires de France, 1957 and 1963.

Pour le centenaire d' Auguste Comte, Paris: Centre de Documentation Universitaire, 1957; second edition, 1961.

Les fondateurs français de la sociologie contemporaine; Saint-Simon et P.-J. Proudhon. 2 vols. Paris: Centre de Documentation Universitaire, 1957.

(Ed.) *Traité de sociologie.* 2 vols. Paris: Presses Universitaires de France, 1957 and 1960.

Dialectique et sociologie. Paris: Flammarion, 1962.

Pour le centenaire de la mort de Pierre-Joseph Proudhon—Proudhon et Marx: Une confrontation, Paris: Centre de Documentation Universitaire, 1964.

The Spectrum of Social Time. Dordrecht, Holland: D. Reidel and Sons, 1964, translated by M. Korenbaum and P. Bosserman.

C.-H. de Saint-Simon. La physiologie sociale, Paris: Presses Universitaires de France, 1965.

Proudhon. Sa vie, son oeuvre, Paris: Presses Universitaires de France, 1965.

Les cadres sociaux de la connaissance, Paris: Presses Universitaires de France, 1966.

Articles and Periodicals

"Kant and Fichte als Rousseau—Interpreten," *Kantsludien,* XXVII (1922), 138-164.

"La philosophie russe du premier quart du XX siècle," *Monde Slave* (August, 1926).

"La philosophie du droit de H. Grotius et la théorie moderne du droit international," *Revue de Metaphysique et la Morale* (1927), 365 ff.

"Le principe democratique et la democratie future," *Revue de Metaphysique et de Morale* (1929), 403-431.

"Les idées maitresses de Maurice Hauriou," *Archives de Philosophie du Droit,* Cahier III-IV (1931), 155-194.

"Une philosophie instituioniste de droit," *Archives de Philosophie du Droit,* Cahier III-IV (1931), 403-420.

"Les fondements et l'evolution du droit d'aprés Emmanuel Lévy," *Revue Philosophique de la France et de l'Etranger,* No. 117 (1934), 104-138.

"Théorie pluraliste des sources du droit positif," *Annuaire de l'Institut International de Philosophie du Droit et de Sociologie Juridique,* I (1934), 114-130.

"Remarques sur la classification des formes de la sociabilité," *Archives de Philosophie du Droit et de Sociologie Juridique,* Nos. 3-4 (1935), 43-91.

"La science des faits moraux et la morale théorique chez E. Durkheim," *Archives de Philosophie du Droit et de Sociologie Juridique,* No. 7 (1937), 18-44.

"La théorie des valeurs de Heinrich Richert," *Revue Philosophique,* (September-December, 1937), 80-88.

"Les variations de l'expérience morale immédiate," *Congrès Descartes,* XI (1937), 39-44.

DIALECTICAL SOCIOLOGY

"Le problème de la conscience collective dans la sociologie de Emile Durkheim," *Archives de Philosophie du Droit et de Sociologie*, No. 8 (1938), 119-173.

"La sociologie juridique de Montesquieu," *Revue de Metaphysique et de Morale*, No. 46 (1939), 611-626.

"The Sociological Legacy of Lucien Lévy-Bruhl," *Journal of Social Philosophy*, V, No. 1 (1939).

"Sociologie de la connaissance et psychologie collective," *Annee Sociologique*, (1940-1948), 463-468.

"Major Problems of the Sociology of Law," *Journal of Social Philosophy*, VI (April, 1941), 197-215.

"Mass, Community, and Communion," *Journal of Philosophy*, XXXVIII, No. 18 (August 28, 1941), 485-496.

"The Problem of Social Law," *International Journal of Ethics*, LII (October, 1941), 17-40.

"Democracy is a Sociological Problem," *Journal of Legal and Political Sociology*, I (1942), 46-71.

"Magic and Law," *Social Research*, IX (1942), 104-122.

"Is Moral Philosophy a Normative Philosophy?" *Journal of Philosophy*, XL (March 18, 1943), 141-148.

"Is the Antithesis of 'Moral Man' and 'Immoral Society, True?'" *Philosophical Review*, III (November, 1943), 533-552.

"La philosophie sociale de Bergson," *Renaissance*, I (1943), 81-94.

"Compte-rendu de MacIver—Social Causation et Sorokin—Socio-Cultural Causality, Space, Time," *Cahiers Internationaux de Sociologie*, II (1947), 172-182.

"La sociologie du jeune Marx," *Cahiers Internationaux de Sociologie*, IV (1948), 3-47.

"Psychologie collective et psychologie de la connaissance," *Annee Sociologique* (1948-1949), 171-175.

"Groupement social et classe sociale," *Cahiers Internationaux de Sociologie*, VII (1949), 2-42.

"La technocratie est-elle un effet inévitable de l'industrialisation?" in Gurvitch, Georges, (ed.), *Industrie et technocratie*. Paris: Librairie Armand Colin, 1949, 179-200.

"Microsociology and Sociometry," *Sociometry*, XII, Nos. 1-3 (1949, 1-31.

"Les dégres de la liberté humaine," *Cahiers Internationaux de Sociologie*, XI (1951), 3-20.

"Response a une critique. Lettre diverte a M. L. Von Wiese," *Cahiers Internationaux de Sociologie*, XIII (1952), 94-104.

"Hyper-empirisme dialectique," *Cahiers Internationaux de Sociologie*, XV.

"Le concept de structure sociale," *Cahiers Internationaux de Sociologie*, XIX (1955), 3-44.

"La crise de l'explication en sociologie," *Cahiers Internationaux de Sociologie*, XXI (1956), 3-18.

"On Some Deviations in the Interpretation of the Concept of Social Structure," in Moreno, J. L. (ed.) *Sociometry and the Science of Man*. New York: Beacon House, 1956, 245-262.

"Pour le centenaire de la naissance de Durkheim," *Cahiers Internationaux de Sociologie*, XXVII (1959), 3-10.

"Continuite et discontinuite en historie et sociologie," *Annales*, No. 1, (1957), 73-84.

THE WORKS OF GEORGES GURVITCH

"Philosophie et sociologie," *Encyclopedie Française,* XIX (1957), 26.15-28.4.

"Le problème de la sociologie de la connaissance," *Revue Philosophique,* Part I (October-December, 1957), 494-502.

"Le problème de la sociologie de la connaissance," *Revue Philosophique,* Part II (October-December, 1958), 438-451.

"Le problème de la sociologie de la connaissance," *Revue Philosophique,* Part III (April-June, 1959), 145-168.

"Dialectique et sociologie selon Jean-Paul Sartre," *Cahiers Internationaux de Sociologie* XXXI (1961), 113-128.

"L'effondrement d'un mythe politique: Joseph Stalin," *Cahiers Internationaux de Sociologie,* XXXIII (1962), 5-18.

"Les variations des perceptions collectives des étendues," *Cahiers Internationaux de Sociologie,* XXXVII (1964), 79-107.

"Avant-propos: les classes sociales dans lemonde d'aujourd'hui," *Cahiers Internationaux de Sociologie,* XXXVIII (1965), 3-11.

Gurvitch Contributed the Following Articles to the Encyclopedia of Social Sciences

Chicherin, B. N.; Fichte, J. G.; Gradvsky, A. D.; "Justice"; Kistyakovsky, B. A.; Korkunov, N. M.; Menger, A; "Natural Law"; Petrazhitsky, L. I.; and Secretan, C.

Unpublished Materials

"Mon itineraire intellectuelle." Originally prepared for publication, 1958. (Mimeographed)

Other Sources

Class lectures, the University of Paris, 1956-1957.
Personal interviews with Professor Gurvitch, 1960.
Personal letters from Professor Gurvitch, 1960-1963.

THE GENERAL BIBLIOGRAPHY

Books

Abraham, Henry J. *The Judicial Process.* New York: Oxford University Press, 1962.

Allport, Gordon. *The Nature of Prejudice.* Garden City: Doubleday Anchor Books, 1958.

Aron, Raymond. *Le développement de la société industrielle et la stratification sociale.* Vol. II. Paris: Centre de Documentation Universitaire, 1957.

Baldwin, James. *Nobody Knows My Name.* New York: Dial Press, 1961.

Becker, Howard. *Through Values to Social Interpretation.* Durham, North Carolina: Duke University Press, 1950.

———. (ed.) *Modern Sociological Theory.* New York: The Dryden Press, 1957.

Bergson, Henri. *An Introduction to Metaphysics.* New York: G. P. Putnam's Sons, 1913.

Bidney, David. *Theoretical Anthropology.* New York: Columbia University Press, 1953.

Bohr, Niels. *Atomic Physics and Human Knowledge.* New York: John Wiley and Sons, 1958.

Boodin, John Elof. *The Social Mind.* New York: The Macmillan Company, 1939.

Bowle, John. *Western Political Thought.* London: Methuen, 1961

Broom, Leonard and Selgnick, Philip. *Sociology.* 2d ed. Evanston Illinois: Row, Peterson and Company, 1958.

Bruyn, Severyn, *The Human Perspective in Sociology.* Englewood Cliffs, New Jersey: Prentice-Hall, Inc., 1966.

Buber, Martin. *Between Man and Man.* Boston: The Beacon Press, 1955.

———. *I and Thou.* New York: Charles Scribner's Sons, 1961.

Bunge, Mario. *Intuition and Science.* Englewood Cliffs, New Jersey: Prentice-Hall, 1962.

Carr, Edward H. *What Is History?* New York: Alfred A. Knopf, 1962.

Childs, Marquis. *Sweden: The Middle Way.* New Haven: Yale University Press, 1936.

Dimock, Marshall E. *The New American Political Economy.* New York.

Durkheim, Emile. *Les règles de la méthode sociologique.* 4th ed. Paris: Felix Alcan, 1907.

Eliot, T. S. (ed.) *Pascal's Pensées.* New York: Dutton Everyman Paperbacks, 1958.

Gross, Llewellyn. *Symposium on Sociological Theory.* Evanston, Illinois: Row, Peterson and Company, 1959.

Haber, William (ed.) *Manpower in the United States: Problem and Politics.* New York: Harper and Brothers, 1954.

Hare, Paul, Borgatta, Edgar F. and Bales, Robert F. *Small Groups.* New York: Alfred A. Knopf, 1955.

THE GENERAL BIBLIOGRAPHY

Heilbroner, Robert. *The Making of Economic History*. Englewood Cliffs, New Jersey: Prentice-Hall, 1962.

Hunt, Elgin F. and Karlin, Jules. *Society Today and Tomorrow*. New York: The Macmillan Company, 1961.

Johnson, Harry M. *Sociology: A Systematic Introduction*. New York: Harcourt, Brace and Company, 1960.

Kluckhohn, Cylde. *Mirror for Man*. New York: McGraw-Hill, 1949.

Lerner, Max. *America as a Civilization*. 2 vols. New York: Simon and Schuster, 1957.

Lewis, Oscar. *The Children of Sanchez*. New York: Random House, 1961.

Lincoln, C. Eric. *The Black Muslims in America*. Boston: Beacon Press, 1961.

Lipset, Seymour M. and Smelser, Neil J. (eds) *Sociology, the Progress of a Decade*. Englewood Cliffs, New Jersey: Prentice-Hall, 1961.

MacIver, Robert M. *Web of Government*. New York: The Macmillan Company, 1947.

Martindale, Don. *The Nature and Types of Sociological Theory*. Boston: Houghton Mifflin Company, 1960.

Mauss, Marcel. *Sociologie et anthropologie*. Paris: Presses Universitaires de France, 1950.

May, Rollo. *Existence*. Glencoe, Illinois: Basic Books, 1958.

Mead, Margaret. (ed.) *Cultural Patterns and Technical Change*. New York: UNESCO, 1953.

Merton, Robert. *Social Structure and Social Theory*. 2d ed. Glencoe, Illinois: The Free Press, 1957.

Merton, Robert, Broom, Leonard and Cottrell, Leonard, Jr. (eds.) *Sociology Today*. New York: Basic Books, Inc., 1959.

Mills, C. Wright. *Marxism*. New York: Dell Publishing Company, 1962.

————. *The Sociological Imagination*. New York: Oxford University Press, 1959.

Muelder, Walter G. *Foundations of the Responsible Society*. New York: Abingdon, 1960.

Niebuhr, Reinhold. *An Interpretation of Christian Ethics*. New York: Harper and Brothers, 1935.

Odegard, Peter H., Carr, Robert K., Berstein, Marver H., and Morrison, Donald H. *American Government: Theory, Politics and Constitutional Foundation*. New York: Holt, Rinehart and Winston, 1961.

Parkinson, C. N. *The Evolution of Political Thought*. New York: The Viking Press, 1960.

Parsons, Talcott. *Eléments pour une sociologie de l'action*. Paris: Presses Universitaires de France, 1955. Translated by M. F. Bourricand.

Pirenne, Jacques. *The Tides of History*. Vol. I. New York: E. P. Dutton and Company, Inc., 1962.

Ramsey, Paul. *Nine Modern Moralists*. Englewood Cliffs, New Jersey: Prentice-Hall, 1962.

Randall, John Herman, Jr. *The Making of the Modern Mind*. Boston: Houghton Miffllin Company, 1940.

Sanders, Irwin T. *Rainbow in the Rock*. Cambridge: Harvard University Press, 1962.

Scheler, Max. *Man's Place in Nature*. Boston: Beacon Press, 1961. Translated by Hans Heyerhoff.

———. *The Nature of Sympathy*. London: Routledge and Kegan, Paul, 1954. Translated by Peter Heath.

———. *Philosophical Perspectives*. Boston: Beacon Press, 1958. Translated by Oscar Haac.

Schilpp, P. W. (ed.) *Albert Einstein, Philosopher-Scientist*. Evanston: The Library of Living Philosophers, 1949.

Seligman, E. R. A. (ed.) *Encyclopedia of Social Sciences*. New York: Macmillan Company, 1930-1935.

Smith, Huston. *The Purposes of Higher Education*. New York: Harper and Brothers, 1955.

Sorokin, Pitirim A. *Social Philosophies of an Age of Crisis*. Boston: Beacon Press, 1950.

The New English Bible. New York: Oxford University Press, 1961.

Timasheff, Nicholas S. *Sociological Theory*. Garden City, New York: Doubleday and Company, Inc., 1955.

Tiryakian, E. A. *Sociologism and Existentialism*. Englewood Cliffs, New Jersey: Prentice-Hall, 1962.

Toulemont, René. *Sociologie et pluralisme dialectique*. Louvain, Belgium: Editions Nauwelaerts, 1955.

Twain, Mark. *The $30,000 Bequest and Other Stories*. New York: Harpers and Brothers, 1935.

Weber, Max. *The Protestant Ethic and the Spirit of Capitalism*. New York: Charles Scribner's Sons, 1958.

———. *The Theory of Social and Economic Organization*. Glencoe, Illinois: The Free Press, 1947.

Book Reviews

Abel, Theodore, Review of *Sociologie et pluralism dialectique*, by René Toulemont, American Sociological Review, XXI (October, 1956), 634.

Aillet, Georges. Review of *Morale théorique et science des moeurs*, by Georges Gurvitch, Archives de Philosophie du Droit et de Sociologie Juridique, VIII (1937), 26-57.

Alpert, H. Review of *Déterminismes sociaux et liberté humaine*, by Georges Gurvitch, American Anthropologist, LVIII (April, 1956), 372-373.

Balandier, Georges. Review of *Dialectique et sociologie*, by Georges Gurvitch, Cahiers Internationaux de Sociologie, XXXIII (1962), 167-169.

Birnbaum, Norman. Review of *Où va la sociologie française?* by Armand Cuvillier, American Journal of Sociology, LX (September, 1954), 199.

Davis, Kingsley. Review of *Elements de sociologie juridique*, by Georges Gurvitch, American Sociological Review, VI.

Faris, Ellsworth. Review of *The Social System*, by Talcott Parsons, American Sociological Review, XVIII, No. 1 (February, 1953), 103-106.

Ford, J. B. Review of *Déterminismes sociaux et liberté humaine*, by Georges Gurvitch, American Sociological Review, XX (October, 1955), 599-600.

THE GENERAL BIBLIOGRAPHY

Goode, W. J. Review of *Industrialisme et technocratie*, edited by Georges Gurvitch, *American Sociological Review*, XV (June, 1950), 444-445.

Halsey, A. H. Review of *Campus U.S.A.! Portraits of American Colleges in Action*, by David Boroff, *American Sociological Review*, XXVII (June, 1962), 419.

House, Floyd N. Review of *La vocation actuelle de la sociologie* by Georges Gurvitch, *American Journal of Sociology*, LX (September, 1954), 198-199.

Lightman, J. B. Review of *Sociology of Law*, by Georges Gurvitch, *American Sociological Review*, VII.

Mueller, J. H. Review of *Traité de sociologie*, Vol. I by Georges Gurvitch (ed.), *American Journal of Sociology*, LXV (July, 1959), 106.

Sorokin, Pitirim, *Sociological Theories of Today*. New York: Harper and Row, 1966.

Swanson, G. E. Review of *Theory of Action*, by Talcott Parsons and E. A. Shils, *American Sociological Review*, XVIII, No. 2 (April, 1952), 125-133.

Timasheff, N. S. Review of *Déterminismes sociaux et liberte humaine*, by Georges Gurvitch, *American Journal of Sociology*, LXI (January 1956), 373.

Tiryakian, E. A. Review of *Dialectique et sociologie*, by Georges Gurvitch, *American Sociological Review*, XXVII (October, 1962), 701.

Weintraub, Philipp, Review of *The Bill of Social Rights*, by Georges Gurvitch, *Social Forces*, XXVI (March, 1948), 343-345.

Wilson, Everett. Review of *Traité de sociologie*, Vol. II, by Georges Gurvitch, *American Journal of Sociology*, LXVIII (September, 1962), 253.

Wolff, Kurt R. Review of *La vocation actuelle de la sociologie*, by Georges Gurvitch, *American Sociological Review*, XVI (February, 1951), 119-121.

Articles and Periodicals

Aron, Raymond. "La societé Americaine," *Cahiers Internationaux de Sociologie*, XXVI (1959), 55-68.

Bain, Read. "The Most Important Sociologist?" *American Sociology Review*, XXVII (October, 1962), 746-748.

Berger, Bennett. "The Study of Man," *Commentary*, XXXIV (December, 1962), 511.

Cazeneuve, Jean, "La sociologie de Georges Gurvitch," *Revue Française de Sociologie*, II, No. 1 (Jan-March, 1966), 3-14.

Combat. January 23, 1957.

Doty, Patricia J. "Complementarity and Its Analogies," *The Journal of Philosophy*, LV (December 4, 1958), 1103.

Merton, Robert. "Now the Case *for* Sociology," *New York Times Magazine*, (July 16, 1961), 19-20.

Pfautz, Harold W. "The Current Literature on Social Stratification, Critique and Bibliography," *American Journal of Sociology*, LVII (January, 1953), 406.

Sarinen, Eero. *Time*, (July 2, 1956), 51.

Schmidt, Paul F. "Ethical Norms in the Scientific Method," *The Journal of Philosophy*, LVI (July 16, 1959), 644.

DIALECTICAL SOCIOLOGY

Stoetzel, Jean. "Sociology in France: An Empiricist View," in Becker, Howard (ed.) *Modern Sociological Theory*, New York: The Dryden Press, 1957, 623-657.

The Altantic Monthly, CCX (December, 1962), 74-142.

Tiryakian, E. A., "Existential Phenomenology and Sociology," *American Sociological Review*, XXX, No. 5 (Oct., 1965), 674-688.

Warriner, Charles W. "Groups Are Real: A Reaffirmation," *American Sociology Review*, XXI (October, 1956), 549-554.

Encyclopedias

Berger, Gaston (ed.), *Encyclopedie Française*, XIX, Paris: Societé Nouvelle de l'Encyclopedie Française, 1957.

Seligman, E. R. (ed.). *Encyclopedia of the Social Sciences*, 3 vols., New York: Macmillan Company, 1930-1935.

Wolf, Abraham. "The Scientific Method," *The Encyclopedia Britannica*, Volume XX (Chicago: The Encyclopedia Britannica, Inc., 1955),

Unpublished Materials

Martin, John Vincent, S.J. "Depth Sociology and Microsociology." Unpublished Ph.D. dissertation, Harvard University, 1957.

AUTHOR INDEX

SUBJECT INDEX

OTHER EXTENDING HORIZONS BOOKS

THE BLACK POWER REVOLT   Collected Essays

WHAT WE WANT is the rallying cry as leading spokesmen explore
Black Power in depth. From the rise of black power to significant
application — from demythologizing black power to pertinent interpretation—the theme is identity: cultural; political; social. Including essays by W. E. B. DuBois, Douglass, Malcolm X, LeRoi
Jones, Floyd McKissick and Stokely Carmichael, this anthology dissects old myths and defines new roles by tracing the emergence of
the concept and its meaning to the Black community.
200 Pages Paper $2.95 1967

SOCIAL WORK AND SOCIAL CHANGE

Sugata Dasgupta

A synthesis of general theory with actual social work techniques
explores the application of these methods within the living framework of culturally diverse communities. The study reveals the practical contributions of an important program of social development as
well as the integration of rational and self-generating means of
democratic change.
256 Pages Cloth $6.95 1967

THE ROLE OF THE PEACE CORPS
IN AMERICAN FOREIGN RELATIONS

Irving O. Ostrowski

Viewing the history of the Peace Corps from its inception to the
present, Professor Ostrowski bases his appraisal on the organization's relevance to modern political and social dilemmas: the power
struggle between competing ideologies; the precarious military balance
between East and West; the Sino-Soviet schism; and the birth pains
of newly independent nations.
100 Pages Paper $1.95 1967

SOCIAL AND CULTURAL DYNAMICS

Pitirim A. Sorokin

This one-volume abridgement of the four-volume masterpiece of Dr.
Sorokin presents for the general reading public a great pioneering
work of inductive sociology. This monumental study analyzes the
events, trends, personalities and philosophical beliefs which have
contributed to the making of today's civilization. A truly remarkable
analysis, this study ranks with the works of Pareto, Toynbee and
Spengler.